EVERYTHING YOU NEED TO KNOW ABOUT (LEGALLY) CARRYING A HANDGUN IN MINNESOTA

Written by

Joel Rosenberg

For

The American Association of
Certified Firearms Instructors

Everything You Need to Know about (Legally) Carrying a Handgun in Minnesota.

Published by American Associaton of Certified Firearms Instructors

First Printing, May, 2003

Copyright (c) 2003 by Certified Firearms Instructors, LLC.
Box 131254
St. Paul MN 55113
(612) 730-9895

10 9 8 7 6 5 4 3 2

Library of Congress Cataloguing-in-Publication Data

Rosenberg, Joel

ISBN 0-9741480-0-8

Everything You Need to Know about (Legally) Carrying a Handgun in Minnesota.

Printed in the United States of America by The First Impression Group, 2700 Blue Water Road, Suite 450, Eagan MN 55121-1429 (651) 683-1125

Written by Joel Rosenberg, with the assistance of Joseph E. Olson and Tim Fleming Grant.

Design, layout, and typesetting by Ellegon, Inc.

Photos by Oleg Volk. Used by permission.

EVERYTHING YOU NEED TO KNOW ABOUT (LEGALLY) CARRYING A HANDGUN IN MINNESOTA

published by

THE
AMERICAN
ASSOCIATION OF
CERTIFIED
FIREARMS
INSTRUCTORS

Introduction:
What This Book Is All About...7
    Carry Laws 7
    Who this book is for 9
    Who we are...11
    Orientation...12
    A carry permit and a handgun are insurance 13
    Humor...14
    Keeping it simple...14
    What a permit changes 14

Chapter 1:
Why Would Anybody Want a Carry Permit? 17
    Getting a carry permit because of a safety concern.......................................21
    Why somebody would not want to have a carry permit...............................22
    "My gun might be taken away and used against me".....................................22
    "There are all those accidental gun deaths"...22
    "Guns are used in suicide more than in self-defense"...................................23
    "Guns are a lousy way to settle personal disputes".......................................23
    Beyond the bad reasons 23
    Is it right for you? 24

Chapter 2:
Staying Out of Trouble 25
    Your Options..26
    Alertness 27
    Avoiding conflict 28
    Avoid the conflict, and avoid the consequences..30

Chapter 3:
Lethal Force, in Law and Practice 31
    Justification...32
    Self-Defense...33
    Situation one: defense of person..37
    Situation two: defense of dwelling...44
    Situation three: defense of property...51
    When the right to use lethal force ends 51
    What isn't required..53
    Defending others 54
    Defensive "brandishing" and reasonable force 55
    The aftermath..56

Chapter 4:
Lethal Force and its Aftermath.. 57
    Threat of force – is it enough?...58
    Talking yourself into trouble..58

Running into trouble...60
When the assailant flees..61
When the assailant surrenders: citizen's arrest.................................63
When the attack continues 65
The physics of a lethal confrontation..65
The physiology of a lethal confrontation..66
The physical effects of a shooting..69
After a lethal confrontation 72
When the police arrive 73
A four-part strategy...74
Why not talk? 78
What the police will do..80
When are you under arrest?...83
Not talking isn't just for you 84
An alternate strategy 85
The one exception...86
After a nonlethal confrontation 87
Getting sued 89

Chapter 5:
Routine Police Encounters

Routine Police Encounters 93
Don't argue..94
Don't volunteer unnecessary information..94
Be polite 95
Don't lie..96
Obey all instructions promptly..96
Don't produce your handgun except on instruction 96
Keep your hands in plain sight..96
Don't consent to a search..97
When a routine encounter becomes something else 99
At the end of the day...99

Chapter 6:
Choosing a Handgun for Carry

Choosing a Handgun for Carry..101
Reliability..102
Pointability 102
Concealability...102
Luggability 103
Caliber...103
Trade-offs, and a recommendation 104
Revolvers vs. semiautos...104
The case for revolvers for self-defense...107
The case for semiautos for self-defense 108
The case against revolvers...109
The case against semiautos..109

Specific choices...110
"Mouse guns" 111
Small revolvers...112
Mid-sized revolvers..113
Full-sized revolvers 114
Compact semiautos 114
Mid-sized semiautos 115
Full-sized semiautos..116
Our recommendation...116
Ammunition...117
Exotic rounds 119
Specific ammunition recommendations 120
Summing up...121

Chapter 7:
The Legalities of Everyday Carry 123
Permitted places..123
Carry at work 124
The parking lot...125
Posting...126
Carrying without a permit 127
Prohibited places 127
Airports...131
Post offices and other federal facilities...132
Churches...136
Carrying and drinking 137
Traveling outside of Minnesota 138
Traveling outside the United States 139
Traveling by air...141
Know the local laws of your destination 141
How to check in a firearm 142
What not to do...143

Chapter 8:
The Mechanics of Everyday Carry.................................... 145
When should I carry? 145
Don't touch the gun...146
Do avoid exposing it unintentionally 147
The belt...147
Carry methods 148
Holsters...148
Belt holsters 148
Inside the waistband 150
Shoulder holsters 151
Pocket holsters 153

Deep cover..155
Miscellaneous carry methods...157
Holsters to avoid...158
Carry without a holster..159
Off-body carry..159
The bathroom..160
Carrying for women...161
Storing when carrying 164
Specifics of Minnesota law 165
Carrying openly...165
Number and type of guns carried 166
Handguns vs. long guns..166
Loaded guns and children...167

Chapter 9:
Gun Safety, On and Off the Range... 169
Basic safety rules..169
Rules for handling guns..172
Safety when shooting...174
Cleaning guns 176
Storage 177
Wash your hands...178
Wear safety glasses and hearing protection..................................179
Gun safety and children 179
Gun accidents...180

Chapter 10:
Shooting, on the Range and on the Street 181
Target shooting vs. self-defense shooting 182
The Weaver...183
The Chapman..183
The Natural Isosceles 184
What could go wrong?..187
Practicing 188

Chapter 11:
Training..191
Where to get training 191
Qualifications 192

Chapter 12:
Applying for a Minnesota Carry Permit 193
Where to apply..193
How to apply 194
What happens next...194
When the permit is granted...195
If the permit is denied 195

Evaluate 195
Negotiate...196
Litigate 199
Finding an attorney 199
The appeals process..200
Chapter 13:
Out-of-state Permits: Not Just for Those From Other States 201
Out-of-state permits 201
Out-of-state permits *for* Minnesota residents..............................202
Pennsylvania 203
Florida...203
New Hampshire...204
Utah...205
Chapter 14:
What to Do After You've Gotten Your Permit 207
Decide on your own personal carry strategy.................................208
Spend time at the range with your carry handgun 209
Recycle your carry ammunition..210
Clean your carry handgun 210
Take additional training 211
Keep up with changes in the law..211
Check out the AACFI website 211
Prepare to renew your permit..212
Support the individuals and groups that made it possible............212
Appendix A: Necessary Equipment 215
Appendix B: IACP "Officer-Involved Shooting Guidelines" 217
Appendix C: Selected Minnesota Statutes 223
Appendix D: Minnesota Legislators Who Supported You..................... 245

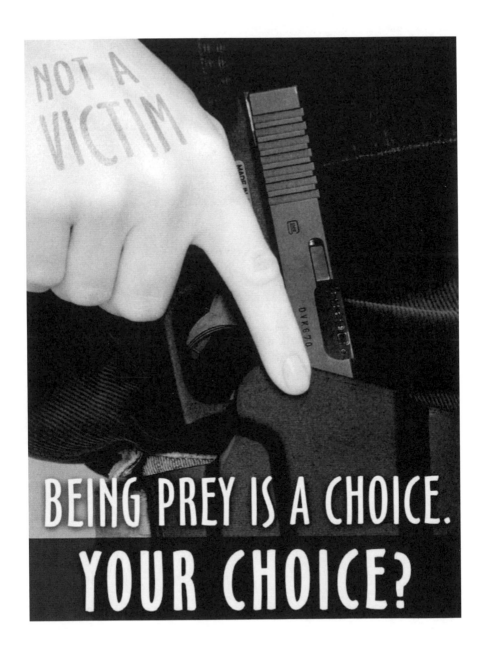

INTRODUCTION
What This Book Is All About

So, you want to carry a handgun in Minnesota?
Are you sure?
Don't be too quick to decide.
There are lots of reasons not to, after all —
particularly if you listen to the often well-
intentioned people who bandy about phrases like
"there's already too many guns on the street,"
"every fender-bender will turn into a gunfight,"
"what if there's a pistol in that overcoat?"

Even if you listen to people in the self-defense-rights movement,
you'll hear that getting a carry permit may not be right — for you.

Because that's what you've got to decide.

Not: *Is allowing citizens to get carry permits a good idea?*

Not even, yet: *Do I want to carry a handgun in public?*

But: *Should I get a carry permit?* After you decide that, then you have
other decisions to make.

Carry Laws

A bit of background, first.

There are, to oversimplify just a bit, three kinds of handgun permit

laws in the United States: "may issue," "shall-issue," and "no-issue."
In "may-issue" states, permits are issued only at the *discretion* of local authorities, who — sometimes in theory and often in practice — are free
to deny permits for any reason, or no reason at all. Until the Minnesota
Citizens Personal Protection Act ("MPPA") was enacted in 2003[1], Minnesota was a "may-issue" state. In some Minnesota cities and counties,
permits were issued to any adult who applied for one. In others (especially in the Metro area), they were issued only to security guards or to
nobody at all.

Seven states are still in this category: California, New York, Hawaii,
Massachusetts, Rhode Island, New Jersey, and Maryland. In these states,
permits are typically issued only to people who have what the authorities consider compelling business needs (e.g., bank guards), extreme
wealth or strong political connections.

In "shall issue" states, any qualifying adult can get a carry permit by
meeting objective criteria: passing a criminal history check, taking the
appropriate training, filling out and filing a form with the local sheriff,
and paying a fee. It's like a driver's license — if you qualify, you automatically receive a carry permit. The three-quarters of the states, containing
the majority of the population, have "shall issue" laws. Minnesota has
joined these states.

The third category is a shrinking handful of "no-issue" states. As of
2007, only two states — Illinois and Wisconsin — are still in this category.
In "no issue" states, carry permits are simply not available, and law-
abiding citizens are barred from carrying handguns to protect themselves (unless they are retired law enforcement officers).

Today, in Minnesota, if a qualified adult meets the objective criteria,
they get the permit. It's not a matter of persuading a government official
that they have a "special" need. Instead, it is a right, just like a driver's
license.

And it's like a driver's license in other important ways: a driver's license *allows* you to drive a car, but does not *require* you to, and both licenses can be taken away if you violate certain laws.

There's an important distinction between getting a carry permit and
carrying a handgun in public. Some people don't plan to ever carry a
handgun, but may choose to get a carry permit anyway. A permit gives

---

[1] After a court decision that the MPPA had been enacted by a defective legislative
procedure, the 2003 Act was re-enacted "retroactively and without interruption" in May
2005.

you the *option* of carrying a handgun;[2] it's not an obligation. But, just as with a driver's license and driving a car, having a carry permit and carrying a handgun is a responsibility you should take very seriously.

It wouldn't be accurate to say that it's easy to get a handgun permit in Minnesota, just as it wouldn't be accurate to say that it's easy to get a driver's license: you have to train and qualify for either one. There's work involved, and some expense—although not a lot—and there should be some careful thought, as well.

And about the only thing we can promise you about carrying a handgun is this—and it's a theme we'll return to regularly in this book: *A gun never solves problems.*

Really.

At best, the *proper* use of a handgun can substitute lesser—but very real—problems for more serious ones. If you so much as brandish a handgun in public—even in an unambiguous circumstance where your only other choice is to be the victim of assault, rape, kidnapping, or murder, and where you've got abundant witnesses to that effect—you can expect to be arrested. If you are one of those rare permit holders who actually fires a handgun anywhere off the range, you're likely to be prosecuted as well as arrested, and quite possibly sued.

Yes, that's better than being assaulted, raped, kidnapped, or murdered. But it's better to avoid the whole problem in the first place—and yes, we'll be returning to that, too.

Who this book is for

While there are quite a few very good books on issues of the carrying of handguns, *Everything You Need to Know about (Legally) Carrying a Handgun in Minnesota* is different—it's about carrying a handgun *in Minnesota*.

Most of the principles involved apply anywhere; staying alert in Minnesota isn't different than staying alert in Oregon, after all. But Minnesota is different from every other state. "Minnesota Nice" is part of our culture, and this book was written with that in mind. Even more importantly, the Minnesota statutes and case law involving the carrying of handguns and of the use or threat of deadly force are different, in signif-

---

[2] You may choose to carry a handgun for defense or hold the license merely to avoid inadvertent crimes when transporting firearms. Or, you may simply want the knowledge that the carry permit course provides.

icant ways, than those of other states.

Just to take one minor example, Minnesota law — unlike that of most states — doesn't distinguish between "open" carry, where a handgun is worn visibly, and "concealed" carry. If you're going to carry a handgun in Minnesota, you should know both what's sensible — which is pretty much the same from state to state — and what's legal.

And it's not just the law as written in the statutes, or the "case law" — the way laws are interpreted by courts. See the footnote about "arresting the gun" in Minneapolis. That's hardly the only issue. We'll get to them.

If you've read about the permit law in Minnesota and wonder what it means, this book is for you — whether or not you decide to apply for a carry permit. That's particularly true if you've been wondering what's involved in getting a permit, and carrying a handgun, both in legal and practical terms.

If you already have a personal safety concern — a stalker, say, or an abusive ex-spouse, or work or live in a bad neighborhood — this book is for you.

If you're considering taking a job where you may be required to carry a handgun as a citizen — a security guard, for example — this book is for you.

If you've been wondering about what kind of training and equipment you'll need, you'll learn that in these pages. Even if you haven't been wondering about the legal, moral, and practical issues, you'll learn about those too.

You *don't* need to be an experienced gun owner, or have even so much as held a firearm, to benefit from this book. You don't even have to like guns.

If you're an experienced gun owner, this book is for you, too. Many people who have owned guns for most of their lives have yet to deal with the laws and details of day-to-day handgun carry.

If you're a police officer who wonders if you should be worried about citizens carrying guns, this book is for you as well. For now, think about this: while there are millions of permit holders in the US, there hasn't been a single — not one — reported incident of a permit holder so much as pointing a handgun at a police officer, although there are numerous reports of permit holders saving police officers' lives. You don't need to worry about permit holders; they're the good guys.

Even if you're a passionate gun-control advocate or think that all handguns should be banned, this book is for you. You should know about the issues involved, as somewhere upwards of 100,000 Minnesotans will eventually have carry permits. If you're worried about that, we hope to reassure you that it's going to be okay[3].

If you're somewhere in the middle, this book is for you. Regardless how you feel about firearms or people carrying handguns in public, some changes have been made, and you should know about them.

This book is also for those people—a small number, we hope—who think that carrying a handgun around in public is fun and cool, who think that Minnesota's permit laws means that they can now strut around in public, pushing people around, not taking nonsense from anybody because, well, they've got a gun.

We hope and expect to talk them out of that.

Who we are

The American Association of Certified Firearms Instructors (AACFI) is dedicated to providing outstanding training in firearms safety, storage, and basic firearms handling, as well as permit-to-carry and advanced-defensive-carry instruction.

Joseph E. Olson, the President of AACFI, is Professor of Law at Hamline University, as well as a longtime political activist involved in 2nd Amendment issues, and a former member of the board of directors of the National Rifle Association. A former federal prosecutor and experienced defense counsel, he's licensed to practice law in Minnesota and California. In addition to being a NRA Certified Firearms Instructor since 1985, Olson is a graduate of the *Judicious Use of Deadly Force* course, the *Lethal Threat Management for Civilians* course, and the *LFI Refresher* course at the Lethal Force Institute; the *Tactical Pistol* course at Gunsite Training Center; the *Urban Rifle* course at Thunder Ranch Training Center; the *Advanced Pistolcraft* course at Chapman Academy; the *Arizona Concealed Carry* course at the Urban Firearms Institute; and the *Nevada Concealed Carry* course at Armed and Safe, Inc. Olson has been issued carry permits in Arizona, Florida, Maine, Massachusetts, Minnesota, New Hampshire, and Washington state. Olson is the President of the American Association of Certified Firearms Instructors, an organization dedicated to training civilians not only on the law and technicalities of

---

[3] If not, you could consider moving to the shrinking number of states and cities where carry permits are difficult or impossible to get. The bad news, though, is that places like these—New York, Chicago, or Washington DC, etc.—top the list of high-crime destinations.

carrying a handgun for personal protection, but on strategies and tactics for avoiding any necessity of the use of a handgun for personal protection. He holds Counselor, Certifier, and Instructor ratings from AACFI.

Tim Fleming Grant, the Vice President of AACFI, is a political activist and marketing professional. Grant's interest in firearms and self-defense began in February of 1996 when his cousin was killed in a drive-by shooting in Golden Valley, Minnesota. After four years of committed part-time work on the leadership team of Concealed Carry Reform, Now!, Grant left his position as National Sales Manager for a division of Norstan and, later, Siemens to focus more time on changing carry laws. As CCRN's lead strategic planner and elections manager, Grant played a key role in developing and guiding the Minnesota Personal Protection Act through the Minnesota Legislature. Grant holds an MBA from the University of St. Thomas, graduate credits from St. Paul Seminary and a Bachelor of Arts degree in Political Science and Economics from the University of Minnesota. He also holds both Instructor and Certifier ratings from AACFI.

Joel Rosenberg has written two *Everything You Need to Know About (Legally) Carrying a Handgun* books for AACFI with the able assistance of Joseph E. Olson and Tim Fleming Grant. Rosenberg is a professional writer of nonfiction, science fiction, fantasy, and mysteries. As one of the very few Minneapolis, MN, residents ever granted a carry permit under the previous law "for personal safety, as needed," he has been licensed to carry a handgun for more than six years. He holds several Instructor ratings from the National Rifle Association and is also a NRA Certified Range Officer.

Like Olson and Grant, Rosenberg owns a few firearms.

None of them has ever so much as pointed a firearm at another human being — much less shot one — and all three of them like it that way.

And, as a special note, the first edition of this book wouldn't have been possible without the assistance of attorney David M. Gross of Faribault, MN.

Orientation

Let's start at the beginning. When developing both the AACFI training courses and this book, we did a lot of reading and research. One of the things that we found irritating about much writing on handgun self-defense matters is that it assumed a lot of familiarity with the issues, and with firearms themselves.

Transportation and cars aren't only for roadway design engineers, mechanics, and automotive hobbyists; medical care isn't just for doctors and nurses; and self-defense and personal safety aren't just for people who already know a lot about firearms.

Whether or not you should apply for a carry permit has a lot more to do with your own personality, morality, and situation than it does with whether or not you know a lot about firearms, or want to know a lot about firearms. A carry permit isn't a necessary accessory for a firearms hobbyist. On the contrary, it's entirely reasonable to have no interest at all in firearms beyond personal protection and choose to take out a carry permit.

While we've not skimped on the needs of more experienced people, our recommendations—where we give them—are largely for people new to the possession and particularly the carrying of handguns.

While we have nothing against other legitimate uses of guns—hunting, target shooting, etc.—the focus of AACFI's training courses and this book is on the day-to-day and emergency issues of people carrying concealed handguns, *in Minnesota*. That's an important distinction—and not just because Minnesota law is different in significant ways from the laws of other states, although that's certainly part of it.

Even people who have owned guns for many years may never have carried one in public at all, much less on a daily basis. They haven't had to think through the many issues involved—and there are a lot of them, from day-to-day matters of how to carry a handgun, to routine encounters with police, to the thankfully rare situations where a handgun must be taken out in public.

And far too many people—including some who have owned guns all of their lives—have picked up a lot of misinformation from television and newspapers. Very few people—even very experienced gun owners—have more than the vaguest idea about the laws involving self-defense or practical matters involving the carrying of a handgun as a citizen.

That's what this book is all about.

A carry permit and a handgun are insurance

Probably the best place to start is this: the vast majority of people who carry a handgun will never have an occasion to take the gun out in public.

That's a good thing.

A carry permit—and the accompanying training and equipment—should be thought of as something like the fire insurance you carry on your home. When you buy fire insurance, you hope and expect that you'll never have to use it, but you also know that, should your house burn down, a good insurance policy will make what will be a horrible incident at least a little less horrible. And fire insurance is only one of the things a prudent homeowner buys in order to protect himself—or herself—and family: smoke detectors and fire extinguishers are every bit as important, and so are good locks on the door.

And so it is with handguns and carry permits. Taking out a permit and buying a handgun for carry are only a small part of seeing to your personal protection.

Which is as it should be.

Humor

While carrying a handgun in public is a serious matter, and must be taken seriously, that doesn't mean that a little humor every now and then is a bad idea. In fact, we think it's essential, and we hope that the occasional touches of humor in this book will be appreciated and not misunderstood.

There are, however, things we don't joke about. One of them is pointing a handgun at a human being. Another topic that we find utterly unfit for jokes is the unsafe handling of firearms.

Keeping it simple

Another part of our orientation is this: we believe in keeping things simple whenever possible. There are sound psychological, legal, and physiological reasons for this when it comes to life-threatening encounters—before, during, and after.

That doesn't mean we've tried to oversimplify issues, honest. Some of the matters touched upon in this book are complicated, and while we've tried to boil them down, the simple truth is that anything involving law or human behavior isn't simple. We've tried to strike a balance here.

What a permit changes

Even before you decide whether or not to take training and apply for a carry permit, you should understand what it does and doesn't change.

Legally speaking, it changes one thing and one thing only: *a carry permit allows you to carry a handgun in public in some situations where it would otherwise be unlawful to do so.*

Period.

It doesn't change the law of self-defense—in or out of the home. It doesn't change whether or not you're allowed to own firearms—although people who aren't lawfully entitled to possess firearms aren't eligible for permits, nor are all persons who may legally possess a firearm certain of getting a permit to carry. It doesn't change the laws involved in keeping handguns at home, or at your place of business.

Let's look at it in a tabular format. (It's not quite as simple as this, granted, but it's a close approximation.)

Rights	Non permit holders	Permit Holders
Owning firearms	Yes	Yes
Carrying loaded/unloaded firearms at home	Yes	Yes
Carrying loaded/unloaded firearms at place of business	Yes	Yes
Carrying firearms, unloaded, in a case, in the trunk of the car	Yes	Yes
Use of lethal force in self-defense	Yes	Yes
Performing citizen's arrest	Yes	Yes
Carrying a firearm in most public places	**No**	**Yes**
Carrying a loaded firearm in the passenger compartment of a car	No	Yes
Carrying firearms into schools	No	No
Acting as a police officer	No	No

The important thing to note is that the *only* significant thing a permit changes is the right to carry a handgun in public.

It's not a "junior G-man badge."

It doesn't change — one way or another — the legal right people have to defend themselves under Minnesota law.

To repeat, the *only* important thing it changes, legally, is the right to carry a firearm in public.

Period.

Of course, it's not quite as simple as that. If it was, you wouldn't need to read on.

And remember: a gun never solves problems.

CHAPTER 1
Why Would Anybody Want a Carry Permit?

Across the United States, millions of people in more than forty-five states have handgun carry permits.

The reasons vary as much as the people do.

Some have them because they need to be able to carry a firearm in order to protect other people or other people's money: bank guards, for example. Some people have permits in order to protect their own money. Many permit holders are small business owners who want to protect both their bank deposits and themselves during the sometimes-harrowing trip to the bank at the end of the day. In rural areas, in many states, some people have carry permits because it enables them to lawfully keep their rifles or shotguns in the passenger compartment of the car or truck, rather than locked in the trunk.

But most people who have carry permits have them for personal protection.

Some are worried about a specific threat, such as a stalker or an abusive ex-spouse. Others are in risky jobs, such as convenience store clerks, pizza delivery drivers, and cab drivers. Others have them without any specific worry — but just as insurance.

People who carry guns lawfully are far less likely to be assaulted or murdered than people who don't.[4]

We emphasize *carry*. Most permit holders will go through their entire lives without taking their handgun out except to put it on or put it away, other than at the shooting range. Very few will ever have to produce it to deter or stop an attack, and of those who do, very few will actually have to fire a shot.

Many people who have carry permits don't regularly carry a handgun in public.

That's understandable.

One of the few universal truths about a handgun is that it never, ever gets lighter as the day goes by and is utterly useless — or worse than useless — in every kind of ordinary situation. A Swiss Army knife, for example, is a tool that can be used to open envelopes and wine bottles, trim fingernails, tighten and loosen screws, or remove splinters. A handgun is useful only in a life-threatening situation, and not even all of those. The rest of the time, it's nothing more than a pound or more of metal to carry around.

The burden of carrying a handgun isn't just the problem of hauling a hunk of metal around. It's also necessary, both for moral and liability reasons, to keep the handgun under control, whether on the body or secured somewhere. If, say, the weight of a Palm Pilot in the shirt pocket becomes annoying as the workday goes on, it's reasonable just to put it in the drawer of the desk. If it gets stolen, that's certainly annoying, but it's not dangerous.

It's obviously very different for, say, a revolver left on a desk.

There are other issues. While Minnesota law doesn't make it unlawful for a permit holder to carry a handgun openly, most permit holders keep their handgun concealed — and we think that's a good thing.

Exposing the handgun can not only startle people, but can also result in the police being summoned to a "man with a gun" call — and that can be not only annoying, but potentially dangerous. You could even lose your permit because of it.

The problems don't stop there.

People carrying handguns have to worry about forgetting that they're doing it and unintentionally violating the law about where a

---

[4] A good web site on personal risk assessment is *www.rateyourrisk.org*, which gives an online scored test compiled by Captain Ken Pence of the Nashville Police Department, based on known risk factors. We recommend that you take this test regularly, and note that your risk score drops *dramatically* if you answer that you lawfully carry a handgun.

handgun can be carried. While it may be forbidden to, say, take a pair of nail scissors or a pocket knife through the security checkpoint at an airport, somebody who forgets he has one of those items really doesn't have anything to worry about beyond losing it. A permit holder who forgets that he or she has a handgun—either on the person or in a briefcase—*will* be arrested. In Minnesota, a permit holder going to pick up his or her children at school has to remember to secure the handgun in the car if it's necessary to go in the building.

"I forgot" isn't a legal defense.[5]

Even ordinary social situations can become difficult at times.

Take drinking, for example. While we certainly recommend against drinking and driving, most normal-sized adults can have several drinks over the course of a social evening and still be able to drive lawfully. The legal limit for blood alcohol content (BAC, as it's called) while driving is .08. For people who carry a handgun, it is half that (.04), and exceeding that limit is a crime.

It is best to refrain from consuming alcohol while carrying a handgun. And, if you are taking medication that alters your behavior or judgment, you probably shouldn't carry a handgun at the same time.

All in all, a lot of the time, carrying a handgun in public is an annoyance, an inconvenience, and just a plain nuisance.

So why would any reasonable person ever want to?

That's easy: it's simply because, on those rare occasions when a handgun is necessary in self-defense, there's no good substitute.

Less violent means—like pepper spray, or stun guns—require letting an assailant get very close, and often don't work. Karate and other self-defense training are fine in theory but, in practice, most martial arts are useful in real life only for the most proficient and healthy people. Improvised weapons—car keys, a heavy flashlight, The Club™—work much better in theory than in practice, as well.

Statistically, the single most effective way to deter or stop a determined assailant is to produce a handgun and be willing to use it if necessary—although most of the time it won't be necessary to actually fire it. While it's a very bad idea to produce a handgun if you're not lawfully entitled and willing to use it, the surveys of Gary Kleck of the University of Florida, probably the most prominent academic studying these issues, show that a tiny percentage of defensive gun uses (DGUs) result in the victim shooting the assailant.

---

[5] Neither is, "oops!"

More generally, there's the overall crime issue. Enough people taking out permits lowers violent crime rates. John Lott's repeated studies have shown that one of the few things that can reliably drive down violent crime rates is the issuance of carry permits.

How this happens isn't quite clear. Those states, like Minnesota, with progressive carry laws, don't seem to see an increased rate of shootings, even justified ones.[6] Since most successful self-defensive handgun uses don't involve shooting at all, and are not reliably reported, it's hard to argue that that's the cause.

Besides, the decrease in violent crime rates typically seriously outstrips even the number of eligible citizens who have taken out carry permits — generally about 2-4% — much less those permit holders who carry regularly.

Research by criminologists confirms that what's happening is that criminals are responding to information about their own risk.[7] The fact that there may be armed citizens present — either as the criminal's would-be victim or as bystanders — persuades some criminals, some of the time, to make different choices because of their increased perception of risk to themselves. In all of Minnesota, there are around two thousand police officers on duty at any given time, most of them in uniform. Having to worry about 100,000 lawfully armed civilians increases a violent criminal's chance of a bad result by *50 times*. The mugger may decide that either moving away or switching to breaking into unoccupied cars is less risky. The abusive ex-spouse may worry more about the possibility of being shot while trying to beat up his ex than he does of the consequences of violating an Order for Protection.

Still, regardless of *why* "shall-issue" laws lower violent crime, the important point is that they *do*.

Beyond this, we come to a more controversial matter. We think that permit issuance is a good thing for society in general, and not only because of its effect on violent crime, but also just for ordinary civility.

---

[6] As the experience of the more than thirty-five "shall-issue" states has shown, all the talk about "blood on the streets," "fender-benders turning into shootouts" and "turning [our state] into Dodge City" has turned out to be the real-life equivalent of Chicken Little crying, "the sky is falling!"

[7] We promise not to drown you in references and statistics in this book, but this one is important. *Armed and Dangerous*, by James D. Write and Peter H. Rossi (Aldine de Gruyter: New York; ISBN 0-202-30331-4), was the result of a study of over 2,000 convicted felons. Of these, two-thirds admitted having been "scared off, shot at, wounded, or captured by an armed victim," and two-fifths of them had decided not to commit a crime because they knew or believed that their intended victim was armed.

As Robert A. Heinlein wrote, "an armed society is a polite society." Granted, Heinlein was writing about fictional societies. Still, in real life, incidents of permit holders so much as brandishing a firearm because somebody has been verbally rude or abusive are just this side of imposs-ible to find, but it's possible that the *fear* of such things has caused some loud and rude people to behave better in public.[8]

No permit holder should ever do anything to encourage that fear, but it's possible that the anti-reform groups, like Sarah Brady's remarka-bly well-financed The Brady Center to Prevent Gun Violence, may have unwittingly ended up making for a politer Minnesota by scaring some ill-mannered, boorish people into behaving better. Permit holders, by and large, help to raise the average level of civility. As you'll see, if you're carrying a handgun, you must take more — not fewer — precautions to avoid confrontations that could escalate.

Getting a carry permit because of a safety concern

It is at least theoretically possible to get a Minnesota carry permit is-sued within hours because of an immediate threat.

It makes much more sense to get a carry permit in advance of a per-sonal safety problem, keep it current, and then make day-to-day deci-sions should a threatening situation appear.

This will be discussed in more detail in a later chapter, but it's im-portant to note that, while carrying a handgun may be an important part of personal protection in such circumstances, it is *never* the only part of it. Those people who have specific personal safety concerns — a stalker, a physically abusive ex, a criminal one may be testifying against in court — should consult both the local police and other safety and legal profes-sionals as to what else needs to be done. An Order for Protection (OFP) or the equivalent order for stalkers is not terribly difficult to get. While it is, in one sense, just a piece of paper, it's a piece of paper that can be very useful in dealing with both the police, if summoned, or in helping to es-tablish the elements of self-defense, should it become necessary.

The most important thing in personal safety under stressful situa-tions is constant personal awareness.

---

[8] Again, to be clear: we're *not* advocating either showing or threatening to show a handgun in order to quiet down a rude or obnoxious person—and, in fact, we *very strongly* advise against doing that. It's not only morally wrong, but it's a dangerous thing to do—and it's a quick ticket to jail, as it should be.

Why somebody would not want to have a carry permit

It's simply a fact that the majority of eligible adults don't—and won't—get carry permits. We've gone into some of the reasons already, but they're hardly the only ones. There are both good reasons and bad reasons why somebody would not want to take out a carry permit, or even own a firearm for self-defense at all.

Some bad reasons:

"My gun might be taken away and used against me"

That's a very serious problem—for police officers. 14% of police officers who are killed are shot with their own firearms. Police have very different exposure to that sort of threat than citizens do. They carry their firearms openly—something that's generally a bad idea for citizen permit holders. And they frequently come into close contact with criminals, often needing to fight with them in order to subdue and arrest them, in the enforcement of the general criminal law. That, as you'll see, is also something you shouldn't do, as someone who is not a licensed peace officer.

That said, the notion of citizens drawing guns in self-defense and having their own gun turned on them is an urban myth. It happens on TV shows a lot—but in real life, a search of Lexis/Nexis reports *no* incidents of that happening. This is understandable: when an assailant is confronted by a firearm, he almost always flees.

Realistically, it's a non-issue.

"There are all those accidental gun deaths"

Every accidental fatality, no matter what the cause, is tragic. But, realistically, firearms accidents are among the *least* common causes of accidental fatalities in the United States. The National Safety Council, a nonpartisan organization, consistently reports fewer than a thousand accidental firearms deaths per year—about a fourth as many as accidental drownings, and about the same number as deaths from falling out of bed. Over the twenty years that the NSC has been measuring causes of accidental death, gun accidents have been an almost invisible cause, and the number has dropped, despite the enormous increase in both the population and the number of guns owned in the United States. Most firearm accidents in the United States are hunting accidents, but the number is consistently dropping due to youth hunter safety courses. It's not a good idea to take gun safety casually—quite the opposite—but if you make a habit of always following the basic rules of firearms safety, your chances of accidentally or negligently injuring—much less killing—yourself or somebody else are zero.

Safety is no accident.

"Guns are used in suicide more than in self-defense"

Well, no, they're not.

Gary Kleck, the foremost academic researcher on the subject, has done studies that show there are roughly 2.5 million gun defense uses every year. (Most of those, as we do keep repeating, involve either showing a firearm or referring to one; few involve actual shooting.) There are roughly 16,000 suicides in the US each year involving a firearm. The experience in both Canada and the United Kingdom shows that when handguns become effectively unavailable, the overall suicide rate is unchanged. People who would have chosen to commit suicide with a fire arm simply substitute other means, like jumping off a building, hanging, taking pills, or ramming a car into a wall.

"Guns are a lousy way to settle personal disputes"

Yes. That's *absolutely* correct.

They're not just a lousy way, they're an *illegal* way to settle any kind of dispute. The only proper reason to point a gun at another human being is because of an imminent threat of death or serious bodily harm. Using guns to settle heated arguments with family, neighbors, or strangers—no matter how serious the arguments are—isn't just unlawful, but it's also rare, at least among permit holders.

Of the millions of permit holders across the nation, it's almost impossible to find one who has used a firearm—even by brandishing it—in such an irresponsible way. And there have been, to date, no cases, anywhere, of a permit holder *lawfully carrying a handgun under a permit* being convicted of murder.

Not one.

Beyond the bad reasons

Probably the main reason most eligible people don't get carry permits is that it's just not something they think about. While we have no opinion as to whether or not you should get a carry permit, we do think it is worth thinking about, no matter which way you decide.

Beyond that, some people believe they're incapable of controlling their temper and would be foolish to provide themselves easy access to a tool that can do a lot of damage in one uncontrolled moment. We think they're making a good choice, all in all. However, a search of newspaper reports has been unable to find a single incident of a permit holder lawfully carrying a handgun who has shot somebody in such a moment.

The same is true for those who have reason to doubt their own mental stability, even if it hasn't reached the point where they've been committed. The myth of the deranged permit holder shooting down innocent bystanders is anti-gun propaganda and nothing more—it just plain hasn't happened. Let's keep it that way.

Still, a carry permit isn't right for everybody.

Is it right for you?

We *can't* decide that for you. What we can say is that qualifying for and getting a carry permit does give you some options that you wouldn't otherwise have. While neither the training nor the recommended equipment are free, they're not terribly expensive, and—and this is the key point—they give you a choice.

Some personal safety problems come about unexpectedly. If, say, you find that you're being stalked, or if muggings outside your place of work become a problem, carrying a handgun may, for you, be a sound part of your personal protection strategy. If you wait until a problem situation arises, it could take up to three months to get a permit.

If you make it a point to complete the training and apply for a carry permit in advance, you'll be able to decide whether or not to carry on a day-to-day basis.

Our recommendation is to read about it, think about it, and do a little soul searching. If you think it might be right for you, take a good training course from the AACFI or other organization whose accreditation must be honored. After that, you might consider applying for a carry permit. But remember that a carry permit makes it lawful for you to carry a firearm in public; it doesn't make it obligatory.

It's up to you.

And remember: a gun never solves problems.

CHAPTER 2
Staying Out of Trouble

Probably the most important thing for a permit holder, or anybody else, to do is to stay out of trouble in the first place.

The advantages of this are obvious: a violent confrontation that you avoid won't get you injured, or killed, or prosecuted, or sued. Many people who have survived lethal confrontations — even without being injured themselves — suffer from all sorts of psychological damage: depression, anxiety, Post-Traumatic Stress Disorder, etc.

On television, the effects are usually understated or solved just before the last commercial. That's fine in fiction, but that's not the way it works in real life.

Even when lethal violence is utterly justified — legally, morally, and practically — it has strong, important, and lasting consequences. While the television myth of the deranged veteran is about as accurate as much television entertainment is (not very), it does point to a real thing: violence, even when entirely legal and state-sanctioned, has negative effects on everybody involved. Those who defend themselves against violent attack are still victims — they are just "victims of a different type".

Bob — not his real name — shot and killed a robber in his store twenty years ago. The Grand Jury returned a "no bill." They said there wasn't any reason to believe that he might be guilty of a crime. While he was sued by the robber's family, his insurance company settled.

Twenty years later, he still takes drugs for depression and anxiety.

Joel Rosenberg, one of the authors of this book, went through a much less traumatic handgun self-defense incident against robbers in his own home just over a decade ago. No shots were fired, and neither Rosenberg, nor his family, nor the robbers were injured — but it was many months before he could sleep through the night, and he and his family subsequently moved. The house just didn't feel safe after that.

The short form is this: being involved in a situation where lethal force is used — even justifiably — is an awful thing, and going to some trouble to avoid it is a good idea for everybody, particularly those who choose to carry handguns in public.

Your Options

In any threatening situation, you will have a maximum of four options. Each option has its benefits and risks, and the specific situation may determine which options are available. Maintaining alertness allows you to keep all options available.

Your first option is to leave. When a situation makes you uncomfortable, the best thing to do might be to leave before any trouble starts. Should you find yourself in *Condition Orange* (discussed below), it's time to make your exit.

Your second option is to do nothing. You may choose to remain in a situation and go with the flow, electing not to take any defensive action at all, and hope that the situation does not escalate to the point where defensive action is required. You may also decide to take cover or hide in some fashion.

Your third option is to act defensively using less than lethal force. Your defensive action may be anything from issuing a verbal command to be left alone, to actions that might be categorized as an assault — striking or shoving an assailant to facilitate your escape, for example.

Your fourth option is to use lethal force. For our purposes, this begins with the threat of lethal force (e.g., brandishing), but most certainly includes firing a handgun or using any other type of force that could cause death or great bodily harm.

Certainly, your goal should be to escape with having to use force, lethal or otherwise. Your ability to do so will largely depend on your level of alertness to your environment. The earlier you recognize a dangerous situation, the greater your opportunity to exercise your first option and leave.

Alertness

The key to avoiding problems is maintaining a reasonable level of alertness, particularly while in public. This is particularly true for avoiding street crimes like mugging, assault, robbery, and rape. Being alert has two advantages: it helps you avoid trouble, and appearing to be alert helps to persuade trouble to avoid you. Generally speaking, criminals are opportunists. As trainer Clint Smith puts it, "If you look like prey, you will be eaten."

Many years ago, Colonel Jeff Cooper developed a simple color code for one's level of alertness, dividing it into Conditions White, Yellow, Orange, and Red.

In *Condition White*, you're unaware of your surroundings and any possible threat. That's a perfectly reasonable state to be in when you're at home with the doors locked. The ultimate example of Condition White is when you're asleep — it would take some serious effort to gain your attention. There's nothing wrong with Condition White; it's a perfectly appropriate level of awareness in safe circumstances.

Condition Yellow is the next step up. It's not paranoia, or even worry, but a deliberate awareness of your surroundings. In Condition Yellow, you make it a habit to pay attention to what's going on around you. You're calm, relaxed, and not concerned about an immediate threat, but looking for things out of the ordinary. When you're waiting at a bus stop, you watch the folks around you, rather than burying yourself in a newspaper or a book. When you're driving, you make it a habit to look in the rear-view mirror and notice if you're being followed. It's not a matter of making major changes in how you live your life; it's a matter of being constantly aware of what's going on around you.

It's possible — and a good idea — to make a habit of keeping your attention level in Condition Yellow whenever you're out in public. And it's not just a matter of personal safety — although awareness is the key to that. Life is just more interesting when you're paying attention to what's going on around you.

Condition Orange is the next step up. Instead of just being aware, you're *concerned* — there's a possible problem. It may be something you're consciously aware of — say, somebody approaching you in an otherwise empty parking lot late at night. Or it may be just a feeling: something's wrong.

Don't ignore these feelings. Human beings are complicated creatures, and feeling that there's a problem could easily be the result of something you noticed subconsciously. Or it could be nothing; it could be something you ate. So you pay even more attention. Condition Orange is the time to figure out what the problem could be, and how to handle it if there is one. Perhaps you're concerned about the person who just got on the elevator you were waiting for—it's not like he's brandishing a knife; you just have a bad feeling. So, you just take the next elevator. Condition Orange isn't a time to panic. It's a time to take reasonable steps to make sure that you don't have to go to the next step: Condition Red.

If you find yourself in Condition Orange, consider exiting and reevaluating the situation. Find a safe place and assess what is happening and whether professionals (i.e., the police) need to be called. Colonel Cooper devised this situational awareness scheme from a military training tool. As citizens, we fortunately have additional options.

Condition Red is a condition we sincerely hope you never find yourself in. You're under attack, and you have to protect yourself, whether it's by defending yourself with anything you have on hand, running away, calling for help—or all of the above at the same time.

We'll get into some of the physiological and psychological implications of Condition Red later on. For the time being, let's just leave it that the best time to figure out how to handle a problem is before it happens, because you're likely to be thinking more clearly, more able to make a plan and act on it, and because it gives you time to avoid the problem if at all possible.

Avoiding conflict

"Alternative Means of Conflict Resolution" can be looked at as a fancy way of saying, "Don't escalate an argument into a fight." It's probably a good idea to cultivate a thick skin in any case, but it gets even more important if you're carrying a handgun.

Consider an ordinary stressful situation: a fender-bender. Some idiot has just backed into you, doing serious damage to your car. You're understandably angry, and the other person is even angrier, although perhaps less understandably so.

The temptation is to leap out of the car and go shout at the idiot. It's an understandable temptation, but *don't*. If he or she is angry and starts shouting at you, you'll find the temptation to shout back almost irresistible—but let it be *almost* irresistible. Just keep calm, stay aware, and make sure that the police have been summoned.

Note that this is good advice for everybody, but it's even more important for permit holders. "Road Rage" shootings by permit holders is another one of those urban myths, and you don't want to be accused of being the first one.

That doesn't mean, of course, that you shouldn't immediately be in Condition Orange. You should be. You should be constantly evaluating the situation: Is the idiot just blowing off steam by shouting and swearing, or does he intend to attack you? Can you calm him down with words, or is it safer just to let him shout for awhile? Will holding up your cell phone and saying, "Let's wait until the police get here — they're on their way," calm him down, or do you need to throw your car into reverse and drive off to get away?[9] Even if, say, he takes a tire iron out of his trunk and starts to approach you, you're much better off backing away than trying to dissuade him by drawing a gun (even if your car is already damaged, you can probably back away faster than he can run).

Let's assume that you do it differently: you leap out of the car, and idiot leaps out of the car, words turn to blows, and it gets to the point where you honestly, truly, reasonably believe that he's going to kill you as he stands over you, prepared to stomp or bash you to death.

You draw your handgun...

Congratulations. With good luck, he'll back down, and you'll both be arrested.

You'll both be charged with assault, and you'll be charged with "intentionally pointing a gun at a human being" under Minnesota Statute 609.66, Subdivision 1. If you're very lucky, your attorney will be able to persuade the prosecutor or the jury that every single one of the elements of self-defense was there, at every moment.

Good luck.

On the other hand, your attorney may point out to you that you weren't a "reluctant participant"[10] in the fight, and that you're guilty, and try to work out a plea bargain with the prosecutor, which will almost certainly leave you without a handgun permit, and definitely leave you

---

[9] However, you must consider that it is your obligation to stay at the scene of the accident and to trade identification information and insurance information; leaving the scene can lead to concerns of "hit and run." On the other hand, if your choice is to run away from a threat, even at the risk of being accused of "hit and run," or letting it escalate into a situation where you need to produce your handgun, you're probably better off running away and *immediately* calling the police for assistance.

[10] This is a legal term, which we'll get to on page 37. For the time being, just take our word for it that if you voluntarily get into a fight, you're in serious legal trouble if you end it by threatening somebody with a gun, and in even more trouble if you actually shoot him.

with a conviction on your record.

Or consider another scenario. You're in a shopping center with your children, and you accidentally bump into a woman who begins shouting expletives at you, using a whole scad of four-letter words.

You could yell back. You could ask her, more or less politely, to watch her language in front of your children, and just maybe she'd immediately realize the error of her ways and apologize, after which you would then apologize for having bumped into her in the first place, and you'd both go merrily on your way.

Care to bet thousands of dollars and at least a night in jail that that's the way it would go?

So don't. Just take your children and walk away.

Beyond being aware of what's going on around you, staying out of avoidable trouble is, fundamentally, a simple, three-step approach:

1. Be nice. If you have to have an unpleasant argument with somebody, do it over the phone.
2. If others aren't being nice, ignore them if you can.
3. If others aren't being nice, and you can't ignore them, leave.

Avoid the conflict, and avoid the consequences

It's really that simple.

And remember: a gun never solves problems.

CHAPTER 3
Lethal Force, in Law and Practice

First of all, relax. You're not going to be buried with a lot of legal jargon in this chapter. That said, when it comes to the lawful use of force, there's just no way around getting into some of the nitty-gritty of the legalities, and we have to deal with those.

Please understand, though, that you're not getting "legal advice" here. While this book was written with the help of some very experienced attorneys, the author is not an attorney and, even if he were, he couldn't give you legal advice without knowing a lot more about you and your specific situation.

The law is never simple. Even when principles are clear and well-developed, the exact facts of each situation (at every moment, even as they change) can cause the legal answer to vary as tiny changes occur. This book discusses principles. Only your own legal counsel, armed with specifics of the law and the facts of your own situation, can give you "legal advice" that you can depend on.

Another thing you'll notice is that in the court cases cited, most of the people accused and convicted were, all in all, pretty bad and stupid people, as were the deceased. Most—not by any means all—criminal prosecutions involve such folks. Most ordinary, law-abiding citizens, with or without carry permits, manage to go through their whole lives without ending up in a criminal court either as a defendant or as somebody testifying against an assailant.

If you do your best to stay out of trouble and are fortunate enough to succeed, you'll never need to know the law about the use of lethal force.

So why bother?

Well, for one thing, learning the law about the use of lethal force is required to get a carry permit in Minnesota. More importantly, you can control your behavior, of course — but not your luck.

Justification

As we've said, the possession of a carry permit doesn't change Minnesota law about the use of force, one way or another.

Under Minnesota law, self-defense is a "justification" defense. In effect, by claiming self-defense in the use of force, you're saying that you did something that is normally illegal, but isn't in this case because your behavior met each and every one of a whole list of criteria.

Pleading "justification" requires the defendant to admit the violation of a statute while simultaneously claiming that the magnitude of the harm avoided by the violation outweighs the harm the statute seeks to prevent. Therefore, the otherwise criminal act was justified in this particular instance, and the defendant is not guilty of the crime.

In simple terms, *lethal* force (that which may cause death or great bodily harm) may be used against another person to repel that other person's use or threatened use of *lethal* force against the victim (and thereby neutralize the threat of death or great bodily harm to the victim). There is a proportionality aspect to any claim that the use of force is justified. This limitation rests on the common law principle that the amount of force used must bear a reasonable relation to the magnitude of the harm sought to be avoided.

Minnesota court decisions further develop this proportionality theme with *express rules* in regard to (1) defense of person, (2) defense of a dwelling or premises, or (3) defense of property. In each situation, the law identifies threats of harm which may justify the use of physical force and expressly identifies the more serious threats justifying the use of lethal force. For example, the actual *use* of lethal force (e.g., discharging a firearm at another person) is justified only where the degree of threatened injury is equally severe. *Remember this principle!* The law carefully specifies the threats which are of sufficient magnitude to excuse the use of lethal force.

Self-Defense

Minnesota Statute 609.06 authorizes the use of *non-lethal* or "reasonable force" as follows:

609.06 AUTHORIZED USE OF FORCE.

Subdivision 1. **When authorized.** Except as otherwise provided in subdivision 2, reasonable force may be used upon or toward the person of another without the other's consent when the following circumstances exist or the actor reasonably believes them to exist:

* * *

(3) when used by any person in resisting or aiding another to resist an offense against the person; * * *.

For our purposes, the key phrase is the last one: "when used by any person in resisting or aiding another to resist an offense against the person." You can use *reasonable* force to "resist an offense" — to protect yourself against someone trying to commit a crime against your person, for example. In Minnesota, force may not be used to resist an offense against only property.[11]

Minnesota Statute 609.065 specifically restricts the use of *lethal* or "deadly force."

609.065 JUSTIFIABLE TAKING OF LIFE.

The intentional taking of the life of another is not authorized by section 609.06, except when necessary in resisting or preventing an offense which the actor reasonably believes exposes the actor or another to great bodily harm or death, or preventing the commission of a felony in the actor's place of abode.

The use of deadly force is further restricted by subdivision 2 of Minnesota Statute 609.06.

Subdivision 2. **Deadly force used against peace officers.** Deadly force may not be used against peace officers who have announced their presence and are performing official duties at a location where a person is committing a crime or an act that would be a crime if committed by an adult.

---

[11] A dual-effect crime, targeting both your person and your property, is treated as the more serious threat; that is, to your person.

Section 609.065 adopts rules for justified taking of life that are similar to those which most states apply to the actual *use* of deadly force, irrespective of the outcome. Minnesota law[12] is consistent with Model Penal Code section 3.11(2) and a majority of states in defining "deadly force" to mean:

> force that the actor uses with the purpose of causing or that he knows to create a substantial risk of causing death or [great] bodily injury. Purposely firing a firearm in the direction of another person or at a vehicle in which another person is believed to be constitutes deadly force. A threat to cause death or [great] bodily injury, by the production of a weapon or otherwise, so long as the actor's purpose is limited to creating the apprehension that he will use deadly force if necessary [i.e., authorized by law], does not constitute deadly force.

Therefore, *only* if the firearm is discharged and a death ensues, do the more restrictive "deadly force" rules of Minnesota Statute 609.065 apply. In other situations, the "reasonable force" rules contained in Minnesota Statute 609.06 provide the sole criteria governing the authorized use of force.

With regard to the use of *deadly* force in resisting an offense, the injury threatened must be of death or great bodily harm (e.g., exposing the victim to an unacceptably high risk of death). This law limits your authorization to use deadly force. Let's repeat that rule: **with regard to the use of deadly force in defense of person, the injury threatened must be of death or great bodily harm**. Memorize this statement.

Self-defense reflects a *conscious* decision on your part to *intentionally* use force, "reasonable" (non-deadly) or deadly, to neutralize a threat. If you shoot by accident, you have no defense; if you shoot by reflex, you have no defense; and if you "didn't intend to shoot," you have no defense.

Thus, there are strict prerequisites for the lawful use of force in self-defense, and *all* of these prerequisites must be present *all* of the time that you're using force.

The first three are the same regarding all situations in which "rea-

---

[12] See also Minnesota Statute 609.066 adopting this definition for police use of deadly force. This is consistent with Minnesota case law applying Statute 609.065, which speaks in terms of "intentional taking of life" (one possible result) rather than in terms of using deadly force (the deliberate act).

sonable" protective force is authorized. Criteria four is variable. It spells out the circumstances under which the deliberate use of "deadly" force as the level of force is seen as the proportional response to a threat.

1. **Nonaggressor.** *You are not the aggressor in the situation.* The situation must be occasioned or developed through no fault of the actor. You can't start—or escalate—a confrontation, and then claim to be acting in self-defense. If you are the "initial" aggressor—if you started the argument that ended up in a situation where you used lethal force—you must have tried to withdraw from the confrontation *and* communicated it to the other person.
    Somebody unwillingly involved in a violent confrontation is often referred to as a "reluctant participant," which nicely describes it.

2. **Imminent threat.** *You must reasonably believe the threat is imminent.* "Imminent" does not mean immediate or instantaneous, but rather that an action is pending.

3. **Danger of death or great bodily harm.** *You reasonably believe that the threat presents a danger of sufficient magnitude to justify the use of deadly force.*

4. **Necessary.** *You reasonably decide that the use of force is necessary to avoid or prevent a threat to yourself or a third person.* If you can solve the problem by less violent means, you must. Minnesota case law requires that, if safe and practical, you must retreat rather that use deadly force. You've got to reasonably believe that the force you use is necessary, as an emergency measure.

All four of these factors must be present in order to lawfully use, or threaten to use, *deadly* force in defense of a person.

Think of your right to use deadly force in self-defense as a chain that you're desperately trying to hang on to, as you're dangling over a prison cell that (obviously) you don't want to fall into. The chain has exactly four links. If any *one* of those links is missing—or if, at any time, any one of them breaks—your right to use or threaten lethal force ends at that very moment, and if you continue, you fall.

There are three preliminary matters you need to understand before we review the major criteria.

1. *You have the burden of "injecting" the legal issue of self-defense into the case.* The defendant, usually through his or her lawyer, has the burden of going forward with evidence to support a claim that the use of protective force was justified. A trial judge's deci-

sion to deny a requested self-defense instruction will not be reversed on appeal absent an abuse of discretion.[13]

2. *You must reasonably believe that every element of the justification defense existed at the time protective force was employed.* This means not only that you (1) actually believed the element of defense existed (e.g., the object in the assailant's hand was a gun) *but also that* (2) you were reasonable in so believing (e.g., the object was silver and was held and pointed in the same manner in which a gun would be handled). The standard is "reasonable belief" — a matter of perception, not fact (e.g., that the silver object turns out to be a cell phone is not relevant).

3. *The ultimate burden of proof never shifts to the defendant.* This means if there is any evidence to support self-defense, the prosecution must prove beyond a reasonable doubt that the use of deadly force was *not* justified.

The key word is "reasonable," which is an external, *objective* standard. It is what a hypothetical reasonable person in your situation would believe. Honesty and sincerity are not sufficient; you also must be reasonable in your belief, or you're committing a crime if you use physical force in self-defense.

That doesn't sound scary, but it should.

In a legal context, whether or not something is "reasonable" isn't a matter of opinion; it's a matter of fact. Matters of fact are determined by a "trier of fact" — usually a jury, and a jury may not only disagree with you, but can also get it wrong. If the prosecutor has any doubt that your belief was "reasonable," he can put you in front of a jury and let your lawyer try to persuade them.

A "reasonable belief" is an objective test. Everyone in the legal process (arresting officer, detectives, prosecutors, juries, and judges) gets to "second guess" whether or not you were reasonable in believing that a particular factual element existed.

---

[13] But a defendant is entitled to a self-defense instruction to the jury if there is any evidence to support each element of the defense theory. In evaluating the evidence, it must be viewed in the light most favorable to the party requesting the instruction, State v. Edwards, 717 N.W.2d 405, 410 (Minn. 2006).

Situation one: defense of person

Let's take these criteria one at a time in the legal context of defense of person.

Non-aggressor / reluctant participant

The classic example of a reluctant participant in a violent confrontation is a mugging victim. You're minding your own business, walking down the street, and somebody shoves you up against the wall and brandishes a knife. Forgetting, for just a moment, what the best way of handling that confrontation is — although we'll return to it — you are, in law and in fact, a reluctant participant. You weren't looking for a confrontation, and have not taken any action that would indicate otherwise.

Compare that to, say, a stereotypical loud bar confrontation.[14] Somebody says something offensive to you. You respond with harsh words, and words turn to pushing and shoving, which turns to him pulling a knife and you pulling a gun.

Neither the police nor the courts are going to think of you as somebody who isn't the aggressor. Who started it? Well, that depends on what the meaning of "it" is, so to speak. Was the other fellow the aggressor when he first made an off-color comment? Is the first person to resort to physical force the aggressor? Or is the aggressor the first person to resort to physical force that could cause "great bodily harm"?

Is this the sort of thing you'd like discussed in court — at your expense, with no guarantee that it'll go your way, with the certainty of conviction and the likelihood of prison time if it doesn't? Judges call this situation "mutual combat." Neither party can claim self-defense here.

It is very unlikely to go your way. After all, you've voluntarily engaged in this confrontation and, while it's escalated far beyond what you've wanted or intended, you haven't tried to avoid it. You're not a reluctant participant and you're in legal trouble, even if the person who pulled the knife backs down.

And if he doesn't, it's worse — for both of you.

Minnesota case law provides that if an aggressor withdraws from the quarrel or conflict and communicates that withdrawal, expressly or impliedly, the right of self-defense is restored.

If, in the example above, when he shoves you, instead of shoving

---

[14] We strongly recommend against getting involved in loud arguments in bars, whether or not anybody's armed. Alcohol and loud arguments don't mix.

back, you raise your hands and say, "I don't want any trouble," and then back away, you've demonstrated that you're trying to avoid a conflict, that you are a "reluctant participant."

It's not just a legal thing, either. You're trying to stay out of trouble, because you'd much rather avoid a fight than win it. Remember that deadly force is a final, unavoidable option to be used only when there is no other choice left.

If you turn to the bartender and say, loudly enough for everybody in the bar to hear, "I'm going to leave now; could you get him to stay here, please?" you've made a further demonstration that, not only are you not looking for trouble, you're actively trying to avoid it, even at the cost of inconvenience, embarrassment, and even humiliation. As required—by statute, case law, and good sense—you've "indicated to the other person your desire" to end the encounter, and made it abundantly clear to the witnesses, as well.

Odds are, you'll be able to get away without having to show a gun. Yes, it will be annoying and embarrassing, and perhaps even humiliating—but that's all it will be; live with it.

Still, if he comes chasing after you after that, then you are, demonstrably, a reluctant participant. You've tried to avoid trouble, and in fact have gone to some effort to get out of the confrontation. You've also created witnesses who can attest to your desire to end the confrontation, which you can use in court if necessary.

And that's, as we keep repeating, the key to both avoiding the necessity of lethal force, and avoiding committing a crime if you can't avoid the necessity. Desperately avoid violent confrontations. If it's necessary to get involved in an angry argument—and sometimes it can be—just do it over the phone, with everybody out of sight and out of reach of each other.

This isn't just a matter of rights. If, for example, you've taken out a valid Order for Protection against your ex-spouse, and you see him walking toward you down the street, legally speaking, it's the ex-spouse and not you who has the legal obligation to cross the street and move away. After all, the court has told him to stay away from you, not the other way around.

So cross the street yourself, anyway.

This has two benefits: it lowers the chances of there being an immediate confrontation and, should one be unavoidable, it helps to demonstrate that you've gone to some trouble to avoid it.

If you're going to be involved in a violent confrontation—and we hope you aren't—do it only as a reluctant participant.

Reasonable belief that there is an imminent threat of harm

The threat must be imminent. "I'm going to go home and get my shotgun and come back to kill you," may be a serious threat. It should be taken seriously. But it's not an *imminent* threat. You have time to call the police, and should do so.

Kevin Jamison describes the concept in these words:

> "It is ...an elastic term 'involving a period of time dependent on the circumstances, rather than a fixed point of time implicit in the concept of immediate or instantaneous.' *** 'Imminent' does not mean immediate or instantaneous, but that an action is pending [or that a course of conduct has commenced]. Thus a subject may pose an imminent danger even if he is not at that very moment pointing a weapon at the actor. The threat cannot be speculative or at a time allowing for some non-hazardous action. However, if an assailant is attempting to grab a weapon, perhaps by grappling with the actor, that qualifies as a pending threat. If a subject is running away from the actor, that would normally preclude use of force. [But] if the subject is running towards cover for a tactical advantage, that is a pending threat."

Reasonable belief that the threatened danger is of sufficient magnitude to justify using deadly force

Probably the most important area for establishing a self-defense claim, the threat criteria, vary by the category of self-defense claimed. In a defense-of-person situation, the Minnesota statute specifies only one type of threat that is serious enough to justify the *actual use* of lethal force. Minnesota statute 609.065 identifies a single threat against which deadly force may be used—"death or great bodily harm."

Unlike some other states, the Minnesota statute does not go on to identify specific crimes that are so often accompanied by an unreasonable risk of death or great bodily harm that the statute presumes it always exists. In other states, such crimes include murder, voluntary manslaughter, rape, robbery, burglary, arson, kidnapping, aggravated battery, and aggravated sodomy. The commonsense implication of this is that the authors of those laws acknowledged that robbery—having property taken from you through violence or the threat of violence—may be, in and of itself, an unspoken threat of great bodily harm. Many robberies, after all, do result in death or great bodily harm, although it is not an inevitable accompaniment of that crime. The authors of those laws intended to place no further burden of proof on the victim than the fact of armed or violent robbery, burglary, or assault as justification for using lethal force in self-defense. In those states, lethal force can be used to defend against arson, for example, even if the victim does not have a separate fear of death or great bodily harm. In Minnesota, the victim can only use lethal defensive force if she testifies to having *a separate* and reasonable fear of death or great bodily harm.

So, let's concentrate on the primary basis for a successful self-defense claim — "death or great bodily harm."

Under Minnesota law,

> 'great bodily harm' means bodily injury which creates a high probability of death, or which causes serious permanent disfigurement, or which causes a permanent or protracted loss or impairment of the function of any bodily member or organ or other serious bodily harm.

Definitions of lesser forms of harm are:

> 'Substantial bodily harm' means bodily injury which involves temporary but substantial disfigurement, or which causes a temporary but substantial loss or impairment of the function of any bodily member or organ or which causes a fracture of any bodily member.

> 'Bodily harm' means physical pain or injury, illness, or any impairment of physical condition.

Notice that the listed non-deadly injuries are determined by the ultimate result (after the event and months in the hospital), not the threat. Luckily, Minnesota courts seem to ignore this "glitch" in the self-defense context.

But, was your situation that serious? The trier of fact decides (ultimately the *jury*, but in fact the police, prosecutors, judge and everyone in the criminal justice system). Needless to say, if they can decide, they can decide wrongly.

Is a broken spine "great bodily harm"? Sure. The loss of a limb? Of course. A beating? A broken arm? A concussion? Maybe, or maybe not — how bad is the beating? Does it cause permanent disfigurement? A protracted loss or impairment?

It's easy to create obvious cases. If you're surrounded by a pack of

Cub Scouts who are threatening to punch you in the thigh, that obviously doesn't qualify. But, if you're surrounded by a pack of St. Louis Athens Park Bloods who are threatening to stomp you to death, that obviously does.

Anywhere in between? It's up to the jury.

The law uses the "reasonable person" test, which is mostly simple common sense. Would a reasonable person, knowing what you knew at the time, be afraid of getting killed or badly hurt right then and there?

Even though it's common sense, it's still something to worry about. Would a *jury*—a bunch of people who weren't there and have only heard evidence in the cool, quiet, safe environment of a courtroom—think that you were in danger of "death or great bodily harm"?[15]

It's best not to find out in the first place.

The threat must be of deadly injury—death or great bodily harm. Fear of being embarrassed or humiliated does not qualify. You're not entitled to use lethal force over words, no matter how offensive the words are. Words only help to justify the use of lethal force when they indicate an imminent action.

And make a note of the "great bodily harm" part. You can't use lethal force to stop somebody from hitting you with a pillow, say. You can't use lethal force to stop lesser bodily harm—bruises and abrasions, for example. You can only use lethal force to prevent death or "great bodily harm"—injuries that make it likely that you'll die, be seriously and permanently disfigured, or crippled for life or at least a long time.

Let's take a couple of examples.

You may well resent somebody throwing a snowball at your car, and even be afraid of the damage that it might do to your windshield, or worried that it might cause you to lose control of the car. But it's hard to argue that a reasonable person would think, even if there are some rocks in it, that a snowball thrown at your car is going to kill you or injure you seriously.

A twelve-year-old boy threatening to throw a punch at a healthy adult is unlikely to kill or seriously injure, even if he connects. Put a machete in his hand and it's a different matter. If you're a healthy, two-hundred pound man, it's not reasonable to think that a punch from a one-hundred-pound woman would kill you or cause great bodily harm, but it's entirely possible that a one-hundred-pound woman could be

---

[15] This lack of tactical appreciation by the trier of fact is why successful self-defense claims are usually buttressed by competent expert testimony.

afraid of being badly hurt or killed by even an unarmed attack by a man twice her size.

This *doesn't* mean that you have to let someone beat you up before you are authorized to use or threaten lethal force. It does mean that, if you do use lethal force, you have to be able to convince a jury that a person in your situation might reasonably believe that he or she was in danger of death or great bodily harm.

Weapons aren't necessary. An assailant doesn't have to have as much as a nail file to be able to kill his victim. According to the US Department of Justice, only 1/3 of violent crimes involved the assailant using a weapon. But that's an important factor, and juries and courts look at all the factors, both alone and together.

Relative size, age, physical impairments, nastiness or multiple attackers are relevant factors.

An important principle of the law is that the perpetrator of a criminal act is required to take the victim as he finds him.

If, say, you're a hemophiliac or have a serious heart condition, it may be reasonable to fear that a single blow might kill you, and it's not legally necessary that your assailant know this in advance—that's his problem. If you're confined to a wheelchair, an immediate threat to dump you into the street in front of a passing car could easily cause a reasonable person in your situation to fear death or great bodily harm.

And what you *reasonably* believe to be true—at the time—is what counts. You don't have X-ray vision and, as a reluctant participant, you're not required to take the assailant as he is, but as he reasonably appears to be, to you, at that time. If it turns out that the machete that the apparent maniac is trying to hack you to death with is really just a toy sword, you're not required to have known that, nor do you need to know that Crazy Bob just likes to scare people with his chainsaw, but never really hurts anybody.

The issue is how a reasonable person in the *same* circumstances (all of them) would perceive the situation, not what the reality is.

Retreat is not practical

Again, common sense prevails. If you can solve the problem by retreating, you should. Close the elevator door; walk—or run or drive—away.

You should retreat only if it's *practical and safe*. You're not required to back away from one attacking gang member into the arms, or knife, of another. You are not required to turn your back on an assailant in the hope that you can outrun a healthy 18 year-old thug. You're not obligated to run away from a knife-wielding assailant and leave your child behind to face his knife, nor are you required to believe the carjacker who says he only wants your car and will see that the infant in the car seat is safely returned later on. As with using lesser force, you have to seriously consider retreat, if only to reasonably and instantly dismiss it as impractical, and you (in practice, you'll probably do it through your lawyer) must be able to explain *why* retreat appeared impractical.

Retreat is *not* cooperation with an assailant. If somebody attempts to force you into a car, you're not obligated to consider that going along with him is retreat. You have every reason to believe that you're being forced into the car to be taken to what the police call a "secondary crime scene," and it would be foolish to go along.[16]

Use of deadly force is necessary

This is actually one of the simpler concepts. If you can handle a threat by some lesser means than lethal force, you're required to. Again, the reasonable person test applies: if all you have to do to avoid the machete-wielding madman is, say, to shut the door in his face or step on the car's accelerator, you're not entitled to use or threaten to use deadly force.

You *are* obligated to consider alternatives, even if only to dismiss them instantly as being insufficient.

And this also means that once you've used enough force to stop the attack, you must *immediately stop* using force. After the "threat is neutralized" (as police witnesses always testify) — the attack is stopped — any force you use is retaliation, not self-defense, and the law does not permit retaliation.

In one case in Minnesota, both the appeals court and apparently the jury were not overly impressed with the accused who claimed self-defense, having stabbed one supposed assailant six times and then shooting him in the back of the head, and stabbing another of his assailants nineteen times, and then breaking her skull with the butt of a rifle.[17]

---

[16] As a simple rule: don't *ever* go to a secondary crime scene. As bad as the present threat may be, it's going to be worse when your assailant controls every aspect of the situation. As one police officer put it, "the secondary crime scene is where we usually find a dead body."

[17] We're not overly impressed, either.

It is, of course, possible that six or nineteen stabs from a knife—or as many shots from a handgun[18]—may not be sufficient to stop a determined assailant. But when it is sufficient—not in theory, but in the actual situation—then the attack has ended, and so does the right to use force in self-defense.

We'll come back to this issue later, but imagine a situation where the hypothetical person standing around the corner hears you shout, "Don't move! Don't move! Drop your weapon! Drop your weapon!" followed by a flurry of bang-bang-bang-bang!, a thirty-second pause, and then another bang! Police, the prosecutors, and a jury might find it quite possible to believe that those first four shots were what were necessary to stop the assailant, decide that the fifth one was excessive, and determine that—regardless of whether or not you were justified up to that point— that final shot was murder, not self-defense.

What was happening during that thirty seconds? If you were fighting with your assailant for the gun, that's one thing and another reason, if appropriate, to keep shouting "Don't move! Don't move! Drop your weapon! Drop your weapon!" If you were standing over him as he lay on the pavement, waiting to see if he'd move and then deciding to give him one final shot, that's another thing.

Situation two: defense of dwelling

While the changes in the Minnesota laws about carry permits haven't changed anything at all about possession of firearms in the home, or the laws surrounding self-defense in the home, we would be neglectful if we didn't mention that there are lesser hurdles for the use of lethal force in the home.

You can't kill somebody just because they're in your home. You can't kill somebody just because they're trespassing in your home. Really.

But there is a different standard for self-defense in the home, which in Minnesota legal terminology is called "defense of dwelling."

First, it's not necessary to fear "death or great bodily harm." What's required, instead, is to reasonably believe that the use of force is necessary to prevent a felony from being committed in the home. But note the

---

[18] The authors know of police cases in which 13 or even 33 handgun shots (out of multiple magazines) were insufficient to neutralize the threat. The "extra" shot was needed to save the officer's life.

word "felony."

Burglary can be a felony, but it may not be. Burglary of a *dwelling* is a felony. Second-degree burglary is committed by entering a dwelling without permission and with intent to commit any crime[19] therein, either directly or as an accomplice. If the dwelling is occupied, the crime is first-degree burglary. Minnesota Statute 609.581 broadly defines "dwelling" to mean a building used as a permanent or temporary residence.

You have to infer the *intent* of the intruder from all the facts and circumstances. The refrigerator repairman rarely (never!) comes in at 4am without knocking on the door, so a midnight intruder is presumably up to no good. Any crime will do but, once again, the test is *reasonable* perception on your part.

Someone trespassing[20] in your home may be innocent of anything other than a mistake. The stranger in the bathroom or the hallway could be your teenage daughter's boyfriend, who she let in without mentioning it. The man who entered your unlocked front door[21] and is standing in your darkened living room might be an Alzheimer's patient who got lost and is confused, or he could be a drunken former occupant of the home who has forgotten where he lives. Someone running in through your front door could be fleeing from an attacker.

If the felony has already been committed and the burglar is attempting to flee, it's *not* lawful to use lethal force to prevent his escape or to apprehend him for the crime. (It's also a stupid thing to do. Let him go.)

The biggest difference, in practice, between self-defense and "defense of dwelling" is that the legal obligation to retreat is absent. You're not legally required to retreat, even if it is practical, when you are inside your own home.

This isn't, however, a hunting license for burglars: all other obligations remain the same, particularly the "reasonable person" test. If there's any doubt in the prosecutor's mind, he can test whether or not your fear or use of force was "reasonable" by putting you in front of a

---

[19] "Crime" means another felony, gross misdemeanor or misdemeanor, but *not* a petty misdemeanor.

[20] Actually, in the examples we give, the person isn't even trespassing in a legal sense. In Minnesota, what turns what we ordinarily think of as "trespassing" into a misdemeanor is the refusal to leave if told to do so, not coming in in the first place. In none of the examples we give has the "trespasser" been told to leave.

[21] No, it shouldn't have been unlocked. But do you always lock your doors? You should, but do you? "Defense of dwelling" isn't a license to shoot trespassers in general, or even burglars. It is, in effect, an alternative defense that your lawyer can use when you shoot someone in your home in self-defense.

judge and jury, with your liberty at risk.

In State v. Carothers, cited as 594 N.W.2d 897 (Minn.,1999), the Minnesota Supreme Court summed it up this way:

> A duty to retreat does not attach to defense of dwelling claims. So long as a person claiming defense of dwelling meets all [our emphasis] of the criteria for making his or her claim—that the killing was done in the belief that it was necessary to prevent the commission of a felony in the dwelling, that the person's judgment as to the gravity of the situation was reasonable under the circumstances, and that the person's election to defend his or her dwelling was such as a reasonable person would have made in light of the danger to be apprehended—the person need not have attempted to retreat from his or her home.

Note that the court used the word "reasonable" repeatedly. If you've been charged with a crime, a jury gets to decide what's reasonable, and they might not agree with you.

See State v. McCuiston, 514 N.W.2d 802 (Minn. App., 1994). McCuiston, a small black man, was being threatened by a drunk, six-foot-tall white neighbor. He retreated to his home—which demonstrated that he was a reluctant participant—sent his son upstairs, and locked the door. He retrieved his shotgun when he heard the neighbor trying to kick his door in, and shouted for his neighbors to call the police. When his attacker tried to force his way into the house, McCuiston shot him, killing him.

At the trial, he described the final moments this way:

> A. Then Mr. Fontaine [the victim]—I said—I told him—I tried to bluff him, I said, 'The police on their way, man. You better go home.' He said, 'Fuck the police and fuck you black motherfuckers and get the fuck out of my way.' And, when he said that, he came at me with both hands.
>
> Q. Did you feel threatened at this point?
>
> A. Yes, sir.
>
> Q. Okay. Exactly how did you feel when you saw Mr. Fontaine coming at you?
>
> A. I had a decision to make. I wasn't about to be no statistic or my child's life wasn't going to be put in danger. I had a decision to

make. Either let him in my house for coffee and doughnuts or keep him from coming in.

At trial, the judge refused to instruct the jury on "defense of dwelling." Despite what appears to the authors to be a pretty clear case of a person being reasonably in fear of being badly hurt or killed, the jury didn't agree. They convicted him of second degree felony murder, and he appealed.

The Court of Appeals court seemed unhappy with the law as it is:

> "... the notion that a person may kill to prevent a felony inside the home may exceed what most people would think permissible under the law. But it is not our role to debate the wisdom or parameters of the statutory language. McCuiston was entitled to an instruction on the use of deadly force to prevent the commission of a felony in his home."

But it is still the law. McQuiston won his appeal. Or look at State v. Pendleton, 567 N.W.2d 265 (Minn.,1997). The Minnesota Supreme Court summed up the case this way:

> In December 1994, the defendant Akeem Pendleton and his fiance Lorraine Wilson were living with Wilson's children in a duplex in Minneapolis. On December 10, a Saturday, at about 5:00 p.m., Wilson's cousin Tony Caine came to the apartment to visit. When Caine arrived, Pendleton let him in. Also present in the apartment were Doug Buckanaga, a friend of Pendleton's from work, and Buckanaga's girlfriend, Angela Bellanger. Pendleton, Buckanaga and Bellanger were socializing in the kitchen while Pendleton prepared a meal. Caine and Wilson were talking to each other at the dining room table.
>
> Wilson testified that she had been having conflicts with her family over various issues, including her relationship with Pendleton and her family's expectation of financial and other support from her. Earlier on the day of the crime, she had asked Caine not to come to her home anymore. On the evening in question, she and Caine were arguing about these problems, as well as Wilson's complaints that Caine took money from her and used her telephone. She described their argument as becoming heated. She eventually got up from the table and went into the bathroom.
>
> At that point, Caine went into the kitchen looking for Pendleton.

According to Buckanaga's testimony, Caine made a comment to Pendleton about his needing to keep his fiance in line and shoved Pendleton. Caine then punched Pendleton in the face a couple of times causing Pendleton to bleed beneath his eye. Pendleton started to fight back, but Buckanaga interfered and pulled Pendleton away. At the time Caine started hitting him, Pendleton had a knife in his hand, which he had been using in his cooking. Buckanaga took this knife away and set it down. Pendleton then went into the bathroom to clean the blood off his face.

According to testimony at the trial, Pendleton came out of the bathroom and asked Caine to leave. By this time, they were both standing in the front room, as were Buckanaga and Wilson. Caine refused to leave the apartment and tried to hit Pendleton again. Pendleton jumped up and grabbed a shotgun out of the ceiling tiles. As Pendleton was taking the gun out of its case, he kept telling Caine to leave. Caine rushed at Pendleton, they struggled with the gun, and Pendleton shot Caine in the shoulder. The struggle continued until Pendleton wriggled free, ran, and drove away with Buckanaga and Bellanger in Buckanaga's truck.

Pendleton and his fiance Wilson both testified that when Caine lunged at Pendleton in the front room, Caine had a knife in his hand. Buckanaga, who was standing in the same room, testified that he never saw Caine with a knife, although he did say that immediately before Caine lunged at Pendleton, Caine was standing with his hand behind his back. The police did find a knife at the scene, but did not seize it, so it was never tested for fingerprints. In his testimony, Caine denied attacking Pendleton and claimed instead that Pendleton had started the fighting.

At trial, Pendleton argued that he acted in self defense because Caine lunged at him with a knife. In the alternative, he argued that he acted to prevent the commission of a felony, either second- or third-degree assault, in his home[22]....

The important point here is in the court's footnote: while both second-and third-degree assault are felonies, neither involves "great bo-

---

[22] Second-degree assault is assault with a dangerous weapon, Minn. Stat. 609.222 (1996), and third degree assault is assault resulting in substantial bodily harm, Minn. Stat. 609.223 (1996). Great bodily harm is more permanent than substantial bodily harm, Minn. Stat. 609.02, subds. 7a & 8 (1996).

dily harm." Pendleton was convicted, and appealed; the Appeals Court upheld the conviction, but the Minnesota Supreme Court reversed it. The court wrote (the emphasis here is ours):

> ...it is clear that one does **not** have to fear great bodily harm or death to justify the use of deadly force to defend against the commission of a felony in one's home....a defendant asserting "defense of dwelling" is **not** required to show that he or she feared death or great bodily harm to justify the use of deadly force in preventing the commission of a felony in the defendant's place of abode.

In both law and practice, the requirements for the use of lethal force in self-defense are lower in the home than outside — but somebody using lethal force in the home is still very much in danger of having to persuade a jury that his decision was reasonable, as the court put it, with the real possibility that the jury might disagree.

The sad but real truth is that, in most cases of serious violence, the victim and the assailant know each other — usually well. A huge proportion of violent attacks are between spouses or domestic partners, with men and women being the victim and perpetrator just about half the time. It's important to note that the right to self-defense and the lack of an obligation to retreat in the home also apply when both the assailant and victim live there. "Defense of dwelling" doesn't apply only to intruders.

In State v. Glowacki, 630 N.W.2d 392 (Minn., 2001), the Minnesota Supreme Court again ruled that a person does not have a duty to retreat in his own home. In this case, during an altercation with his girlfriend that she, according to Glowacki, had started, he "kicked her, placed his hands around her throat, and threatened to kill her."

At Glowacki's trial, the judge had instructed the jury that Glowacki had a duty to retreat, to leave the room, or even the house, rather than defend himself.

Glowacki was convicted, and the case was appealed, eventually landing in the Minnesota Supreme Court. The Supreme Court ruled that the trial judge had been wrong, that Glowacki didn't have any obligation to retreat in his own home.

This didn't help Glowacki, though.

The Supreme Court ruled that, while he didn't have a duty to retreat, and the judge had been wrong, it also ruled that the force he used was unreasonable under the circumstances, and that the wrong instruction by the judge was a "harmless error." The jury had convicted Glowacki of fifth-degree domestic assault, fifth-degree assault, and disorderly conduct, and the convictions and sentence stood. Force—whether with a handgun, a baseball bat, or bare hands—is not the way to settle domestic disputes.

In practical terms, self-defense in the home, as elsewhere, should be avoided if at all possible. Think of it as labeled "use only if necessary."

As mentioned previously, Joel Rosenberg was forced to deal with intruders in his home one night. While under Minnesota law, Rosenberg would have been legally permitted to go chasing off into the rest of the house after them and threatening lethal force to prevent theft (the intruders were, at the very least, committing burglary, a forcible felony, and it was reasonable for him to arrive at that conclusion under the circumstances), it would have been foolish to do so, and he was right not to have.

Once the burglars had retreated down the stairs, and Rosenberg knew his wife and daughter were safe, actually using deadly force might have been considered "retaliation" rather than "self-defense." That's when a jury of his peers (who were not there) gets to second-guess his decision later and determine if it was "reasonable."

"Defense of dwelling" is a legal defense; that doesn't make it a good idea.

Rosenberg's family was safe, and chasing the perpetrators would have been stupid.

There are tactics for what is called "clearing" a house—going from room to room to make sure that there are no intruders there, and dealing with the threat if they are—but these are advanced issues that require lengthy and careful training, and they're always risky.

Even then, Clint Smith, a nationally known trainer and proprietor of Thunder Ranch, a well-known training center, says, "The more you know about tactics, the less you'll want to use them."

The best and simplest procedure in the case of a home invasion is to retreat with your family to a relatively safe location, call 911, and wait there for rescue to arrive, following the 911 operator's instructions to the letter. The *only* time that you should even *consider* confronting the invaders is if you must do so to see to the safety of a family member.

That exception aside, if it's necessary to "clear" the house to be sure the intruders have left, let the police do it. They've got the training and the body armor, and it's their job.

Situation three: defense of property

Unlike some other states, only *reasonable force* (such as the display of a handgun) is authorized in Minnesota in response to the fear of losing property or damage to it. In the words of Minnesota Statute 609.06:

> 609.06 **AUTHORIZED USE OF FORCE.**
>
> Subdivision 1. **When authorized.** Except as otherwise provided in subdivision 2, reasonable force may be used upon or toward the person of another without the other's consent when the following circumstances exist or the actor reasonably believes them to exist:
>
> * * *
>
> 4) when used by any person in lawful possession of real or personal property, or by another assisting the person in lawful possession, in resisting a trespass upon or other unlawful interference with [e.g., theft] such property;... .

A threat *solely* to property *never* justifies the actual use of deadly force. If a thief insists on taking your property, you cannot stop him by discharging a firearm. You have to let him go. And file a police report.

When the right to use lethal force ends

As we've said, the requirements for using lethal force in self-defense should be thought of as a chain. If any one of the links is missing or breaks, the chain no longer works, and the use of lethal force must end, even if all the requirements were met up until that moment.

If the prosecution can show that even one is missing, the use of lethal force isn't self-defense anymore, and you're guilty of a crime.

Remember that chain? Again: if one link breaks, it's useless.

The obvious case in which the right to use lethal force ends is when the assailant either shows that he's chosen to stop attacking, or is unable to continue the attack. No matter how scared and adrenalized you are, if the reason to fear immediate death or great bodily harm ends, so does the right to use force to prevent that. Pursuit and apprehension is the function of the police.

"Citizen's arrest" is another justification defense that we'll talk about in the next chapter. In short, if your assailant chooses to run away, get a good physical description and call the police but, above all, let him get away from you.

The right to use lethal force must be present at every moment that lethal force is used or threatened

This is one of the more difficult concepts. A court looks not just at the whole incident in context, but at *each* time segment in isolation. If you fail any test at any time, you're guilty.

Consider a hypothetical attempted knifing. You're walking down the street, minding your own business, and somebody you didn't notice leaps out of an alley and comes at you with a knife, screaming that he's going to kill you.

So far, so good—to the extent that an attack can be "good." You're a reluctant participant. You're reasonably in fear that he'll kill you. Nothing short of deadly force will stop him; he's running faster than you can, and you've every reason fear that if you try to run away backward, not only will he catch you, but you could easily fall, leaving you even more vulnerable. Retreat is not a sensible option.

Shouting, "Don't move! Don't move! Drop your weapon! Drop your weapon!" you draw your pistol and fire one shot to his center of mass. But he keeps coming, still attacking, so you—still entitled to use deadly force—keep shooting.

Your second shot doesn't stop him, but your third shot, in this hypothetical scenario, hits him in the kneecap, and he falls to the ground three feet away from you. Now he's crawling toward you, knife in hand, still apparently intent on knifing you, perhaps even saying so.

Can you continue to shoot?

Absolutely *not*.

It is no longer "necessary" to use lethal force to avoid or prevent great bodily harm to yourself. Less lethal options have opened up. Your moral obligation (also a legal requirement in most states) to choose alternate means of defense, if practical, has never gone away. It wasn't practical up until this moment, as he was running at you, and turning your back or running backward would have been foolhardy. Now, even though he still intends to kill you, and nothing less than lethal force can stop him if you stay there, you do have the ability, in complete safety, to take three steps to the side and out of danger.

You don't have to like it.

You just have to *do* it.

What isn't required

Appearances can be deceiving, but that's your assailant's problem, fortunately. You're not required to know what the truth is; you can act on your perceptions if a reasonable person in your situation (with those perceptions) would have reasonably believed they faced a deadly threat. In fact, technically, it doesn't matter what the reality is, but what it appears to be to a reasonable person in your position.

You're not required to know that the assailant has just changed his mind and is now trying to run past you, or that the third shot you fired is going to cause him to collapse in the next half second. A reluctant participant, as mentioned above, isn't required to have X-ray vision, or to actually have been harmed in order to justify the use of lethal force. In fact, the issue of *actual* harm — real or potential — is not relevant. What justifies the use of lethal force is the reasonable belief (fear) that you are about to suffer death or great bodily harm.

Even in the example of a hemophiliac, somebody who has been struck is not entitled to use lethal force if the assailant appears to be breaking off the attack. If the threat ends — no matter what damage has already been done — so does the justification for using lethal force in self-defense. Lethal force isn't allowed in retaliation for an injury.

It's not necessary to have actually been physically harmed in order to be reasonably in fear of death or great bodily harm; the threat suffices to authorize defensive action.[23] The threat must be imminent, but "imminent" is a term with flexibility in it.

The assailant who has, for example, dropped his handgun on the floor but is lunging for it so he can continue the attack is making a credible threat. So is the one who has momentarily turned his back without breaking off the attack; there is no legal requirement as to which direction an assailant must be facing.

Further, there is no specific space limitation. You are not required to wait until an assailant actually comes into close enough proximity to cause harm — it's the imminent *threat* that justifies the use of lethal force. It's a standard part of both police and advanced self-defense training to demonstrate — using mock guns and a rubber knife — what is called the "Tueller Drill." This drill is named after a former Utah Deputy Sheriff, Dennis Tueller, who would regularly demonstrate that, even with advance warning, a healthy assailant with a knife in hand is regularly able

---

[23] Thus both the defendant and the trier of fact may consider what the defendant knew of the aggressor's violent nature, reputation for violence, customary carry of weapons, etc.

to reach and strike even an alert victim if he begins within twenty-one feet.

Demonstrating the Tueller Drill—with a rubber knife and a toy gun[24]—is a useful thing to try. Have a friend take up a "low-ready" position with a toy gun. (A low-ready position is where he's holding it with both hands, with his finger off the trigger, and with the barrel pointed generally down and to the front.) Pace off twenty-one feet, rubber knife in hand. The moment you start moving—but not before—your friends will try to shoot you with the toy gun before you touch him or her with the rubber knife. [25]

Few, if any, will be able to do it.

Imminent doesn't necessarily mean "within reach."

You are also not required to stop *until* the threat has stopped. As we'll discuss in a subsequent chapter, a single shot may not stop the attack, and the reasonableness of continuing to shoot doesn't end until the assailant either demonstrates that he's decided to stop attacking or is observably unable to. [26]

If you are entitled to use deadly force, you are entitled to do so until the threat stops, no matter how many shots it takes.

Defending others

You have no duty to intervene in a situation involving a third party unless you have a protective relation with that person (such as parent-child).

The rules for defense of another are *identical* to those for defense of yourself.

In State v. Granroth, 200 N.W.2d 397, 399 (Minn. 1972), the Minnesota Supreme Court held that "justification for homicide in defense of another parallels defense of self." That is the majority position in America. Criminal law scholar Wayne R. LaFave puts it this way: "so long as the defender [actually and] reasonably believes that the other is being

---

[24] *Don't* use real firearms for this sort of thing, even if you're absolutely sure they're unloaded. *Please* use a toy gun. If you want to make the Tueller Drill more exciting, you can use paintball guns and full paintball safety equipment. That's probably not necessary—as it is, the Tueller Drill is very persuasive.

[25] Twenty-one feet is not a bright line. A successful attack could be threatened from a greater distance depending on the circumstances.

[26] If you do continue to shoot after either of these two things happens, you're committing a crime. Don't do that.

unlawfully attacked, he is justified in using reasonable force, including deadly force if necessary, to defend [that person]." The problem arises in properly (reasonably) perceiving the facts when you are not involved in the action.

What if the person you think is the victim is actually the original aggressor? For example, say you witness two people rolling out of a doorway, fighting.

You have no way of knowing how the fight started, and who—if either—is a reluctant participant, and you have no right to make an assumption that because one is black and the other white, one is a man and the other is a woman, one is well-dressed and the other scruffy-looking, that one person is a reluctant participant and the other isn't. The scruffy-looking one may be an undercover police officer attempting to subdue a suspect. For that matter, for all you know, the scruffy-looking one may be a police officer using unjustified force on somebody who hasn't done anything wrong at all.

How can you know who is the "initial aggressor" and who is the victim? You can't. If the person you think is the victim isn't—if you're wrong—he or she doesn't have the right of self-defense, and you're going to have to be able to persuade the jury that your mistake was one that any reasonable person would have made.

Lots of luck.

Police have to get involved in such things—it's part of their job. Permit holders are not police officers.

You do, however, have the right to whip out your cell phone and dial 911. Do that instead.

Defensive "brandishing" and reasonable force

"Brandishing" may be defined as a threat to cause death or serious bodily harm by the production of a weapon or otherwise, so long as the actor's purpose is limited to creating an apprehension that he will use deadly force *only* if necessary. See Model Penal Code sec. 3.11. It does not involve the actual discharge of a firearm, for example. Nor does it constitute the "use" of deadly force.

In Minnesota, brandishing is governed by the rules for use of *reasonable* force set forth in Minnesota Statute 609.06 (see page 223). This is the usual American rule. As criminal law scholar Wayne R. LaFave says,

"merely to threaten death or serious bodily harm, without any intention to carry out the threat [unless necessary], is not to _use_ deadly force, so that one may be justified in pointing a gun at his attacker when he would not be justified in pulling the trigger."

This is a common example of the necessity criteria in action prohibiting greater force when lesser force will do. If the assailant continues the attack, the _use_ of deadly force (i.e., firing the gun) will be necessary and, therefore authorized. An imminent threat is often not instantaneous. If the threat (even of death or great bodily injury) can be neutralized by a mere counter threat, that is certainly allowable if safe for the defender, even if never mandatory. 98% of successful defensive gun uses involve mere brandishing. The defender demonstrates that she is capable of using deadly force, and the encounter ends as the assailant flees. Even criminals can weight the odds of their _own_ injury.

Although seldom heard of by the public except in homicide cases, justification defenses like self-defense apply to all crimes. Thus, self-defense may be pleaded if, as a consequence of a brandishing incident, you are charged with assault[27] in the second degree (a felony), with intentionally pointing a gun at or toward another person (a misdemeanor) or with reckless handling or using a gun so as to endanger the safety of another (a misdemeanor).

The aftermath

Even assuming that you are entirely on sound legal and moral grounds after having shot somebody, your troubles aren't over. You've got to deal with the aftermath of it all, and it's going to be pretty stressful, even at best. And that's the subject of the next chapter.

And remember: a gun never solves problems.

---

[27] Minnesota statute 609.09, subdivision 10 defines "assault" as:
(1) an act done with intent to cause fear in another of immediate bodily harm or death; or
(2) the intentional infliction of or attempt to inflict bodily harm upon another.

CHAPTER 4
Lethal Force and its Aftermath

If the law about how limited the right to use lethal force is hasn't frightened you yet, read on.

Lethal force in real life doesn't work the same way as it does on television and in the movies. Somebody who is shot isn't thrown backwards several feet, or even several inches. Bullets don't go precisely where the shooter wants them, even under the best of circumstances, and even when they do hit their target, a single handgun bullet often doesn't stop somebody.

And, most importantly, the use of lethal force may — and should — end the immediate threat, but it doesn't end the problem.

Again, we refer to the introduction: *a handgun does not solve problems, ever.*

The aftermath of even a justified self-defense shooting can be dangerous, both in terms of physical risk, and very serious dangers of both criminal prosecution and the threat of a civil lawsuit. It's vital that you understand all that before you even think about carrying a handgun in public.

Anybody who is seriously considering getting a carry permit should also consider developing a relationship with a good criminal lawyer, as a form of insurance. The odds of you actually having to make an urgent call to your lawyer are small, but in the unlikely event that you need to either threaten or use lethal force, you will need the services of an attorney. Having a number or business card in your wallet is just plain sensible.

That's not just true in the unlikely event that you find yourself standing, firearm in hand, over the dead body of an assailant—it's also true if you have to take out your handgun and successfully *deter* an attack. Doing that, we hope, will solve the immediate problem of being beaten, raped, or killed.

But...

Threat of force—is it enough?

We hope so.

But that doesn't mean that it solves all of your problems.

While you should never take out a handgun in a situation where you are unwilling to use it if necessary, statistics show that the vast majority of armed confrontations do end without a shot being fired, much less an injury or fatality. The most detailed research on this subject has been performed by Gary Kleck of the Florida State University School of Criminology and Criminal Justice, who estimates that roughly 2.5 million defensive handgun uses occur every year. Even if every one of the 100,000 domestic gunshot injuries of all sorts every year were the result of defensive gun uses (and, of course, they're not—most are the result of criminal activity), that would mean that fewer than five percent of armed confrontations result in somebody being injured.

In practice, the vast majority of the time, should you actually draw or display a gun, that action will end the immediate confrontation. Your assailant will, in the vast majority of instances, either surrender or, more likely, flee.[28] No shots will be fired.

Both possibilities, as well as the possibility of having to actually fire a shot, must be addressed. We'll get to them shortly. But before that, let's talk about what you say, as well as what you do.

Talking yourself into trouble

From the moment you begin to act in self-defense, you have to protect yourself not only from the immediate consequences of being the vic-

---

[28] It's happened twice to one of the co-authors of this book. To you, the victim, the assailant's flight *is* a successful defensive gun use.

tim of a violent crime, but from the legal system as well, and everything that you say and do is of vital importance.

From that moment, you're no longer a citizen.

You're a suspect. You can be a smart suspect, or a stupid one; it's your choice.

Attempting to stop an assailant by saying something out of the movies is yet another way to cause yourself trouble. Clint Eastwood's Dirty Harry character can say, "Go ahead; make my day," when attempting to persuade somebody not to attack him. He's both a police officer, and fictional, and the scriptwriter will keep him out of trouble. You're neither fictional nor a police officer, and you can't depend on a scriptwriter.

The general rule is to not only assume, but to *hope*, that anything you say can and will be repeated later, and repeated accurately, whether by witnesses that you can see, or ones out of sight.

So keep it short and simple; make it easy for witnesses to get it right. The longer the sentence is, the more likely it can be misheard, misunderstood, and misinterpreted.

Sentences should be kept short, and repeated, loudly. **"Don't move! Don't move! Drop your weapon! Drop your weapon!"**

Ideally, anything you say when confronted with an assailant is something you would *want* to be repeated later, even if it's overheard by somebody around the corner or next door.

Keep it loud, and simple, and hope that it's overheard.

Instead of, for example, "Go ahead; make my day," somebody attempting to deter an attack would be much better off shouting, "Don't move! Don't move! Drop your weapon! Drop your weapon!" If you shout that while holding a handgun, it's going to be understood to mean, "Don't attack me or I'll shoot you." Wanting to say that is understandable, but it could cause trouble later on. What if that hypothetical person standing around the corner misses the first part of the sentence and only hears, "...I'll shoot you"? Do you really want him saying to the police, "Gee, I don't remember exactly what he said, but it was something about shooting..."?

Keep it short, and repeat it. Loudly. Hope that people overhear it. Imagine there's a video camera trained on the scene, and you want it to record each and every thing you say and do.

Trying to be too clever is a mistake. To call for the police while asking the assailant to stop — "Police, stop!" — might be misconstrued by the assailant as a claim that you are a police officer (of course, you're not claiming that; you're merely attempting to summon a police officer while telling your assailant to stop attacking you). The combination of that and producing a handgun is likely, although not guaranteed, to deter him, but it's also likely to get you into trouble later.[29]

Do you want the hypothetical person around the corner saying that you claimed to be a police officer?

No.

So don't do that. Instead, shout "Don't move! Don't move! Drop your weapon! Drop your weapon!" And once the imminent threat is neutralized, "Somebody call 911! Somebody call 911!" and hope that any witnesses hear just what you've said.

Running into trouble

In the case of flight, as mentioned before, an assailant's decision to flee the scene ends the immediate threat and also ends the right to use or threaten lethal force in self-defense. (A retreat, as previously mentioned, is different from moving away from you to resume the attack—say, by retrieving a dropped weapon, or seeking cover or concealment to continue the attack.)

While the temptation to chase somebody might be understandable, don't do it. If you're unlucky enough to actually catch up with your assailant, you are no longer a "reluctant participant," and any use of lethal force will be treated as though it were an attack, not a defense. That breaks the "reluctant participant" chain of the self-defense argument.

Besides, remember that hypothetical person around the corner? Do you want him seeing you chasing your assailant? What if a police car pulls up just as your assailant rounds the corner, running away from you, and you have a drawn handgun? What's the police officer going to think? See the discussion of the physiological consequences of a lethal confrontation on page 66—what happens if you can't hear the officer's command to stop and drop your weapon?

It won't be good for you.

So don't chase him.

If your assailant flees, he's no longer an imminent threat, either. That breaks another link in the chain. A threat must be "right f...ing now" in order to justify lethal force. A fleeing assailant saying, "I'm going to

---

[29] And it's just as bad of an idea to shout, "Stop! In the name of love!" hoping that the criminal will think you were shouting "Stop! In the name of the law!" while the witnesses realize that you're only shouting out the lyrics to one of your favorite songs. Don't try to be clever.

come back and kill you," while it should be taken seriously, is not an *imminent* threat, no matter how seriously it may be meant or understood. Fleeing ends the present threat.[30]

It does not, however, end the implications of a confrontation.

One of three things will happen when you produce a handgun in a self-defense situation: your assailant will flee, he'll surrender, or he'll continue to attack.

Each of these is different, but each has much in common. Let's look at them one by one.

When the assailant flees

Again, *let him.*

More than that, *encourage him.* A fled assailant is the easiest situation to handle, and the one that's least likely to cause you serious danger or legal trouble.

You can encourage him to leave without saying something that you may not want repeated. Shout "Run away!" rather than "Run or I'll shoot you." Throw him your extra wallet (see *Appendix A*). If he keeps it, let him explain to the police later on how he came to have it, and why he fled the scene.

Don't place yourself between him and the nearest exit from the situation. If you happen to find yourself there, move aside and let him go. Again, this is the easiest situation for you to handle, and you owe it to yourself to make it as easy on you and your family as possible.

And that happens when he flees. (His flight is what triggers the deterrent effect of concealed-carry legislation. You just know that at the next meeting of the local Thugs & Muggers Club, he will tell his buddies that there are people out there who have guns!)

Still, you can't just consider it all over. You've threatened deadly force (you've likely pointed a gun at another human being) and both that person and any witnesses may tell the story very differently from how you do, or how it happened.

The temptation to just walk away — or run away — will be strong, but it's risky. What if your cry of "Drop your weapon! Drop your weapon!" drew the attention of somebody from a nearby house, and the only thing

---

[30] Unless the assailant is merely running away to gain tactical advantage; for example, cover or concealment from which to continue the fight, another weapon, or the assistance of an accomplice.

that somebody saw from a window was you pointing a gun at your assailant, just after he stopped and before he fled? Who threatened whom, from that observer's point of view? When he called 911, what do you think he said?

So you've got to take action. You've defended yourself from a life-threatening event, and now you've got to defend yourself from the legal system. This is particularly true if your local police department has the policy of "arresting the gun.[31]" If so, you're definitely going to be arrested, and it's a lot better for you if it happens without you fleeing, and with you having made a quick phone call to 911.

So immediately call 911 — "I've been attacked at Ninth and Elm. I successfully defended myself and the assailant has run away. The assailant was a tall, thin white man with black hair, a blue jean jacket, red plaid shirt and tan pants. He ran down Elm to the south. I'm safe now. My name is John Jones. My phone number is 888-444-3333. Is anyone coming to investigate this incident? ... If not, I'm going home now and you can call me later." Then immediately get off the phone and call your attorney, since you've had to produce your handgun, even though you've not fired a shot.

If there's going to be a police report — and the odds are there is going to be one — your attorney will make sure that all that you need to say, and nothing more, is on the record.

Naturally, common sense has to apply. When the police arrive, they should find you with your ID and permit in hand, and your gun holstered. Your story should be very short, and entirely factual: "A man attacked me; here's his description. I defended myself and he ran away, I'm very scared and upset, and (finally) I need to talk to my attorney."

Why? They'll ask. "You were the victim, right? All you have to do is talk to us. Let's just clear this up right away."

Don't start gabbing. You are in no condition to protect yourself from confusion in the investigation.

"**I need to talk to my attorney,**" is <u>all</u> you need to say at that point, although you may have to repeat it. And then, *you say nothing at all*, until you've talked to your attorney.

---

[31] While the gun will be seized and taken into evidence, that's not what it means to "arrest the gun." It means to arrest the person using a gun, no matter how obvious it is that it was self-defense. Police departments in both Minneapolis and St. Paul have this as a very real, if unwritten, policy.

When the assailant surrenders: citizen's arrest

Ideally, the assailant flees, and it's hard to recommend too strongly that you should let him, or even encourage him, to do just that. Let him explain why he fled. If he's never located (odds are, he'll go to some trouble to avoid being found), your attorney will have that fact to work with when talking to the prosecutor in an attempt to get your charges dismissed, if you've been charged.

That said, the assailant may surrender, forcing you to hold him for the police, perhaps at gunpoint.

Minn. Stat. 629.37 makes citizen's arrest possible:

> A private person may arrest another:
>
> (1) for a public offense committed or attempted in the arresting person's presence;
>
> (2) when the person arrested has committed a felony, although not in the arresting person's presence; or
>
> (3) when a felony has in fact been committed, and the arresting person has reasonable cause for believing the person arrested to have committed it.

The relevant statute is Minnesota Statute 609.06:

> "Except as otherwise provided in subdivision 2, reasonable force may be used. when the following circumstances exist or the actor reasonably believes them to exist ... when used by a person not a public officer in arresting another in the cases and in the manner provided by law and delivering the other to an officer competent to receive the other into custody."

If the assailant isn't convicted, there's a real chance of being sued for "false imprisonment" or some such thing, and the sorts of immunities that police have won't be applied to the likes of you and me.

Moreover, there's some real physical risk, and not just from the perpetrator. If the police roll in on a situation responding to a "man with a gun" call and see you holding a gun on somebody else, are you willing to bet your life that they'll see you as the "good guy"? Or, will they think that you're a robber, about to execute an innocent party?

Further, remember what we said in the introduction: a carry permit is not a "Junior G-man badge."

The most important principle remains: even a lawfully armed citizen is not a police officer and takes huge risks—legal and physical—when using or threatening force to arrest somebody.

Should an assailant stop attacking, your right to use or threaten lethal force has ended *at that moment*, and you must immediately summon the police to arrest the assailant—even if doing so permits the assailant to flee. Police are protected by both law and custom when they use and threaten force to make an arrest; citizens aren't.

Nor are citizens required to engage in all the other things police do, both in fiction and in reality, when they arrest somebody. It's not necessary to advise the surrendered assailant of his constitutional rights, nor is it necessary—or safe—to attempt to search him for other weapons or contraband. The way to think of such a situation is not as an arrest—although, technically speaking, it is—but as simply asking him to stay until the police arrive.

If he attempts to flee, it's not lawful for a citizen to use lethal force in order to prevent that, although it's not necessary to mention that you're not going to shoot him for running away, if you've chosen to hold your assailant at gunpoint until the police arrive.

Since we hope you'll take our advice, the one situation where you're likely to actually have to deal with the problem is when your assailant forces it on you.

Say you've deterred an attack by producing your handgun, and your assailant, a career criminal who has been arrested many times, "knows the drill." Instead of running away, he surrenders: he raises his hands, clasps them behind his head, and kneels down. "Don't shoot me," he says. "I give up."

You're kind of stuck with him at that point.

While under most circumstances it be would illegal to hold somebody at gunpoint, in both theory and practice it is reasonable to—with the finger off the trigger—move the gun to the low ready position (pointed toward the ground at a 30-45 degree angle) and require the assailant to lie face down on the ground with his legs spread and his arms straight out at a 90-degree angle to his body with his head turned so he can't see you (he'll probably be familiar with the position). Then move away from him. This gives you a time and space zone so that you can, if you wish, holster your firearm while continuing to dominate the situation. If he moves on you, you can draw again. Secure the scene and the assailant, then stop.

The thing not to do is go beyond that.

One of the most dangerous things police do is to gain physical control of a suspect. It requires, among other things, holstering the gun (the suspect might grab it) and getting intimately close, well within range of grasping hands or a hidden knife. This is why police will do almost anything they can to avoid controlling a suspect by themselves. There's always one officer out of grabbing range with a gun in hand, while the other moves in to handcuff the suspect. Most police officers have special holsters that make it difficult for somebody to snatch the gun out, and those who do train extensively in using them. Few holsters for concealed handguns have such features.

Remember the Tueller Drill. The sort of close proximity that police move to when affecting an arrest is necessary for them to be able to secure the suspect. It is neither necessary nor wise for a citizen who is simply holding the assailant for the police to do any such thing.

While there's nothing illegal about a citizen carrying handcuffs (it's considered a bit strange, but it's not a crime), trying to put them on a surrendered assailant is just asking for trouble. Massad Ayoob, a nationally recognized self-defense trainer, recommends that his students carry handcuffs routinely, and if it becomes advisable to handcuff a suspect, just toss the cuffs toward the former assailant and say, "Put them on; you know how."

Again, while it may be possible to detain an assailant for the police, it's simpler, safer, and just plain better not to: if an assailant has surrendered, make sure that you are not between him and an escape route (like the door). If he chooses to run, *let him.* Let the police chase him down, and let him explain why he fled.

If you keep him, just as when he's fled, unless you're very lucky, you'll be on your way to the police station, in handcuffs, and need to call your lawyer.

More about that later.

When the attack continues

The last, and most dangerous (and, thankfully, very unlikely) possibility is that you'll actually need to use deadly force: shoot an assailant in order to prevent him from killing or seriously hurting you.

It doesn't work in real life the way it does on TV.

The physics of a lethal confrontation

Newton's Laws apply in real life. Firing a shot sufficient to lift an assailant off his feet and knock him back several feet would have a similar effect on the shooter. In Hollywood, the effect is accomplished by a harness attached to the actor being shot and several burly grips yanking on the rope attached to it.

In real life, this simply doesn't happen. Newton's Laws are not repealed on the street. Even if your first shot stops the attack—and it might—it won't be anything as dramatic as your assailant flying backward. He might appear to stumble or fall—almost certainly forward. It's possible that your first shot will physically incapacitate him immediately—unlikely, but not impossible—and it's certainly possible that it will change his mind.

Or, quite possibly, he'll simply continue with his attack.

The physiology of a lethal confrontation

Adrenaline has both physical and psychological effects, and the threat of a violent confrontation is almost certain to cause a massive adrenaline dump with a huge complex of effects—on both the assailant and the victim.

Vision tends to narrow—the so-called "tunnel vision" effect—where it becomes difficult or impossible to see anything besides the threat. Pain is also diminished. More than a few people who have been shot did not even notice until later.

Strength goes up. This is why light triggers on self-defense weapons are such a bad idea. What feels like simply resting a finger on the trigger may be something entirely different. It's also why you *must* keep your finger off the trigger until you're ready to shoot. Tapes of real-life shootings—usually involving police officers and bank guards—almost always show the shooter with a near-spastic grip on the firearm, something the shooter is probably not aware of at the time, or maybe even later.[32]

Dexterity drops, as does the ability to perform complex tasks. This is why easy-to-operate handguns are better for self-defense than more complicated ones.

The perception of time also changes, in what's known as the tachypsychia (literally, the *speed of mind*) effect. Things may seem to happen in slow motion, or to speed up. This is one of the many reasons not to be

---

[32] There are cases where people involved in self-defense shootings have had such a spastic grip on the handgun that they've been unable to release it, even later, and have had to have it pried out of their hands.

too quick to talk to police afterwards—you might honestly say that a confrontation took two or three minutes when it really only took a few seconds. Police officers and prosecutors aren't always very sensitive to the difference between an honest mistake and a lie.

Auditory exclusion is also common. Most hunters will report not being bothered by the loud report of a rifle when they've shot at game, even though that same *bang!* will often be uncomfortable even when wearing hearing protection on the range. The same is even more likely to be true during a violent confrontation. The sound hasn't gotten any quieter—it's just that your mind is processing it differently.

The ability to feel pain drops. As most hunters who have fired a high-powered rifle at a deer can tell you, they usually don't notice the strong kick of the rifle's butt against the shoulder.

Other things that can happen include "psychological splitting" or an "out-of-body" sensation, where you perceive that your body is moving faster than your mind can, or vice versa, or even that you're watching the whole incident from outside yourself.

Physiologically, when under attack, your senses and physical responses depend on your most innate survival skills and your training. You may remember Maslow's Hierarchy of Needs from high school psychology. Next to maintaining our physiological needs (breathing, eating, and maintaining body temperature) is safety. Your response to an attack will be as innate a response as you may ever experience. Your training and muscle memory of what to do in response to an attack will take over. So, the more you train, the better your response to an attack will be. An attack situation doesn't provide enough time for a great deal of rational decision-making, so your training in threat assessment and response will take over.

According to Artwohl and Christensen[33], your cognition also changes when you are in what they call a "high-arousal state:"

> "Experiential thinking is the kind of thinking that will automatically kick in whenever you perceive a threat and your body is flooded with natural drugs that induce the high arousal state. Under threat conditions, experiential thinking will dominate and reduce or even eliminate your ability to think in a rational, creative, and reflective manner. It's effortless, automatic, lightning quick, action-oriented,

---

[33] Dr. Alexis Artwohl, Loren W. Christensen, *Deadly Force Encounters: What Cops Need to Know to Mentally and Physically Prepare for and Survive a Gunfight* at 45-46 (Paladin Press, 1997).

and much more efficient (but not necessarily more accurate) than rational thinking. It's experienced as much more compelling than rational thinking...

Experiential thinking is also what you do when you follow your gut instinct. There is nothing mystical about gut instincts, sixth sense, or intuition. Our brain is an incredible computer constantly analyzing subtle bits of information to reach conclusions, information that may not be obvious to our conscious awareness. You know your conclusion is right, but you can't explain exactly how you know that (of course, your conclusion could also be wrong).

Experiential thinking does not follow a step-by-step process to reach a conclusion but reaches it quickly without your knowing how it got there. You must rely on this type of thinking when you don't have enough time or information to reach a carefully reasoned, logical conclusion."

The aftermath of a violent confrontation can also bring out more than a little ugliness, particularly if the assailant was a member of a different racial or ethnic group from the victim. Even people who would never consider using an ethnic or racial epithet under normal circumstances may find themselves thinking—or saying—such things. People who even rarely use such words almost certainly will, in the heat of the moment, and that's asking for trouble later on.

All of these effects apply to both the victim of the attack and the assailant, and must be taken into account. The sort of pain that would normally stop somebody in their tracks may well have no immediate effect on a determined assailant. This is why defensive measures like pepper spray are much more effective on volunteer test subjects than real-life assailants.

It's entirely possible for either the assailant or the victim—or both—to continue fighting even after being seriously, and perhaps even fatally, wounded. One video, available on the Internet, shows a bank robber struggling with a guard for several long seconds after being shot in the heart, only to flee and drop dead in the parking lot outside the bank—and, again, he had been shot in the *heart*.

This is why the legal principle that lethal force is justified until the threat ends is so important.

If the assailant continues the attack—even if the wounds he has already received will later prove fatal—it is not only lawful to continue shooting, it is necessary.

The right to use lethal force ends when the attack stops, but it does not end *until* the attack no longer represents a threat of death or great bodily harm. If it becomes necessary to shoot an assailant, it's necessary to continue shooting until the attack stops, and then immediately stop.

It may take one shot for that to happen, or it may take many shots.

And you may not even see the shots landing. On a well-lighted pistol range, a sharp hole against a target will be easily visible at close range, but violent confrontations rarely take place in well-lighted areas. Even in good light, a wound may be hidden by the pattern of the assailant's clothing, even if it immediately starts bleeding.

The physical effects of a shooting

There's no way to discuss the effects of a shooting without discussing some awful facts.

The most important one is that shooting somebody in order to physically stop an attack requires doing a lot of damage to another human being, damage that is entirely likely to be lethal. We wish this weren't so; it would be very nice to have a Star Trek phaser pistol, which could simply and reliably stun an assailant. But such things are, at least at present and for the foreseeable future, artifacts of science fiction, not of reality.

Handgun bullets are not as effective as the fictional phaser. They're more damaging, but they are not necessarily immediately incapacitating. If the first shot stops the assailant, it's likely that it's because he's changed his mind, not because he's unable to continue.

The only time that a single shot can be reliably counted on to immediately stop an assailant is in the unlikely event that it severs the spinal cord. If that happens, the nerves will be unable to carry information below the cut or break, and the attack will stop. The assailant will simply collapse, as his brain will no longer be able to send information to his muscles.

But, that said, the spinal cord is less than an inch across, and in the case of a frontal attack, except where it goes through the neck, it's protected by the rest of the body in front of it and is simply too small to be a realistic target. Even the sort of person who, at the range, can put as many rounds as he cares to in a target's bull's-eye won't be able to reliably hit such a small target during an attack.

The brain is not much better as a target, in practice. Sufficient damage to an assailant's brain will, of course, end his ability to continue the attack. But the skull is thick, and the head is a small target under the best of circumstances, much less during a frightening confrontation where the person being attacked will literally be unable to concentrate on his handgun's sights, focusing instead on the assailant. Also, the head may be moving from side to side.

And if the bullet misses, it will go on until it hits something. The odds of you being attacked in front of a tall earthen berm, where you don't have to worry about a bullet doing anything other than burying it in the ground, are very small.

This is why almost all self-defense instructors teach that defensive shots should be aimed — or, most likely, pointed — at the assailant's center of mass (or COM; roughly speaking, the spot on the chest just about four inches above the bottom of the breastbone), and that the victim should continue to fire until the threat ends.

There are a lot of important body parts in the chest — the heart and lungs, for example. But, as actual videos have shown, even a shot to the heart may take a long time to actually stop an assailant.

Some gun writers talk about "double-taps" — firing twice, then re-evaluating. Some police officers are trained to do that, and there have been cases of police officers firing twice, hitting twice, and then reholstering their handguns only to find that they're still under attack.

The reason why most police — like most well-trained citizens — are taught to keep firing until the attack ends is because that is precisely what is necessary. And then — and *only* then — the shooting must stop.

After the confrontation, it's important for your attorney to be able to assert that you fired only as long as it was legally permissible, and then immediately stopped. One shot may stop the attack, while three may be insufficient.

"Why did your client shoot his assailant four times?" the prosecutor might ask your attorney.

"Because the first three shots didn't stop the attack," will be the answer. "The fourth did — that's why he didn't shoot five or six times."

The only reasonable thing to do, should shooting be necessary, is to keep shooting toward the center of mass *until* the threat has ended, and then immediately stop.

You don't want the hypothetical witness around the corner to hear *bangbangbang*, followed by a thirty-second pause, and then a final *bang*. Your lawyer is much more likely to be able to defend *bangbangbangbang*.

Firing toward center of mass also has other advantages. With a handgun of decent accuracy, it's easy, after very little training, to make tight little groups in targets at self-defense ranges. When adrenaline is pumping, your eyes are inexorably fixed on the assailant, you're literally unable to focus on the sights, and your hands are shaking, it becomes much more difficult to do that, even in good light, which is absent in most defensive shootings.

A center of mass shot permits you to miss the target by the maximum possible distance and still hit the assailant, and not have the bullet go beyond the assailant.

It's hard to think about this while in fear of your life, but you do have to consider where your bullets might go if you miss. A missed shot can travel a long way, and can easily hurt or kill somebody innocent.

And there's another reason to keep firing: most self-defense shots miss.

Statistics bear this out. Depending which study you believe, shots fired on the street by presumably well-trained police miss the intended target as much as 92% of the time.

In the much-publicized Amadou Diallo shooting in New York City, in which four very highly trained police officers fired forty-one shots, at close range, at a man they mistakenly believed was shooting at them, fewer than half the shots actually hit their intended target. These were carefully selected police officers who had gotten out of their cars fully prepared, both in terms of training and intention, for the possibility of being involved in a violent confrontation. The reason they fired more than forty shots wasn't out of some ill intent, as far as could be determined, but because they didn't believe the threat had ended before that.

And again: these were highly trained police officers, members of an elite squad, with hundreds of hours of training and many years of street experience, who were ready for trouble. They were shooting at somebody who, as it turned out, wasn't even shooting back at them—and still, at close range, *more than half of their shots missed.*

All four of them were charged, and all were acquitted. Many people believe that one of the reasons they got off was because at least one of them was overheard shouting "Gun!" While there was no gun found on the unfortunate Mr. Diallo, who was actually reaching for his wallet containing his identification, shouting "Gun!" made it clear that the police honestly believed they were facing a criminal with a gun in his hand, who was about to shoot them. They were wrong—he didn't have a gun—but that's what they thought, and that's why they were acquitted.

This leads to the key point: when a life-threatening confrontation is unavoidable, it's necessary to first survive it on the street, and then be prepared to survive the investigation that will start immediately after.

The physical consequences of a successful self-defense shooting are just the beginning of the victim's problems. While still recovering from the trauma of the experience, it will be necessary to deal with the police, just as it will be if the assailant flees or surrenders.

It's going to be long and uncomfortable, and there's just no way around it.

After a lethal confrontation

The immediate problem of being killed by the assailant ends when he either flees, surrenders, or is no longer able to attack because he has been sufficiently damaged. But other problems are just beginning.

As soon as you take out a firearm in a confrontation—much less actually pull the trigger—you have become a suspect, and are going to remain one at least until the investigation is concluded. You may be a defendant in a criminal case, or in a civil lawsuit—or both.

Your immediate concern should be to call the police and an ambulance. Even if you have injured or killed somebody in self-defense, there is an obligation to see that aid is rendered. Any failure to do so will not be looked on favorably by the police, the prosecutors, or the courts.

The next concern should be to avoid being shot by the police when they arrive on the scene. After that, it's necessary to see to your defense from both prosecution and, if at all possible, a successful lawsuit.

Let's take each of these in turn.

Firstly, *don't* run away, except if necessary for safety—that's true when the assailant flees, and it's just as true if you had to shoot him. Running from the scene of a shooting will be taken by police, prosecutors, and courts as a sign of guilt and should be avoided, just as an attempt to conceal any evidence will be. Let the assailant run away if he can—you stay put, if you can.

Further, modern forensic science is increasingly good, and gun shop advice to "if he drops outside your front door, just drag him back in" should be politely ignored. Don't plant a weapon in the assailant's hand, either. Messing with evidence of any sort is not only illegal and immoral, it's bad strategy, too. *Leave the evidence alone.*

The first thing to do is call 911, or have somebody else do so.

This conversation should be kept *short* and factual. "I need the police and an ambulance at the following address..." is ample. After that, it's best just to get off the line. There's no need to have your excited reporting of the details of the shooting preserved as evidence on the 911 recording.

This requires a firm intention — the 911 operator will instruct you to stay on the line and keep talking. That's what they are trained to do, which is understandable. The more information police and emergency services have, the better they can do their jobs — but an important part of the job of the police, in practice, is to obtain evidence for a prosecution.

When the police arrive

There are several principles involved in being prepared for the arrival of the police.

The most important one is this: *after using or threatening deadly force, the police are not your friends.*

That's worth repeating. *After using or threatening deadly force, the police are not your friends.*

They won't see themselves as your friends — although it may suit an investigator to portray himself as sympathetic — as they'll be coming into the situation cold, possibly knowing nothing more than that they've been summoned to the scene of an attack. In high-crime urban areas in particular, police see the aftermath of many shootings, and few of them are done in self-defense.

Physicians have a saying: "when you hear hoofbeats, think horses, not zebras."

That works for police as well. When they hear reports of a shooting, they think about assault and attempted murder, not a justifiable case of self-defense. Same for when they hear about somebody pointing a gun at somebody. It's understandable. From a police officer's point of view, assault, robbery, attempted murder, and murder are the "horses," and defensive gun uses are the "zebras."

Which is one of the reasons that it's important to be as non-threatening to the police as possible when they arrive on the scene. If it's safe to do so — if the assailant is unable to resume the attack, or has fled — the gun should be holstered. If not, it's important to remember to keep it pointed in a safe direction, with the finger away from the trigger. If possible, somebody else should be sent to meet the police when they arrive, to tell them there is no present danger, to describe the victim — "She's a small, black woman wearing a white coat, and she's the victim. The assailant is lying on the floor" — and to repeat that there is no present danger.

And remember your hands. Police officers love to see hands. At this point, your hands should be visible and empty, if at all possible. Remember the unfortunate Mr. Diallo—he went for a wallet that the police officers honestly mistook for a handgun.

Most of what you should do is just common sense. Follow police directions as to what to do. Cooperate immediately[34] but without any sudden movements that can be misinterpreted.

What is also true but needs to be thought about, as it isn't obvious, is to be verbally cooperative: say specifically what you are doing. "I'm putting my hands behind my head, as you've told me," for example.

When it comes to action—as opposed to discussion—compliance is mandatory. Be as calm as you can be, and utterly polite and cooperative. After all, you've called the police to come to preserve evidence in your defense.

Beyond that, it's necessary to protect yourself from the legal system, and that largely consists of two things: saying as little as possible and, without delay, consulting with a good attorney who is experienced in criminal matters.

As an aside, how you are treated by the police is very likely to be directly proportional to the age and experience of the first officers on the scene. Older and more experienced officers will be able to assess your situation using their years of experience. They also have refined interrogative experience. That said, as the scene is assessed, senior officers (especially beat officers) will figure out what happened fairly quickly. If a "wet behind the ears" rookie is running the scene, be ready for by-the-book treatment.

A four-part strategy

Massad Ayoob, a reserve police captain and well-known trainer of both citizen permit holders and police officers, recommends a four-part strategy: "He attacked me," followed by "I will sign a complaint," "there's the evidence," and finally—and most importantly—"I need to talk to my lawyer before I say anything else," after which you should say

---

[34] This is one of the reasons that your defensive handgun *must* be reliable, both in terms of it firing when you pull the trigger, and of not firing when you don't. The police officer should tell you to "put the weapon down", but if he or she says, "Drop the gun!" that's not a time for asking for clarification; you have to be able to drop the gun without it making a loud bang, or there will be other loud bangs, and you won't like it very much.

nothing more, except to repeat that last statement. (As a matter of law, a demand to consult with an attorney can't be used as evidence of guilt. Don't expect that the police will treat it that way, though.)

With one modification, which we'll get to shortly, this is probably the best approach, *if you are sure that you can stay with it.* Giving police favorable information concerning your exercise of self-defense[35], and other objective information that they're going to find out anyway, won't do any harm and may — may — prevent an arrest.

Let's take these each in turn.

"He attacked me"

It's not a problem to say that you were attacked. It doesn't, in and of itself, admit the use of deadly force, but it's an important part of the justification for it. Justification is what is called in law an "affirmative defense." In this case, it assumes that the victim has used deadly force — something that otherwise needs to be proven beyond a reasonable doubt. Absent the ability to prove that lethal force was used, the issue of justification never needs to come up.

Going beyond "he attacked me" to "so I shot him" is an admission that, if you need to make it, you can make it later on the advice of an attorney.

Legal theory aside, though, there's no major disadvantage to admitting that you've shot somebody, if you have. Your gun is there, the person you shot is there with the bullet or bullets in him, and the paraffin tests that the police will perform will prove that you fired a handgun.

Still, it's best not to start talking. You might not be able to stop. The only reason why you might want to say it is if you're in that rare situation where you think that you may not be immediately arrested. By admitting that you've actually shot your assailant, you make it possible for the police to let you go home if they want to, rather than having to hold onto you.

Still, they probably won't let you go home; they'll almost certainly arrest you, and part of their job is to try to get you to talk to them.

Don't.

There is no advantage[36], and much disadvantage, to discussing any of the details of the incident then and there.

Anything you say about the exact details of the attack can and will

---

[35] "Exculpatory information," as the lawyers say.
[36] We repeat: there is *no* advantage to discussing this then and there.

be examined for possible vulnerabilities and compared with later statements, and can easily be used to suggest that you have changed your story, rather than that you've said the same thing in different ways. If you tell what happened then but leave out an important element, it's likely that you'll be accused of "conveniently" remembering it later — that you're lying.

Just to make it worse, any normal and innocent inconsistency can and likely will be used to suggest that the victim is lying. You could honestly say, then, that the whole thing took two minutes, when a witness might say it took three seconds — that can be used against you. Your immediate memory might not be accurate. It's entirely possible that, focused as you were on the attack, you could think that you shot twice but actually shot six times. That could be interpreted as lying, and trying to — foolishly — mislead the police about the number of shots you fired.

As can any understandable statement about emotions.

"I'm very upset," could be interpreted to mean either, "I'm very upset because I had to properly use deadly force in self-defense," or "He upset me, so I shot him."

And there are questions you can't answer without the answers being used against you, like "Were you angry at him?" If you say yes, then it can be argued that you shot him because you were angry at him. If you say no, then you're a liar — how could anybody not be angry at somebody who tried to kill him.

The simple way to avoid any possibility of either misinterpretation or being accused of lying is to say as little as possible.

What you *don't* say *can't* be used against you, thanks to your Fifth Amendment right against self-incrimination.

"He attacked me" is all you need to say on that subject before talking to your lawyer.[37] That will, you hope, get the police on the right track.

"I will sign a complaint"

This doesn't really mean what it says. Writing out and signing a complaint needs to wait for the advice of your attorney. If the police officer responds by saying, "Fine, just write down what happened," the only safe response is, "I'll be happy to, just as soon as I've talked with my attorney," and repeat that as many times as necessary.

Saying "I will sign a complaint" *isn't* a commitment to talk further.

---

[37] Although if you want to add, "and I acted in self-defense," that probably wouldn't be a bad idea. But leave it at that and go on to the next step.

What it does, however, is permit the police, if they choose, to see you as the victim and not arrest you. It doesn't force them to, of course. There is no way to force them to do so, and trying too hard is counterproductive.

Police understand that the perpetrator signs a confession, and the *victim* signs a *complaint*. By saying, "I will sign a complaint," you're say-ing to them—in language they understand, if not necessarily believe—that you're the victim.

If they don't want to arrest you, this helps to give them justification for it.

Realistically, the police *will* arrest you most of the time. The only thing they know for sure is that there has been a shooting, and they have every reason to believe that the victim has shot somebody. Whether or not it was a justified shooting is something they are likely to leave to others. But there's no reason, after all, to insist on being arrested.

"There's the evidence"

Police officers are humans, and humans can make mistakes. Shell casings from the assailant's handgun can be stepped on; a knife can be overlooked; or a baseball bat, tire iron, or claw hammer might not even be seen as a weapon and not taken into evidence even though the assai-lant's fingerprints on it can be very important. It's vital from your point of view that none of the evidence be overlooked or damaged. Gathering evidence is what the police do.

Evidence isn't just physical evidence—it's perfectly reasonable to point to witnesses, or to suggest that somebody in a nearby building might have overheard the confrontation.

The behavior of the assailant may also be important evidence. Was his behavior erratic and possibly drug induced? Had he been drinking? Are there prescription drugs on his person?

What you want to project, without going into detail, is that you were defending yourself and expect the evidence to support your claim.

But that doesn't mean to keep talking. You need to immediately go to the next step:

"I need to talk to my lawyer, and I do not consent to any search"

This is the most important part of the formula, and you're likely to need to repeat it. As you can see, this is a slight variation on Ayoob's four-point strategy: explicitly saying that you don't consent to any search.

This fourth step is the part that can't be skipped. Those who are concerned that if they start talking, might have trouble stopping, should just skip right to this step and stop there.

Again:

"I need to talk to my lawyer, and I do not consent to any search."[38]

Why not talk?

Ayoob, who among other things trains police officers who investigate police-involved shootings, recommends that any interview with the officer take place at a later time, for fear that an officer who has been involved in a justified shooting will say something—perhaps something innocuous in context, or a heated exclamation showing how angry the officer is—that can be used later on to suggest that he acted improperly.

Ayoob isn't alone in this.

IACP, the International Association of Chiefs of Police, strongly recommends that police officers *not* be interviewed immediately after a shooting:

> ...the officer can benefit from some recovery time before detailed interviewing begins. This can range from a few hours to overnight, depending on the emotional state of the officer and the circumstances. *Officers who have been afforded this opportunity to calm down are likely to provide a more coherent and accurate statement.* [emphasis added]

Not only is a later statement likely to be "more coherent and more accurate," but it's likely to be *less harmful* to the officer involved. The IACP also recommends that police officers involved in a shooting be given a few paid days off on administrative leave ("Make sure the officer understands this is an 'administrative leave,' not a 'suspension with pay'") as a way to help cope with the great stress and trauma of having been involved in a shooting. It *is* stressful, which is why the IACP adopted a whole series of guidelines to avoid creating what the IACP calls a "'second injury'...created by insensitively and impersonally dealing with an officer who has been involved in a critical incident."

The entire list of recommendations that the IACP adopted is included in this book, starting on page 217. As you'll see, the police chiefs' association acknowledges how incredibly stressful and horrible it is to be

---

[38] There are many situations, arrest being one of them, where police can search you without your permission. Don't physically resist a search, but don't give consent, either.

involved in a shooting.

And since that's true for professional police officers, how could it be less so for citizens?

By way of contrast with the IACP's recommendations for officer-involved shootings, police officers are trained that in citizen shootings, their goal is to get the putative perpetrator—that would be you—talking, and to keep him talking, in order to gather evidence that can, if necessary, be used to prove that the shooting was a crime.

You're unlikely to be offered the same gentle and considerate treatment that police officers are.

"Arrest 'em all; let the prosecutors sort it out," is how one police officer puts it.

Realistically, there is nothing you can do to avoid the likelihood of being arrested after a shooting, and what you need to focus on is minimizing the damage.

This is not something that is likely to be mentioned, much less emphasized, by the police at the scene or the detectives who will investigate the shooting later. One common investigative technique is for an officer to portray himself as one who is sympathetic to the suspect—again, that's you—who only needs a few questions cleared up before closing the whole matter. It's a simple play to the victim's need for security and certainty in a stressful, strange, and uncertain situation.

In the wake of a shooting, this is almost certainly not true, and talking to a policeman before consulting with an attorney is, whatever police assurances one receives to the contrary, a risky proposition of dubious possible benefit.

So don't do it.

Just repeat "*I want my lawyer,* and *I don't consent to any search,*" and see what they do. Try to figure out what they're up to, but regardless of what you've figured out, just keep saying, "*I want to speak to my lawyer,* and *I don't consent to any search.*"[39]

A common technique is the "good cop, bad cop" technique popularized on television, where one officer appears to be actively hostile, while the other affects to be sympathetic and eager to hear the suspect's "side of the story." Standard police procedure is, in most cases, not to record such conversations, and should the matter come to court, the officer's recollection of the exact words may not be accurate either through honest error or a strong desire to get the bad guy—you.

---

[39] Think of it as a mantra.

Do you want to bet your freedom that any inaccuracies are going to be in your favor?

As the late Darrell Mulroy, a Minnesota self-defense trainer, put it, "There are two kinds of witnesses in court: prosecution witnesses, and defense witnesses. Guess which ones the cops are?"

What the police will do

While physical abuse and some forms of intimidation are illegal and rare (but not unknown) there are forms of intimidation and influence that courts have not only said are completely legal, but which are part of police officers' training.

And these are the sorts of things that a law-abiding citizen has probably not run into before.

Here's an example. If you are thought to be lying to police, you can be prosecuted (you can ask Martha Stewart about this), but the police have almost unfettered authority to lie to you. Police statements like, "You may as well confess now; we just spoke to Bob, and he says that you [whatever]" are very common, and often very effective. After going through the shock of surviving a lethal confrontation, you're unlikely to be in any shape to sort out truth from fiction, and almost certainly won't be able to make a careful, detailed statement including all of the elements of self-defense.

David Kopel, a leading civil rights attorney specializing in advocacy for self-defense issues, points to the research of Richard A. Leo, Ph.D., J.D., Associate Professor of Criminology, Law and Society, and an Associate Professor of Psychology and Social Behavior at the University of California, Irvine.

Leo's research shows that police routinely use "techniques of neutralization" in an attempt to get you to talk, and to keep you talking.

These can involve telling you that the interrogator thinks you haven't done anything wrong, that the assailant deserved what happened; that you have committed a crime, but only a minor one—say, that your assailant was just lightly injured and is, even at this moment, being booked—and that all the investigator needs is for you to write out and sign a complaint.

Any or all of that could be true.

Any or all of that could be false.

You don't know.

You shouldn't talk.

The investigator could think that you've committed murder and wants to get more evidence. He may believe that the person you shot deserved it in a moral sense, but you're still guilty of a crime for having shot him. And it's entirely possible that the hypothetical assailant, instead of now being booked, is lying dead in the morgue, and the police are gathering evidence that will be used to prosecute you, and would love for you to help them with that.

There's no way to know, and until your lawyer tells you otherwise, you simply should not say anything, except "I want to speak to my attorney, and I don't consent to any search." If you find that you have to keep repeating that, fine. If you shorten that to "lawyer," that's fine, too.

The relationship between police and suspects is not symmetrical. While citizens are not permitted to lie to the police, the police, in fact, *are permitted to lie* to suspects and frequently do. They can, with utter impunity, say that if you talk to them you will not be arrested, and then arrest you after you talk.

They can, and likely will, explain that it's in your best interest to get your side of the story on the record without getting lawyers involved ("It'll look bad if you don't talk now, Bob[40]") and that, instead of calling a lawyer, letting you explain what happened is something they're doing as a favor to you, even though they know it isn't. An officer can say that you're not under arrest, but you still have to accompany them to the police station.[41] The investigator can take a statement under an explicit or implicit promise that there will be no arrest, then immediately arrest you.

There are all sorts of things investigators can do. If they have two suspects, they can put both of them in the back of a police car and leave them alone to talk to each other, with the hidden video camera in the front of the car taping the conversation.

Again, it's the job of police investigators is to get as much information as possible to support a charge and conviction, and then let the prosecutor sort it out later.

And there's another asymmetry to the whole thing.

To the extent that an interrogation is a battle of wits, the opponents

---

[40] They'll probably use your first name a lot. They might either ask you to use their first name—by way of suggesting that you're just friends, talking over a problem—or insist that you call them by their rank, as a means of gaining a psychological edge.

[41] That's untrue, by the way. If a reasonable person in your situation would think that you can't leave, or have to go with them—as opposed to "volunteering" to stay, or to go with them—then you *are* "under arrest."

aren't equal.

The police investigator is experienced at this. He interrogates people on a daily basis, and may have been doing it for decades.

You've gone through your entire life without being the subject of a police interrogation at all. Most likely, the closest you've been to one is watching one on television.

Getting involved in this is like somebody who has never picked up a tennis racket going out on the court with a professional tennis player except, in the case of a police interrogation, there's a lot more to lose than a tennis game.

It's actually much worse than that. When you go into a tennis game, you're not frightened half out of your wits. The minutes and hours after you've been forced into a defensive gun isn't a time when you can coolly and calmly answer questions or explain yourself, and it certainly isn't a time when you'll be thinking about all the implications of the various laws involved.

Realistically, anybody involved in a handgun self-defense *will* need the help of an experienced criminal attorney and must not talk with the police, except as above, before consulting with one. There is no way you can avoid the necessity and cost of a good lawyer. No way. Any attempt to "do it yourself" is just going to cost you money (if you are lucky) or years of freedom (if you botch the job). Leave your defense to the professionals!

If it turns out—and it might—that a police interview is in your interest, the attorney can and should supervise the interview. Many criminal attorneys will simply refuse to have their clients take an interview at all and submit a sworn statement instead.

Finally, your assailant is unlikely to consider whether your lawyer will be immediately available when he attacks you. It is possible that your attorney will be in court, at a dinner party, playing golf or at the kid's hockey game. If you are attacked late in the evening, call the "person who loves you the most" and will move heaven and earth to get you representation immediately. Getting someone familiar with the legal system and whose head is much clearer than yours is the important thing.

After a shooting, trying too hard to avoid being arrested (e.g., by cooperating with the police investigation) is just asking for trouble.

This is your security blanket: *"I need to talk to my lawyer, and I do not consent to any search."* Keep repeating it until the police allow you to speak with your lawyer. Never, *ever*, consent to any search.

Experienced criminal law specialists advise that there is no upside to consenting, none at all.

When are you under arrest?

If police officers have said, "I'm placing you under arrest," it's fair to assume that you are. But, even if they haven't formally made that statement, you might be.

Take a hypothetical case: you're sitting in a room at a police station, behind a table, with two plainclothes detectives on the other side of the table between you and the door. A third, uniformed officer is standing in front of the door, glowering at you. Are you under arrest, or are you voluntarily chatting with the police and free to leave at any time?

Asking, "Am I under arrest?[42]" is the obvious thing to do, but it won't do any good. Feel free to try it.

"Why *should* you be under arrest? Have you done something wrong?" is the standard comeback—and both an attempt to change the subject and an invitation to talk, and, as the police say during the standard "Miranda" warning, "Anything you say can and will be used against you."

If you're under arrest, you have the right to talk to your lawyer. The police must make a telephone available for you to call him or her, and can't question you further after you've demanded to talk to your lawyer unless you choose to waive that right—something they will be only too happy to let you do.

If you're not under arrest, you still have all those rights, of course, but the police don't have to do anything to help you, because you are—at least in theory—free to walk out the door and go wherever you want, and the court will take anything you say as a voluntary admission.

Can you walk out that door?

There's only one way to make your custodial status clear: try to leave.

In that situation, if you get up—slowly—and quietly but firmly say, "I'm going to leave now," and walk toward the door, perhaps saying, "Excuse me, I need for you to step aside so I can leave" to the officer standing in front of the door, one of two things will happen: either you'll be allowed to leave—in which case your first task is to contact

---

[42] Do ask, "Am I free to leave?" rather than "Am I under arrest?" Whether or not you're free to leave is a question of fact; whether or not you're "under arrest" is a legal conclusion. You should take legal advice and ask for legal conclusions from your attorney, not from a police officer.

your attorney—or you'll be informed that you're under arrest, in which case you still must continue to demand to speak to your attorney, and never consent to any search.

And did we mention that you must not talk to *anybody* (paramedic, spouse, cellmate...anybody) before talking to your attorney?[43]

Not talking isn't just for you

Not talking to the police doesn't just apply to you—you think of yourself as the victim; the police think of you as the suspect—it applies to your family as well.

If the victim and the shot perpetrator knew each other, the police will proceed on the assumption that there was a previous history of problems between the two and attempt to find out details about it. Anything said by a family member—say, that you and your assailant once had harsh words with each other—can easily be used as evidence against you. Family members should be instructed, in advance, that they are not to open the door to policemen who do not have warrants, and to always explain that:

1.   They will be happy to have a conversation with any investigators as soon as they've talked to their attorney, and
2.   They do not consent to any search.

And then, simply, they must not talk further until their attorney tells them otherwise.

Yes, this all sounds paranoid.

Most of the time, if you're a law-abiding citizen, the police are, in practice, allies. They're the folks you call when you hear a suspicious sound in the alley outside your house at night. When you encounter a policeman working overtime at the local supermarket, you know he's there to protect you as well as everybody else, and you probably give him a smile and a nod. Even when a police officer stops you for having a turn signal out or a minor traffic violation, he's doing his job, and it's just not a big deal. You may not be happy about it, but you don't treat the police officer as somebody who is endangering your freedom.

And you're right not to. Most of the time. Under ordinary circumstances.

---

[43] That particularly applies to whomever the police lock you in the cell with. It's common practice to put a "snitch" in the cell with a suspect to try to get him to talk. If you find that your cellmate is a good listener, talk about football, say. *Don't* talk about your case or your situation.

But after using or threatening deadly force, everything changes. To the police officer, you're no longer an ordinary citizen—you're a suspect, and, once again:

After you use a gun in self-defense, the police are not your friends.

This may sound paranoid, but for anybody who is the subject of a police investigation, paranoia of this sort is simply good policy. The risks of talking are huge, and the benefits—while a competent police investigator will try his or her best to make it appear otherwise—are minimal at best.

We do keep repeating this, and we hope we're not boring you, but this is so important that it probably can't be repeated too often:

In the aftermath of a defensive gun use—particularly in a shooting—the most important thing to do is to repeatedly request an attorney and make no other statements, regardless of the temptation.

If you're utterly sure that you can follow the four-point plan, go ahead. But do remember that the fourth point—the *request* for the lawyer, the *refusal* to consent to any search, and *not talking after*—is the most important part of it.

An alternate strategy

That said, there is an argument to be made for talking, at least a little. But, in order to use this strategy, it's necessary to have a degree of self-control beyond what most people have under normal circumstances, much less after having just been involved in a terrifying situation.

If you're not sure that you've got such self-control, it's best to just repeat demands for a lawyer, and leave it at that.

Most people should just leave it at that.

Still, many people will—whether it's wise or not—choose to talk to the police after an attack. If you're going to ignore our advice and do that, do so only using the following principle: give only objective facts that the police are going to discover anyway, and ignore other questions.

"I live here" is an objective fact. "This is my garage," ditto. "He attacked me," or even, arguably, "I shot him." Even "I said, 'Stop attacking me!' and 'Drop your weapon!'" are objective facts, if that's what you said.

When it goes beyond reporting objective, verifiable facts to answering subjective questions ("Were you angry at him?") or addressing other matters ("Have you had arguments with him before?"), then it's time to shut up, and stay shut up.

Those are *lose-lose* questions.

Just about the only thing you say that can't be used against you is, *"I want to talk to my attorney,* **and** *I do not consent to any search."*

Again: *After using or threatening deadly force, the police are not your friends.*

The risk of this strategy is that once you start talking, you will keep talking and, as they say, "anything you say can and will be used against you in a court of law."

The one exception

Having painted the standard picture — and tried to talk you out of talking to the police — it's important to note that there is one time, and *only* one time, when it is definitely in your interest to talk to the police, although you won't have to say much.

That's when you've got a situation where all of the following elements apply:

1.   You haven't hurt, much less killed, anybody.
2.   You have a police officer who appears sympathetic. That, in and of itself, isn't terribly important (appearing sympathetic can easily be part of a hostile interrogation), but it's necessary.
3.   The police officer has made it abundantly clear that all he wants is a simple "yes" to a detailed, sympathetic question that establishes each and every one of the elements of self-defense.

This will only happen, if it happens at all, in an utterly unambiguous situation, and very few examples of the use or threat of lethal force will appear so very clear to police officers. If, as is very likely, the questioning goes beyond that single request for a simple "yes" to a sympathetic question, the only safe answer is "I want my lawyer."

A real-life example is worthwhile.

Tim and Serena live in a high-crime neighborhood where muggings are common. One night, Serena heard the sounds of a struggle outside and went to the window to find Tim on the ground, surrounded by a pack of muggers who were apparently attempting to kick him to death.

This sort of thing, alas, wasn't rare in their neighborhood.

She retrieved their shotgun from the closet while she called 911 and, thinking it likely that Tim wouldn't be alive by the time the police arrived, she pumped a round into the chamber and stepped outside, screaming at them to stop.

They didn't. She fired a single shot in the air, the kicking instantly ceased, and the assailants fled. (Contrary to the myth, they didn't try to take the gun away from her. They just ran away.)

When the police arrived, the sergeant in charge listened to Tim's statement while the paramedics treated him and loaded him into the ambulance. The sergeant made some notes on his report, and turned to Serena.

"Let me see if I've got this straight, Ma'am," he said, nodding his head. "Fearing that your husband, who you knew to be a reluctant participant in this confrontation, was in immediate danger of death and/or great bodily harm (as indeed he was!), you may have fired one shot in the air in an attempt to deter the perpetrators from murdering him, and then ceased firing the moment they ended the attack?" He kept nodding as he talked. "Is that correct, Ma'am?"

"Yes, sir," she said.

He smiled and stopped nodding. "Thank you, Ma'am; have a good night," he said, as he handed her back the shotgun.

While perhaps Tim's talking to the police and the paramedics could be criticized, Serena's action was spot on. She gave a simple "yes" to an unambiguous, friendly question, and the encounter ended there.

If the question had been less detailed—"So you shot because you thought your husband might be hurt?"—or if the police sergeant had asked for a further statement, the only sensible thing for her to do would have been to say, as many times as necessary, "*I want to talk to my lawyer, and I do not consent to any search.*"[44]

If he'd been really sympathetic to her situation, he would have understood why. If not, then she didn't want to be talking to him at all.

After a nonlethal confrontation

The same principles apply to the majority of defensive handgun uses in which no shot is fired. If anything, these situations can be more complicated. While in the case of a successful defensive shooting, the assailant is either dead or seriously injured and unlikely to be able to immediately or ever spin the situation to his advantage, if the assailant has simply fled—or is still on the scene, uninjured, when the police arrive—he won't be at that disadvantage.

Another actual case from another state (the names have been

---

[44] Yes, we know that this sentence is becoming repetitive. However, it is your lifeline— burn it into your brain.

changed) is worth looking at.

Bob carried a handgun daily to protect the large sums of cash that his business requires that he carry about with him.

One day, he was involved in a small traffic accident in which the driver of another car backed into him, causing no serious damage to his car, but jamming him up against the curb. The other driver came out of the car with a tire iron, saying, "I'm going to beat your head in," and added some colorful expletives as he moved toward Bob.

Believing, reasonably, that he was in immediate danger of having his head beaten in, and retreat not being practical, Bob drew his handgun and pointed it at the assailant, at which point the assailant broke off the attack, retreated to his own car, and drove off.

Bob, thinking that the incident was over, simply drove home. There was, shortly, a knock on his door, and two uniformed police officers asked if they could come in to talk to him, which he agreed to. They asked him some details about the incident, which he answered thoroughly and honestly, if somewhat heatedly, at which point they asked if he could produce the gun that he had been carrying and the carry permit under which it was legal for him to carry it.

He produced both; the policemen seized both, and promptly arrested him on felony charges, at which time he finally contacted an experienced criminal attorney. After some negotiation with the prosecutor's office, his attorney managed to get the charges reduced to a misdemeanor, provided he pled guilty, surrendered his carry permit, and made no attempt to have his handgun returned to him.

Bob made several mistakes and was fortunate enough to have gotten off so easily.

His first mistake was not immediately calling the police. It's an understandable reluctance. After all, he had done something unusual and potentially serious: he had drawn a gun and pointed it at somebody. But that reluctance permitted the aggressor to get in the first complaint to the police. It's called "the race to the courthouse," and he let his assailant win it by default.

His second mistake was not calling his lawyer.

Beyond that, he let the police in and talked to them. This was a particularly bad idea. If an interview with the police had been in his interest — and, all in all, it might have been — that interview should have been conducted under the supervision of his attorney.

He had no obligation to open the door to the police or to answer their questions at all — much less produce his handgun and permit while at home, in an interview that he shouldn't have granted in the first place — and his attorney could have advised him to that effect.

Again: after an armed confrontation, the most important thing to do is to *ask* for a lawyer, *refuse* to consent to any search, and then to *say nothing* more until after talking with your attorney.

If you remember nothing else from this book, do remember that.

Getting sued

As if being almost certainly arrested and quite possibly charged with a crime isn't bad enough if you use your handgun in self-defense, there's also the risk of being sued.

That said, for once, we do have some good news: Minnesota law protects victims against being sued by criminals who have attacked them. Section 611A.08 of the Minnesota Statutes was written specifically to protect victims:

> 611A.08 Barring perpetrators of crimes from recovering for injuries sustained during criminal conduct....
>
> Subd. 2. Perpetrator's assumption of the risk. A perpetrator assumes the risk of loss, injury, or death resulting from or arising out of a course of criminal conduct involving a violent crime... and the crime victim is immune from and not liable for any civil damages as a result of acts or omissions of the victim if the victim used reasonable force as authorized in section 609.06 or 609.065.
>
> Subd. 3. Evidence. Notwithstanding other evidence which the victim may adduce relating to the perpetrator's conviction of the violent crime involving the parties to the civil action, a certified copy of: a guilty plea; a court judgment of guilt; a court record of conviction as specified in section 599.24, 599.25, or 609.041; an adjudication as a delinquent child; or a disposition as an extended jurisdiction juvenile pursuant to section 260B.130 is conclusive proof of the perpetrator's assumption of the risk.
>
> Subd. 4. Attorney's fees to victim. If the perpetrator does not prevail in a civil action that is subject to this section, the court may award reasonable expenses, including attorney's fees and disbursements, to the victim.
>
> Subd. 5. Stay of civil action. Except to the extent needed to pre-

> serve evidence, any civil action in which the defense set forth in subdivision 1 or 2 is raised shall be stayed by the court on the motion of the defendant during the pendency of any criminal action against the plaintiff based on the alleged violent crime.....

All in all, the law is favorable toward those who have to use force to defend themselves against a criminal attack. A conviction of the attacker is, as the law says, "conclusive proof"[45] of the attacker's "assumption of risk."[46] If your attacker sues you, you may even be able to get court costs and attorney's fees. If he sues you while his criminal case is pending, your lawyer can have the action "stayed" — put on hold — until it's decided.

However, if your attacker isn't charged and convicted, you don't have that "conclusive" proof, and may be forced to provide that "other evidence" the statute talks about, and have a judge or jury decide if it's good enough.

Also, notice that what's allowed is "reasonable" force, and remember that if there's any question about what's reasonable, a jury gets to decide.

On the other hand, consider the criminal's problem in trying to get a lawyer to take the case. He's either got to come up with thousands of dollars for lawyer's fees or get a lawyer to take the case "on spec" (where the lawyer doesn't get paid unless his client does). Both are likely to be difficult. Few criminals have thousands of dollars to throw away on lawsuits, after all, and getting a lawyer to take a case "on spec" usually means that the lawyer expects to win in court or receive a large settlement. The chances of the criminal winning the case are likely to be small[47].

It's not impossible that, even if he can find a lawyer to take his case, your lawyer could persuade the judge that no sensible jury could possibly determine that the force you used wasn't reasonable, and the case

---

[45] And, from a legal standpoint, proof doesn't get a whole lot better than "conclusive."

[46] When the law talks about "assumption of risk" here, it's just a legal way to say that getting hurt or killed is the attacker's problem. If he didn't want to take the risk, he could have skipped attacking you.

[47] But not necessarily zero. After being acquitted of attempted murder in New York in the famous "subway vigilante" case, Bernard Goetz was successfully sued by his attackers. While New York State doesn't have as strong a legal protection for victims as Minnesota does, the jury in that case found that the force Goetz used was "unreasonable." Part of what worked against Goetz was that he had talked for hours with the police, without a lawyer.

could be dismissed.

Still, all in all, the same principle applies to worries about lawsuits as it does to worries about being arrested: if you really do need to show or use your handgun to prevent you from being killed or badly injured, at that moment you'll almost certainly be thinking about survival rather than legal repercussions. If you don't survive the confrontation, you won't have any of those problems, granted.

It's better to survive.
Then call 911.
And then, *call your attorney.*

And remember: A gun never solves problems.

Chapter 5
Routine Police Encounters

Most people who carry a handgun will never encounter a deadly threat or be involved with the police in a serious criminal matter. Realistically, outside of the range, most permit holders will never take their guns out other than to put them on and put them away. And that is, of course, a good thing.

Still, permit holders will encounter police officers on a routine basis, as everybody does, whether it's the police officer on overtime at the local drugstore or the one who has pulled you over for an out-of-order turn signal.

This chapter deals with ordinary police encounters, ones where issues of deadly force, police investigations, and the threat or reality of arrest are *not* involved. In cases where *any* of those are, it's necessary to immediately switch to "I want to speak to my attorney, and I don't consent to any search" mode.

It's important to know that the Minnesota Personal Protection Act provides for a statewide, computerized registry of permit holders through the state driver's license database. In Minnesota, a permit to carry must be presented to a law enforcement officer upon request.

A permit to carry may also be recorded on any vehicles registered in the permit holder's name. When the police run your plates — something they routinely do if they've stopped you — they will easily discover that you have a permit. They won't know, of course, if you are armed, but they may well assume that you are.

This is important not only for you as a permit holder to know, but for anybody who happens to be driving your car. If, say, a husband of a permit holder is driving his wife's car, the police may assume that he is armed. Police officers who are not familiar with the exemplary record of permit holders are likely to be nervous. Your task is to get through ordinary encounters without getting into trouble.

The rules are generally straightforward:

Don't argue

There are few times and places to argue with police. The roadside isn't one of them, nor are other routine encounters. Not arguing doesn't mean agreeing—that you're not going to argue with the officer about, say, whether or not you were speeding doesn't mean that you need to admit you were traveling ten m.p.h. above the speed limit. "I don't want to talk about that," is a perfectly legitimate thing to say. The time to correct the officer in his or her misunderstanding of either facts or the law is later, at leisure, and with witnesses, if at all.

Don't volunteer unnecessary information

Under the MPPA, a permit holder has no general obligation to display their permit card or to inform a police officer that he or she is armed, *unless* asked.

If asked, there's no option: you must comply.

While people new to carrying a handgun assume that everybody has X-ray vision and can spot the gun immediately, that's simply not the case. If the policeman doesn't ask, there's no reason at all to tell him or her during a routine encounter that you are carrying, and every reason not to, unless he asks.

The obvious exception to this occurs if the policeman is, shortly, going to see the gun.

Say you're carrying your handgun in a strongside holster, and you've been asked to produce identification. Retrieving your wallet will reveal your gun, so it's a good idea, if not legally required, to inform the officer beforehand and ask for instructions.

"My driver's license and my carry permit are in my right hip pocket; my handgun is on my right hip. What would you like me to do?" for example.

(Remember to keep your hands visible. Police officers love to see hands.)

Even better, in a traffic stop, would be to have your driver's license, registration, and insurance card in hand before the officer arrives at your window, and your permit in your shirt pocket.[48] If the issue of being armed doesn't come up, don't mention it. Just hand over your license, registration, and insurance card when asked.

Still better is to be sure that you can, if needed, produce identification without revealing that you're armed. Those people who carry a handgun in a hip holster can learn to carry their wallet on the side opposite the handgun. Getting used to this can take a week or so, but it can save you from potential grief.

Again: the MPPA requires a permit holder who is carrying a firearm to (1) show the permit and photo identification to a police officer and/or (2) state whether they are presently armed, "upon lawful demand."

Be polite

Consider the problem that a police officer has, if he or she has rarely if ever encountered a permit holder. Some officers are going to be nervous, and while there's no need to be overly familiar, simple politeness — particularly in something like a traffic stop — will help to reassure the officer that you're not going to be a problem, whether the handgun issue comes up or not.

In many ways, the success of Minnesota's right to carry law is in understanding and appreciating the issues of all involved. Permit holders do not deserve or want to be harassed. Law enforcement officers want and deserve to be safe in the company of permit holders. The general public wants to know that permit holders and law enforcement both respect the law.

---

[48] In the case where you're driving your own car—a car that's registered to you—the moment that the police run your plates through the state computer system, they'll be able to get your name and address, and may find out from the database that you have a carry permit. In that case, be sure to have your carry permit out, *whether or not you've got your handgun with you*, with your hands clearly in view, before they reach the car. They may well assume that if you're registered as having a permit, you're also armed.

Don't lie

Generally speaking, there is no legal obligation to talk to police, but there are various statutory and practical penalties for lying. If an officer asks if you are armed, answer honestly. This is one of the few times when you should volunteer information. Before admitting that you are armed, mention that you have a carry permit. "I have my carry permit in my wallet, and yes, officer, I am carrying a handgun on my right hip."

Obey all instructions promptly

Again, this should be obvious. If you're confused, politely ask for clarification. When you're obeying instructions, *say* what you're doing. "I'm getting my wallet out now, as you've told me," for example. Make it utterly clear that you're cooperating with the officer's commands.

Let's make it clear—the instructions you will be obeying have to do with physical actions. If the officer instructs you to provide information, you are being questioned, and you should refuse to answer until you can speak to your lawyer.

Don't produce your handgun except on instruction

Almost invariably, when a police officer decides to take possession of somebody's handgun, the officer will choose to retrieve it himself. That's what they're trained to do. Realistically, officers who don't choose to do that won't bother to retrieve your firearm. In the unlikely instance that a police officer asks you to produce the firearm yourself, obey the instruction, say you're obeying the instruction, do so promptly but without quick or jerky motions, and, of course, be sure to point the gun in a safe direction at all times, with your finger away from the trigger.

Don't offer to turn over your handgun before the officer asks you to do so, because you don't want to give up your Fourth Amendment rights by "consenting" to a search.

Keep your hands in plain sight

Again, this should be largely common sense. The idea is not to make the police officer nervous, and they can, even in ordinary confrontations, become very nervous about things like quick movements and hands in pockets. As they say, "cops love to see hands."

Don't consent to a search

Police officers will, from time to time, ask your permission to search you or your car. Just say no. Be polite, but firm.

Consenting to a search is one of those break-even-or-lose propositions. There's nothing to gain, after all. It's also humiliating, and there's no reason to volunteer to put up with being humiliated.

That doesn't mean, of course, that you won't be searched — just don't consent to one. *Never, ever consent to any search.* There is no possible good outcome for you.

Legally speaking, a full search is different from being "patted down" or a "pat-down search." A pat-down search is just what it sounds like: the police officer pats on your clothes, attempting to see if you have a weapon. They don't get to stick their hands inside your clothes or pockets — they just pat you some.

In Terry v. Ohio, 88 S.Ct. 1868 (US, 1968), and in subsequent cases, the United States Supreme Court gave police broad latitude in conducting pat-down searches. They have much more latitude in pat-downs than when conducting full searches, but even pat-down searches are not something that a police officer can do just because he or she feels like it.

Often, police officers want to search people they stop, even for minor traffic offenses. But, if there's "no additional suspicious or threatening circumstances[49]," they can't even pat you down — unless they ask you for permission and you say "yes."

So don't. Just politely say, "No," and be prepared to repeat it. Don't consent to a search of your car, either. Many people we know have refused consent, and the police officers simply turned to other matters. They knew that saying no was a matter of right and weren't offended.

If you do consent to a search, anything that a police officer suspects might be contraband in your car — whether or not it is — is likely to result in you being arrested. Anything that is contraband in the car — whether or not it's yours, whether or not you put it there, whether or not you had the slightest idea that it was there — will result in you being arrested and charged.

Oh, and a small but perhaps crucial point is that you can change your mind and *withdraw your consent* to a search at any time. So if you wise up as they paw through the contents of your glove compartment,

---

[49] While there's yet to be a court decision on this, having a police-issued permit and handgun on your person isn't likely to be considered a "suspicious or threatening circumstance" by the courts.

you can just say, "Officer, I've thought more about my constitutional rights and I now revoke my consent to any search of myself and my belongings. Please stop immediately." The Fourth Amendment exists for citizens to use.

Here's a real-life case in point. As usual, the names have been changed:

Bill was stopped for a minor traffic violation. He was traveling about ten miles per hour above the speed limit, and the police officer asked permission to search his car.

Bill didn't like the idea of having his car searched, and shook his head.

"Well, if you don't have anything to hide, you won't have a problem," the police officer said, and asked again. This time, Bill agreed, and the officer searched his car.

He came up with a small bag of marijuana hidden under the front seat. It wasn't Bill's — Bill doesn't use illegal drugs — but he had, several weeks earlier, lent his car to his younger sister, who did, and who forgot that she left the marijuana under the seat.

Bill was arrested, and it took quite a long time — and a lot of money spent on lawyers — to clear it all up. If his sister hadn't been willing to swear out an affidavit that the marijuana was hers, he would likely have been convicted.

Even if you don't lend your car to drug-using relatives, you really don't have any way of knowing for sure that there's nothing in there that could cause a problem. Has something fallen out of the pocket of a passenger? Did the parking valet at the restaurant forget something in the car?

Are you sure? Are you willing to bet thousands of dollars and your freedom on that?

No.

It's the same for rental cars. Even though rental companies clean them, anybody who regularly rents cars has found things in it that weren't his.

If you're asked to consent to a search and you say "no," granted, the officer may not be happy. He may tell you that he can make you wait there until he gets a search warrant or they may call a dog to sniff the car. Most likely that won't happen — the fact that you don't give permission for him to search your car isn't evidence that will persuade a judge.

Instead of arguing with him, it's best just to say that you need to call your attorney: "My cell phone is in my pocket, and I need to call my lawyer." Why? He'll ask. "Because I need to talk to my attorney, since you're not letting me leave."

Most likely, he'll finish writing the ticket and send you on your way. And, if he does get the warrant and doesn't turn anything up — and he won't if you're right about there being no contraband in the car — his supervisor will wonder why the resources were used to search such a poor prospect of criminal activity.

Importantly, not consenting to a search is a very different thing than physically resisting.

We shouldn't have to say it, but we will anyway: *don't offer physical resistance to police.*

If they've asked permission to pat you down, and you've said "no," they might decide to do it anyway. Don't say "yes." Say, "I'm *not* consenting to any search, but I'm not going to offer any resistance at all."

When a routine encounter becomes something else

As mentioned above, it is not unknown for what was a routine encounter to become something else. This can happen without any warning, and without you necessarily having done something wrong, or done anything at all. You could be minding your own business, driving down the street at a time when somebody with a similar description driving a similar car has just robbed a bank.

When a routine encounter becomes non-routine, it's necessary to immediately transition into a defensive mode and behave just as you would after a situation where you'd used, or threatened to use, deadly force. For that, go back to the chapter *Lethal Force and its Aftermath* commencing on page 57.

When the encounter turns sour, immediately lawyer up. Don't wait; there is no downside to immediately saying, *"I need to talk to my lawyer, and I do not consent to any search."*

At the end of the day

Remember, police officers want and deserve to be safe in the company of permit holders. The general public wants to know that permit holders and law enforcement both respect the law.

Over time, police officers will learn that permit holders pose no threat to them. They will learn that permit holders are some of their biggest supporters and strongest allies. Permit holders must be willing to take the time for this learning curve to take place. It's a process; let it happen.

You don't have to offer information, but we know of occasions when volunteering that you're a permit holder and are carrying a firearm has led to favorable treatment in a traffic stop.

And remember: a gun never solves problems.

CHAPTER 6
Choosing a Handgun for Carry

If the law about how very limited the right to use lethal force can be, and the advice as to how awful even a confrontation you "win" is going to be haven't frightened you off yet, read on.

Perhaps you already own a handgun that you're considering as your carry gun. Your instructor — see *Training*, start-

ing on page 191 — should be able to advise you. Or perhaps you have a knowledgeable friend to give you some good advice.

But do think about it carefully.

The necessary characteristics of a handgun carried for personal protection are different than one used for target shooting or even for home defense. A good home defense gun can be a lot larger and heavier than a gun most permit holders would be willing to carry. And, while target shooting is most often done with the careful use of sights, almost all self-defensive shooting — regardless of how you've been trained — is what's called "point shooting," where the gun is thrust out at the assailant. Very few people who are in a life-threatening situation are able to look at any-thing except the threat—you'll look at, say, the knife-wielding assailant, and not the sights.

A gun carried for defense should have the following characteristics.

Reliability

The reason for this is obvious. There are two horrible ways that a self-defense handgun can fail: it can fire without putting a finger on the trigger, or it can fail to fire when the trigger is pulled. Guns that can go off when dropped aren't acceptable. Neither are guns that won't fire re-liably, each and every time the trigger is pulled.

Should you find yourself in a situation where you need your hand-gun, it absolutely, positively must work. Reliability is the most impor-tant characteristic.

Pointability

The sights on a self-defense handgun, as we've said, will almost cer-tainly not be used in a real-life defensive situation—your eyes will be locked on the assailant. For that reason, a self-defense handgun must naturally point well for you, whether or not it does for anyone else. At realistic self-defense ranges, the bullet should go where you're pointing without your having to adjust your grip or use the sights. This requires careful selection and possibly some modification of the grips. Just be-cause a handgun points well for your instructor, your wife, your hus-band, or your best friend doesn't mean that it points well for you.

Weight affects pointability too. A gun that is too heavy for you will be slow to deploy, fall off point, and negatively affect your grip.

Your self-defense handgun needs to become an extension of your hand. When holding it properly, with your index finger pointed down-range along the frame, the barrel and your finger should be pointed at exactly the same spot.

Concealability

The inadvertent showing of a handgun, either accidentally or in those few locales where you can carry openly, might cause a panicky person to make a 911 "man with a gun" call. *You want to avoid this.*

Over time, this will change. Even so, there are many advantages to carrying concealed, and few to carrying openly. One of the reasons that uniformed police officers are all-too-often shot with their own handguns is that they must carry openly.[50] Citizen permit holders should almost always carry concealed, which is in their own best interest and everybody else's. Widespread deterrence depends on criminals not knowing who is carrying, so they have to be concerned about everyone. When deciding on a firearm for carry, consider how you will carry it, and how you will conceal it.

How concealed is "concealed" depends on your situation—how you dress, and how bad you think an inadvertent display would be in your situation. There'll be more on that in *The Mechanics of Everyday Carry*, starting on page 145.

Luggability

One of the few absolute truths about carrying a handgun is that it never, ever gets lighter as the day goes by.

It doesn't get smaller, either. Accounts abound of permit holders who start off carrying, say, a full-sized .45, and eventually give up on carrying their handgun at all. In an emergency, even the smallest handgun in the hand is going to be much more useful than a .44 magnum left at home. As many wags have said, "the first rule of a gunfight is, have a gun.'" (They're wrong, of course. The first rule of a gunfight is, "avoid it if at all possible.")

Caliber

While almost all successful handgun defenses don't require any shots being fired at all—and since most permit holders will never have to take their handgun out in public, much less shoot anybody—it could be argued that caliber isn't important. In most cases, it won't be. Most assailants, when faced with a .22 pistol, won't care to find out what getting shot with even a small bullet feels like.

That said, forget the myths about "stopping power." Even the largest, most powerful handguns cannot reliably be counted on to stop an

---

[50] The main reason, of course, is that police officers have to involve themselves in dangerous situations that citizen permit holders don't. A permit holder who is told, "Hey, I think there's a gangbanger making trouble in the alley," will call 911 as he walks away. A police office may have to go in and find himself or herself in a dangerous or ambiguous situation.

assailant with a single shot—even if it hits. That's even more true for smaller caliber handguns, simply because they make smaller holes and the bullets carry less energy. Carry the largest caliber with which you can accurately hit a target 21 feet away every time. Accuracy is essential with every bullet (after all, you want every shot to end up in the target, not somewhere else), but it is crucial with small caliber rounds. A .32 caliber bullet leaves a wound channel much smaller than a .45 caliber bullet. In order to cause sufficient damage to make the assailant's body take him out of the fight, vital organs have to be struck. That's more certain with accurate shots fired into the center of mass.

Trade-offs, and a recommendation

Obviously, there are trade-offs between concealability, luggability, and caliber. Bigger caliber handguns are generally larger and heavier than smaller caliber guns. Smaller handguns are much easier to conceal.

Our recommendation is this: carry the largest-caliber, most powerful handgun that you can reliably control, accurately shoot and reasonably conceal, and that isn't so heavy as to be an annoyance. If it's too much of a problem hauling it around, you will leave it at home. There's nothing wrong with deciding to leave your handgun at home (when you have a carry permit, it's up to you whether or not to carry on a day-to-day basis), but that should be a decision based on some better reason than "it's just too heavy and bulky."

Revolvers vs. semiautos

In the gun community, the discussion of the revolver vs. the semiauto often resembles a religious argument. We're agnostic on the issue; there are real advantages to either platform.

Let's start with basic definitions. A revolver is a handgun with a rotating cylinder that holds the ammunition (the cylinder acts as an attached magazine). Each time the hammer is cocked back, the mechanism inside the frame rotates the cylinder, bringing a new cartridge in line with the firing pin and barrel. Revolvers can be single-action, double-action, or double-action only.

In a single-action revolver, it's necessary to pull the hammer back manually in order to rotate the cylinder. Only after that will a pull on the trigger cause the revolver to fire. Single-action revolvers are not good choices for self-defense.

A double-action revolver, like the one at right, can be fired in two different ways: by pulling the hammer back manually and then firing it with a fairly light pull on the trigger (just like a single-action revolver), or by simply pulling the trigger, which requires a stronger and longer pull. This will simultaneously rotate the cylinder and cock the hammer, and then release the hammer, which fires the round. From 1890 through 1990, the double-action revolver was the predominant police tool for dealing with deadly encounters.

A double-action-only (DAO) revolver can only be operated by pulling the trigger, which rotates the cylinder, cocks the hammer and then releases it, firing the round.

A semiautomatic pistol works on a different principle. A round is first chambered in the pistol. When it's fired, the recoil or gas pressure causes the slide of the pistol to move backwards rapidly, which also cocks the hammer. When the slide springs forward again, another round of ammunition is stripped from the pistol's magazine and automatically chambered. The reason it's called a "semiautomatic" pistol rather than an "automatic" is that, as with the revolver, each shot requires a pull on the trigger. Semiautos, as they're usually called, can be single-action, double-action, or double-action only, although those terms mean slightly different things for semiautos than they do for revolvers.

The mechanism of a single-action semiauto requires that the hammer be manually cocked — pulled back — before the first shot.[51]

After that, when the pistol is fired, the slide automatically recocks the hammer before it comes forward to chamber a round.

A double-action semiauto has two kinds of trigger pulls. Like the double-action revolver, firing the first round requires a long, heavy pull

---

[51] This can be done either by pulling the slide all the way back and releasing it—"racking" the slide—or, if a round has already been chambered and the hammer lowered, by manually pulling the hammer all the way back.

on the trigger—this cocks the hammer and releases it. Firing the first round recocks the hammer and enables the pistol to fire with a short, moderate trigger pull (like a single-action semiauto) on the second and subsequent shots.

A DAO semiauto is operated in the same way as a DAO revolver: every shot requires exactly the same firm trigger pull, which both cocks the hammer and fires the round.[52]

The world of semiautos gets very complicated not just because of the firing mechanism, but because of their various safety systems. All modern firearms have safety mechanisms—frequently more than one—that are intended to prevent the gun from firing if there is no finger pulling the trigger back.

Where it gets complicated is when there's "more than one" safety mechanism. Many semiauto pistols have external safety switches that must be put into the correct position before the pistol can fire. That's particularly true for single-action semiautos, which are typically carried "cocked and locked"—a round chambered and ready to fire, the hammer pulled back, and the safety switch in the "safe[53]" position, preventing the pistol from firing until it is moved to the "fire" position. Just to make things more complicated—as anything involving firearms tends to be—some semiautos have safety switches that are "safe" when pushed up, and others when pushed down.

And if that isn't complicated enough, there are additional safety mechanisms in some pistols. Some have what are called "magazine safeties" that—at least in theory and usually in practice—prevent the pistol from being fired when the magazine is removed, even if a round is chambered and the trigger is pulled.

We'll get back to the discussion of safety switches shortly, but we do want to emphasize two things. First, you must be completely familiar

---

[52] There are all sorts of hybrid and specialty actions. The Glock pistols, for example, have what they call a "Safe Action," where the internal striker is cocked whenever a round is chambered, but where the trigger pull is stiff enough to feel like a DAO semiauto—and the same trigger pressure will always fire the round. While, technically, they're not DAO—because the internal firing mechanism is cocked by the slide going back—in practice, they operate in the same way that true DAO semiautos do.

[53] We're using "scare quotes" around the word "safe" deliberately. As we discuss in *Gun Safety, On and Off the Range*, starting on page 169, it's horribly *unsafe* to rely on a "safety" switch to prevent a gun from firing, for two reasons: you might be wrong about the position that the switch is in, or the switch might fail. Whatever good can be said about external safety switches, they are in no way, form, or manner a substitute for safe gun handling. Ever.

with the features, including the safety features, of any handgun you carry for self-defense. Secondly, and most importantly, we need to repeat what we put in the footnote here, and what we discuss further in *Gun Safety, On and Off the Range*, starting on page 169:

A safety mechanism, no matter how reliable you think it is, is never, ever a substitute for safe gun handling.

The case for revolvers for self-defense

A lot of good things can be said about revolvers for self-defense. They are reliable, simple to operate and, by and large, less expensive than equivalent-quality semiautos.

Because almost none have external "safety" switches, there's no danger of the revolver failing to fire because the switch is in the wrong position, as there is for some semiautos. While semiautos need more frequent maintenance and oiling to function reliably, revolvers need very little. In the event that a round fails — and this can happen, even with high-quality, modern ammunition — all you need to do with a revolver is pull the trigger again, bringing a new round underneath the hammer, and firing it.

Small, or "snubby" revolvers also carry well in a pocket, with or without a pocket holster. They're relatively nose heavy and tend to stay in the proper position (with the barrel down and the butt up), and they are easily reached. When you reach into your pocket for a handgun, you want to immediately grab the butt, not the barrel. While most revolvers suitable for daily carry hold five or six rounds, citizen self-defense shootings rarely involve more than one or two rounds being fired, although they certainly can.

We've been unable to find a case of a citizen dying in an otherwise survivable self-defense shooting because five rounds weren't enough, and we've looked long and hard for one.

Another advantage of revolvers involves their grips. Aftermarket grips of various sizes and shapes are available for almost all revolvers, causing them to point differently in different folks' hands.

The odds are very good that, even if the original manufacturer's grips don't allow a given revolver to point well for you, there is an aftermarket grip that will. While there are aftermarket grips for many semiautos, generally they don't affect how semiautos point nearly as much, simply because the shape of the grip is constrained by having to hold the magazine.

When it comes to making a handgun safe, double-action and DAO revolvers are easy. If you simply release the cylinder latch and swing the cylinder out, the revolver simply cannot fire until the cylinder is closed—and that's easily visible, even to an untrained eye. If you remove the cartridges and leave the cylinder open, it's easy to see that the revolver can't fire now—not only because the cylinder is open, but because it is unloaded as well.

The case for semiautos for self-defense

With all the advantages of revolvers, you might wonder why anybody would want to carry a semiauto. That's understandable; revolver enthusiasts often wonder the same thing. Still, as good as revolvers are, there are some real advantages to semiautos.

For one thing, semiautos tend to be flatter and slimmer than revolvers, and therefore can be concealed more easily. For another, certain semiautos point better for some people. As we've said, for a handgun you're going to carry for self-defense, the single most important feature after reliability is that it point well for you.

Revolver enthusiasts point to the fact that many semiautos have external safety switches, and that's true. It's also true that under the stress of a life-threatening attack, people can—and have—failed to put the safety switch in the right position. But it is easy to find a semiauto without an external safety switch.

If you choose a semiauto, we recommend that it be simple to operate and have no external safety switch that can be left in the wrong position during a stressful, life-threatening situation. In such a situation, you'll have enough trouble remembering that you in fact are carrying a handgun and don't need to worry about whether or not a switch is in the correct position. You'll have more than enough to think about at the time.

Still, some semiautos with safety switches can be—and often are—safely carried with the safety switch off. The only thing that's necessary, in that case, is to remember to leave it alone.

Another advantage of semiautos is ammunition capacity. While citizen self-defense shootings rarely involve many (or any) shots being fired, there's no disadvantage in and of itself to have more rounds available. Even some very small semiautos can carry seven or eight rounds, compared to the typical five or six of revolvers. And reloading a semiauto can be done much more quickly than reloading a revolver.

The biggest advantage, though, is that for some people, a given semiauto will point better than any revolver. One of the authors of this book very much likes the Kimber Pro Carry .45 — despite its complicated manual of arms — simply because it points better for *him* than any other firearm he has tried. While he usually carries a snubby revolver in a pocket holster, he occasionally carries the Kimber. Then again, he has spent many, many hours practicing with it and believes — and sincerely hopes — that the proper operation of it would be second nature to him.

Let's hope he never has to find out.

The case against revolvers

While, generally speaking, revolvers fail more rarely than semiautos do, on the rare occasions that they do, fixing the problem is a job for a gunsmith. It's not something that can be done by an ordinary permit holder, particularly not quickly or under the stress of an immediate threat.

Another downside is that most revolvers have a heavier trigger pull than comparable semiautos. For the arthritic, or those with less hand strength, a revolver may not be a good choice, especially since a self-defense shooting will likely involve firing in double-action due to time constraints. This can cause the shot to miss or be less effective at stopping an attack.

Further, some people find that, no matter how much they try to find the right set of grips, they simply can't find one for a given revolver that makes it point well for them.

It can also be argued that the capacity of a suitable carry revolver is less than ideal, and that's true enough. All other things being equal, it's better to have eight or ten rounds than five or six, although how much better isn't at all clear.

The case against semiautos

The main case against semiautos comes down to reliability under stress. To fire more than one round from a semiauto, it's necessary that the slide go back far enough to strip off another round of ammunition from the magazine, then slide forward fast enough to properly chamber it.

A lot can go wrong with that process. If the slide is dirty or rusted, friction may prevent that from happening. If, as the slide is going back, something interferes with it — say, a misplaced thumb or the body of the shooter—that can prevent it, too. There's also the phenomenon known as "limp-wristing," where the shooter's arm doesn't maintain a steady enough position for the slide to function properly. When the shooter's wrist gives, it soaks up some of the energy that the slide needs to strip off and chamber the next round.

And then there's the magazine itself. If the magazine isn't quite right—if it's been damaged, hasn't been properly inserted, or doesn't fit the pistol quite properly—all sorts of jams and failures can happen.

Another trouble spot is the ejector, which is the small mechanism in the pistol that is intended to fling the spent case away after a cartridge is fired. Most of the time, with a quality pistol that's properly maintained, it does just that. Still, the phenomenon known as a "stove-pipe," in which the spent cartridge manages to get trapped in the ejection port, isn't unknown, and anybody carrying a semiauto should be able to clear such failures quickly and without more than half-thinking about them.

Making sure that a semiauto is reliable is more time- and ammunition-consuming than it is for a revolver. If you put a few cylinders worth of ammunition through a given revolver, you can be reasonably confident that it will function reliably. Because a semiauto's operation is dependent among other things on the interaction between the gas pressure and recoil that the cartridge generates and the physical technique of the human operator, it's vital to put at least a couple hundred rounds of ammunition through your semiauto before you trust your life to it. And it shouldn't be just any ammunition, but the ammunition that you're going to carry for self-defense. If you've decided on 115-grain Winchester Silvertips as your personal protection ammunition for your Glock 26, you really should put at least 200 rounds of that very ammunition through it—with the same magazines that you're going to carry it in—and then clean, lightly oil, and retest the pistol before trusting it.

Specific choices

We're not in the business of endorsing or condemning manufacturers. That said, if we're going to try to tell you everything you need to know about carrying a handgun in Minnesota, some advice about kinds and models of handguns that are and aren't suitable has to be part of it. Let's take the different kinds in turn.

"Mouse guns"

This is the somewhat derisive term often used to describe small-caliber semiautos. There was a time when guns that could easily be concealed in a hand or a pocket were limited to .25 ACP and .22 LR, but that's no longer the case.

The Kel-Tec P-32 at right, for example, in .32 ACP, is small, lightweight and flat, and can easily be concealed in a hip pocket, most shirt pockets or, if necessary, a hand. It weighs only 6.6 ounces unloaded, and about 9.4 ounces with a fully loaded magazine.

Handgun manufacturers are designing a wider variety of small handguns these days, many shooting 9mm or 40-caliber ammunition. These handguns are designed for personal protection carry. The advantages of such guns are that they are small and easily concealable. The disadvantages are that they aren't intimidating to look at and, in an actual shooting, it's likely that most or all of the rounds the gun carries will be needed to stop a determined assailant. Also, as a general rule, the lighter and smaller a handgun is, the harder it is to shoot as the ammunition gets more powerful. A very small, very light 9mm will take some practice.

That said, concealability may be a very large factor for some people. Many people whose mode of dress makes concealing a larger handgun difficult or impossible will find one of these diminutive firearms easy to carry, and they'll conceal very well in a pocket holster. And while no handgun ever gets lighter during the day, less than ten ounces really isn't a lot to haul around. Many guns of this size fit well into the category of "backup" guns, or secondary firearms carried along with a larger firearm.

Small revolvers

Small revolvers, such as the Smith & Wesson Centennial revolver at the right, the Colt Detective Special or Cobra, or the various Smith & Wesson clones from Taurus and Rossi, come in several calibers, as does the slightly larger and heavier Ruger SP-101. They are somewhat larger than the "mouse guns," and they do weigh more.

All of these guns can chamber the .38 Special round—a reasonable choice for self-defense—and the guns of newer manufacture are also rated for the so-called "+P" .38 rounds, which build up greater pressure and therefore send the bullet out of the barrel faster. Some small revolvers are even available in the powerful .357 Magnum cartridge. New gun owners may not be aware that any revolver chambered for a .357 Magnum can chamber and shoot any .38 Special round, +P or not.

The alloy-framed "Airweight" guns and the more expensive titanium- or scandium-framed "Airlight" models can weigh less than twelve ounces. Aside from the expense of the "Airlight" models, the only drawback to these light guns is the recoil. A round that is comfortable when fired from a heavier gun is often punishing in a light one. This is more of a range problem than a self-defense consideration—under the adrenaline dump of a life-threatening situation, you're unlikely to be conscious of the recoil. An ultralight revolver isn't likely to be much fun to shoot at the range, though, and you might have to endure some discomfort in order to fire enough rounds to be completely confident that it will point and shoot accurately for you.

These revolvers come in both double-action and double-action only (DAO) models. Both can be fired by a fairly firm squeeze on the trigger, which both cocks the hammer and fires the gun. But the double-action revolver also makes it possible to cock the external hammer manually and fire the gun with a much lighter trigger pull, thereby, at least in theory, making better accuracy possible.

That possible advantage does come with some trade-offs. If the hammer is pulled back and the gun is not fired, it becomes necessary to lower the hammer manually before reholstering it. While that can be done safely, it's not something that's suitable for shaky fingers.

Secondly, while it's a mistake to so much as rest a finger on the trigger of a gun unless it's pointed at a target and to be immediately fired, there are real-world instances of negligent discharges by people who apparently have done just that with a cocked double-action revolver. It is best, by and large, to avoid the whole problem.

All in all, our recommendation, particularly for those new to carrying, is to stick with a DAO revolver, like the one on page 112, for personal protection. Careful selection of grips can make these guns point well for almost any hand shape and size. Grips need to be chosen not only for shape but also for functionality. Wood is far prettier than rubber, but rubber grips are easier to hold onto, particularly with sweaty hands. On the other hand, rubber grips can grab onto clothing and cause your concealed firearm to become visible. Grip choice is one area among many that involves compromise.

If you have a standard double-action revolver, it can be converted to DAO by any experienced gunsmith. Failing that, simply never cocking the hammer manually can serve almost as well, in practice, although there are some legal risks. In one case, a prosecutor claimed that the accused cocked and shot his DA revolver negligently—which is manslaughter, a felony—rather than by deliberate action in self-defense.[54]

Mid-sized revolvers

Mid-sized revolvers like the Smith & Wesson K-Frame series or the hammerless .44 Special at the right are, generally speaking, on the largish side for carry and concealment, but are by no means impossible for that purpose. This is particularly true for models with shorter barrels. The main problem with them is their weight. The Smith & Wesson Model 65, for example,

---

[54] This was the famous Luis Alvarez case in Miami. In 1982, Alvarez, a police officer, shot Nevell "Snake" Johnson, while holding him at gunpoint. A riot ensued. Alvarez was charged with manslaughter and eventually acquitted in what was, at the time, the longest criminal trial in Florida. By the time the trial was over, all Miami Police Department revolvers had been converted to DAO.

weighs two pounds. On the plus side, some mid-sized revolvers can, like the Taurus Model 66, be chambered for up to seven rounds. But, realistically, carrying one of these with adequate concealment can be a challenge.

Full-sized revolvers

Full-sized revolvers are generally unsuitable. They're large and heavy, and the combination of their size and the bulging of the cylinder makes them significantly harder to conceal than anything smaller. However, it's not out of the question to conceal a full-size revolver, such as a Smith & Wesson L-frame or Ruger GP-100, especially if you have a cover garment.

Compact semiautos

Compact semiautos like the Glock 30 (billed by its manufacturer as a "subcompact" pistol, and shown next to the Kel-Tec .32 for comparison) are often good choices, particularly for those who find that they can point-shoot more accurately with a semiauto than with a snubby revolver.

The small Glocks and other compact semiautos are available in a full range of calibers, up to and including the very powerful 10mm Glock 31.

New and experienced shooters alike often find the Glocks a good choice because of their robust manufacture and simple operation. The only external safety on a Glock is a tiny trigger-on-the-trigger, so it's unnecessary to worry about the safety switch being in the wrong position.

Also in the compact category are guns like the Smith & Wesson 3913, the Taurus Millennium Pro series, the Kahr pistols, and some of the smaller Sig Sauers. The Smith & Wesson semiautos do have an external "safety" switch, which is a disadvantage, but they can be safely carried and properly holstered with the safety switch in the "fire" position.

These pistols are, for most people, too large for regular pocket carry—at least as we recommend considering—but they can conceal reasonably well for most people using other carry methods. In a pinch, many of them can be carried, at least for a short period of time, in a large enough pocket.

Mid-sized semiautos

Mid-sized semiautos are also frequently a good choice for those who can count on wearing a covering garment.

The Colt Commander and its clones, like the Kimber Pro Carry, puts seven or eight rounds of .45 ACP in a very flat and concealable package. The manual of arms of such guns makes them a questionable choice for anybody but experienced shooters, however. They need to be carried either with the hammer back and safety switch on, with the hammer down on an empty chamber, or with the hammer down on a loaded chamber. The first carry method requires remembering to push the safety switch down with the thumb in order to fire, the second requires racking the slide, and the third requires thumbing the hammer back. All are easy to do on the range, but could become problematic in a stressful situation.

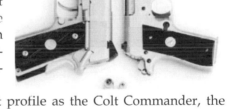

The Para Ordnance LDA series of mid-sized pistols are a much better choice for carry for all but the most experienced users. The compact-sized LDA is shown on the left in the picture, with a Government Model .380 for size comparison.

While they have the same flat profile as the Colt Commander, the LDA pistols can be carried with the hammer down on a loaded chamber and the safety switch off, and still be fired by a firm pull on the trigger.

For newer permit holders, the simplicity of operation of the mid-sized Glocks, such as the Glock 19 or 23, or other simple-to-operate pistols like the Sig P239 at right, can make them a good choice. The Sig pistols have an external decocking lever rather than an external safety, making them prime candidates for carry in this category.

Any of these guns can easily be concealed under a jacket or vest, particularly with an inside-the-waistband (IWB) holster.

Full-sized semiautos

Full-sized semiautos push the limits of what's reasonable to carry, but are by no means beyond them. The classic 1911A1 and similar pistols are very flat, conceal surprisingly well, and can be a reasonable choice for experienced shooters.

A better choice for new permit holders who want to carry a full-sized semiauto is a larger Glock, such as the Glock 17 at the right, or any of the full-sized Sigs. These are recommended because they don't have external safety switches.

While the full-sized Berettas, like the Model 92 and similar offerings from Taurus, are fine firearms, they are both big and thick, and concealing them can be difficult.

Our recommendation

Weighing both the pros and cons, we recommend that new permit holders carry a five- or six-round double-action only (DAO) revolver, chambered in .38 Special, in one of the lightweight alloy frames if you are comfortable with the recoil. These are very simple to operate, and the DAO action prevents any concern about lowering a cocked hammer. Among the good choices in this category are any of the alloy-framed Smith & Wesson Centennial revolvers (such as the 642), the Taurus "CIA" model 850 revolver, the classic Colt "Detective Special" or the lightweight "Cobra" converted to DAO.

The lack of an external hammer makes these revolvers easy to retrieve from a pocket holster without fear of the hammer snagging on the pocket. As you'll see in *The Mechanics of Everyday Carry*, starting on page 145, we think pocket holsters have a lot to offer.

For new permit holders who prefer semiautos, we recommend considering the small Glock, Sig or Kahr pistols, none of which has an external safety switch. These aren't the only good choices, but we think they are among the best ones.

Choosing a self-defense handgun, as we've said, is a serious matter. It's worth some time giving thought to it, discussing it with knowledgeable people — including your trainer — and trying out many different handguns to see which works best for you.

Ammunition

Beyond the issue of caliber and handgun comes the matter of ammunition. There are scads of manufacturers making very good commercial ammunition, some of it specifically designed for personal protection.

Generally, ammunition can be divided into two categories: solid point (usually called "hardball") and hollowpoint, which has a cavity in the nose of the bullet. You'll see both in the illustration here.

Hollowpoint ammunition's primary advantage is that it is less likely to overpenetrate—exit an assailant's body—or ricochet off a hard surface like concrete or a brick wall, continuing in some random direction. Remember that you are responsible for every bullet that leaves your gun, and a prosecutor or judge will not listen long to your excuse that you did not really mean to kill someone two blocks away from where you were attacked.

Hollowpoint ammunition will, at least in theory, quickly expand inside an assailant's body, creating additional damage that will aid in stopping him quickly. A 9mm Parabellum hollowpoint, by this theory, will quickly expand to be larger than a .45 ACP hardball round, thereby doing more damage and stopping the assailant even more quickly than a .45 ACP round would.

That said, there's some question as to how reliably that actually happens.

Even in tests—where bullets are fired into a gelatin medium that is intended to approximate human flesh—hollowpoint ammunition often fails to expand. Even when it does, it often does so only after traveling as much as eight inches or more. In real life, where the cavity of the hollowpoint may become filled with threads of clothing on the way in, it may be even less likely to expand.

And then there's the question of the ballistic gel itself. In order to be a useful way to compare bullet performance, ballistic gel has to be uniform in its composition—but an assailant won't be. How accurately shooting into ballistic gel actually simulates shooting into human flesh is a matter of some debate. A real assailant, for example, will have not only clothing, but bones that can deflect or slow a bullet. As Clint Smith, director of Thunder Ranch, says, "The only thing consistent about small arms ammunition is that it is inconsistent."

Our attitude is to prefer hollowpoints, on the grounds that they at least might expand, but—following what's suggested by the research of Martin L. Fackler—we consider penetration and bullet diameter to be of more importance. This is why we recommend carrying the most powerful, largest-caliber handgun you can reasonably conceal and reliably control.

While there's much good to be said about the very large-cavity .45 ACP hollowpoints (usually called "Flying Ashtrays," produced by CCI and other manufacturers), some semiautos won't feed them reliably. For hollowpoints, it is even more critical to make sure well in advance that your gun will feed them every time. At minimum, you should fire 200 rounds of your carry ammunition without a single jam or failure to fire before considering it suitable for carry.

Following on Dr. Fackler's research, we recommend hardball for those carrying .32 ACP handguns, on the grounds that even the hardball ammunition in these relatively low-powered guns is going to have enough trouble penetrating far enough to cause injury sufficient to stop an attack.

As to what kind of ammunition is good, and what can be defended in court, opinions and myths abound.

Many respected self-defense professionals claim, for example, that a permit holder risks problems in court by carrying handloaded ammunition.

Realistically, both a police investigation and a court case are likely to be far more about whether the use of deadly force was justifiable—at every moment that deadly force was used, as previously discussed—than it is about such peripheral matters as the flavor of ammunition used. We recommend against handloaded ammunition in self-defense weapons, not only or even primarily for liability reasons, but for quality-control ones.

While it's not necessary to use the same loadings as your local police department requires its officers to carry, that's probably not a bad place to start, at least for those carrying guns in the same caliber as their local police department.[55]

We recommend, particularly for new shooters, either carrying the same loadings as the local PD or any of the good commercial ammuni-

---

[55] To find out what ammunition your local police department issues or requires, just call and ask. As of this writing, for example, the St. Louis Police Department requires that their officers carry 9mm+P 115-grain Federal rounds in their service weapons.

tion designated by the manufacturer as "for personal defense." In the unlikely event that your selection of ammunition ever becomes an issue, you're probably better off with something labeled a "personal defense" round than, say, the no-longer-manufactured "Black Talon," about which there was much misleading press. Although with a new name, "Ranger SXT," that round is still immensely popular with police departments.

Among the good candidates are Winchester Silvertip hollowpoints, Federal "Personal Defense" rounds, Cor-Bon ammunition, Remington "Golden Sabers", and Speer "Gold Dot" loadings.

Exotic rounds

Just as a failure of a bullet to penetrate far enough into the body can make it fail in stopping an attack, overpenetration—where a bullet goes through what it's aimed at—can be a serious problem for the more powerful rounds. This is why handguns are a much better choice for personal defense than rifles in most cases, the problem of carrying a rifle in public aside. All but the most carefully selected rifle rounds are problematic for personal defense. A bullet that goes through an assailant will continue on, and there's no guarantee that one or more walls will stop it before it buries itself in some innocent body. "Hardball" rounds tend to overpenetrate more than hollowpoints.

One attempt to solve the overpenetration problem is pre-fragmented rounds, such as the "Glaser Safety Slug" or "MagSafe" rounds. The "bullet" consists of some amount of very small lead shot held in place with epoxy, with a copper casing around it all. Upon hitting anything solid— whether a wall or flesh—the "bullet" immediately fragments, dumping all of its energy into the flesh or the wall, and not overpenetrating.

That certainly works well in theory, and may work well in fact, but there are reasons to believe that such rounds many not penetrate far enough into an assailant's body to do the sort of damage necessary to stop the attack.

We recommend keeping things simple and avoiding exotic ammunition, particularly in semiautos. The cost of running several hundred rounds of Glasers through a semiauto—something that's necessary to ensure it will function reliably—is prohibitive for almost everyone.

Specific ammunition recommendations

There are many good choices for self-defense ammunition. Some recommendations, by caliber, are shown in the following table.

Handgun	Recommendation
.32 ACP semiauto *(Seecamp, Kel-Tec, etc.)*	• Winchester, Federal or Remington 71-gr solid-point ("ball") ammunition • Winchester 60-gr. Silvertip • Speer 60-gr. Gold Dot
.380 ACP semiauto *(aka, 9mm short, 9x17, 9mm Kurtz)*	• Federal 90-gr. Hydrashok • Cor-Bon 90-gr. JHP or 80-gr. DPX • Speer 90-gr. Gold Dot • Remington 102-gr. Golden Saber
9mm Makarov *(aka, 9x18)*	• Cor-Bon 95-gr. JHP • Hornady 95-grain HP/XTP
.38 Special *(older guns not rated for +P rounds; also useful for people sensitive to recoil)*	• Winchester 110-gr. Silvertip • Federal 110-gr. Hydrashok • Hornady 125-gr. HP/XTP
.38 Special +P *(newer guns; also a good choice for .357 Magnum handguns for those who prefer less recoil)*	• Speer 125-gr. or 135-gr. "short barrel" Gold Dot +P • Federal 129-grain +P Hydrashok • Remington 125 grain +P Golden Saber • Cor-bon 110-gr. DPX or JHP +P • Any good commercial "FBI load"—158-grain +P semi-wadcutter hollowpoint
.357 Magnum	• Federal or Remington 125-gr. JHP • Winchester 145-gr. Silvertip • Remington 125-gr. "medium velocity" JHP* or Golden Saber • Speer 125-grain or 135-gr "short barrel" Gold Dot.
9mm Parabellum *(aka, 9x19, 9mm Luger)*	• Remington 115 gr. JHP, 115-gr. +P JHP, or 124-gr. +P Golden Saber • Winchester 115-gr Silvertip or 124-gr. Ranger +P • Cor-Bon 115-gr. DPX or JHP +P • Federal 115-gr. JHP or 124-gr. Hydrashok • Speer 115-gr., 124-gr., 124-gr. +P, and 124-gr. +P "short barrel" Gold Dot.

Handgun	Recommendation
.40 Smith & Wesson	• Winchester 155-gr. Silvertip • Remington 165-gr. Golden Saber • Federal 155-gr. Hydrashok • Cor-bon 150-gr. JHP
.45 ACP	• Federal 185-gr. or 230-gr. Hydrashok • Cor-Bon 185-gr. Sierra JHP • CCI Lawman 200-gr. "flying ashtray" JHP • Remington 185-gr. +P or 230-gr. Golden Saber • Cor-bon 160-gr. or 185-gr. +P DPX

Summing up

It would be easy to say that for a self-defense weapon, it's your choice — and it is.

Beyond that, though, it's hard to argue against the recommendation of a snubby revolver in .38 Special, particularly for those new to carry, and probably for many experienced gun owners.

There'll be more reasons for that recommendation in a subsequent chapter.

And remember: a gun never solves problems.

CHAPTER 7
The Legalities of Everyday Carry

Before turning to the details of how to carry a handgun in public, it's necessary to return to the law — this time about the legalities of carrying a handgun in public.

Relax: this is much simpler than the law on lethal force.

A few preliminaries need to be addressed.

Minnesota law requires a permit holder to possess both a permit and a valid ID (driver's license or state identification card, although a US passport should do) while carrying a handgun in public. Should your permit or ID be stolen, it's best to replace it before carrying a handgun in public.[56] Under the law, police officers are entitled to give a citation to a permit holder who is carrying without the permit and ID — and to take the firearm — although the citation will be dismissed if the permit holder proves that he or she had a valid permit at the time of the violation. In that case, the firearm will also be returned.

Permitted places

Generally speaking, as in much other law, that which is not *specifical-*

---

[56] Minnesota carry permits are intangibles, like a patent, represented by the permit card. Loss of the plastic card does not mean loss of your *permit*, and you are still authorized to carry a handgun on or about your person in a public place.

ly prohibited is permitted. A permit holder can carry a handgun most places, including public places, except where specifically prohibited by law or by proper notice from the property owner or renter.

Carry at work

Special attention should be paid to the issue of carry in the workplace.

Firstly, there is nothing in Minnesota law that forbids a permit holder from carrying his or her handgun at work.

A permit may not even be necessary. Under Minnesota Statute 624.714, Subdivision 9, a permit is not required "to keep or carry about the person's place of business, dwelling house, premises or on land possessed by the person a pistol."

The definition of "the person's place of business" has not been established in court, and until there is a decision by the Minnesota Supreme Court as to what this phrase means, we cannot assume that it includes a workplace where you're employed, but which you do not own.

And if you are required to own it? Does it include employees of a publicly held corporation who own some stock in that company? How about a four-way partnership?

Until sufficient test cases work themselves through the court system, there's simply no way to know if you're breaking the law by carrying without a permit at work. We caution against it; test cases are for other people.

While it is certainly lawful for permit holders to carry at their place of employment—unless it's a specifically banned area, like a school or prison—that doesn't mean you won't be dismissed for doing so, whether or not there is a specific written policy forbidding it.

Yes: it's lawful, but you can be fired for it anyway.

The MPPA permits employers to set regulations about employees' behavior in the workplace, except for parking lots. As a general rule, such regulations ought to be announced in advance. However, as Minnesota is an "at will" state, an employer can, under most circumstances, terminate an employee for any reason (or none), with little or no recourse by the employee. The fact that an employer has not specifically prohibited carry at work may not prevent him or her from firing you for doing so—although if you're fired for that reason, you should immediately contact an experienced attorney.

It's best to quietly investigate the employer's policy, and then make your decision based on what you think the actual risks are. Keeping quiet about your ownership of guns and particularly about your having a carry permit expands your options. You should assume that if anybody at work knows you have a permit, everybody does.

From the point of view of a permit-holding employee, policies on carry in the workplace should be explicit, and ideally allow permit holders to carry.

While there are no pending court cases as of this writing, it's possible that an employer who forbids his or her employees from carrying in the workplace assumes the responsibility of defending them from attacks that could be deterred or stopped with a carried handgun. All in all, employers would be wise not to forbid permit holders from carrying at work, and allow the law take its course.

That said, it's the employer's call. Employers have very broad latitude to prescribe or prohibit behavior while the employee is, as the lawyers say, "acting in the course and scope of that employment."[57]

The parking lot

One of the many virtues of the MPPA is that it cleared up the issue of parking lots. In terms of permit holders and carried handguns, parking lots and ramps are considered public spaces, even if they're owned by an employer. Employers have no right to forbid permit holders from carrying in parking lots.

Still, despite the MPPA, one Minnesota employer specifically prohibited not only carry of any gun on their property, including the rented parking lot, but also the possession of so much as a single gun part or cartridge, even locked in the trunk of a car, and said that they would fire any employee who violates that policy. Whether they will change this policy remains to be seen.

We expect there will be one or more test cases on this.

Employees of that company and those with similar policies should, if they plan to carry to and from work, consider parking outside of the employer's owned or rented property and storing the gun locked in the trunk of the car—and consult an attorney should doing so result in any harm to them.

Another option—which we do not recommend is simply to ignore a

---

[57] In plain English, roughly: while actually at work for the employer, whether on-site or off-site.

company policy against carrying, and carry very discreetly. The risks of being caught and fired have to be weighed against the risks of being unable to defend yourself.

It's a lousy choice, granted.

We don't want to understate the risks of losing your job. Employers have great latitude not only in areas like hiring and firing, but also in searching their property. An employee's desk or locker can be searched without any form of warrant or notice and, to some extent, this even applies to the employee's person.

It won't be easy to find another job after you've been fired for "carrying a loaded, concealed handgun."

Employers are legally entitled to set almost any rules they want in the workplace, even if that means banning all handguns.

A more sensible employer attitude, in the opinion of the authors, would be to permit carry in accordance with the law. In fact, the best thing would be to encourage it, as it would create a safer workplace. However, there is no law requiring employers to be sensible.[58]

Posting

Minnesota law does not make it illegal for a permit holder to carry a handgun in either public or private places simply because it has been posted. That said, property owners do have the right to set limitations on what people can do on their property. Someone who has been asked not to bring a gun into the building, either by direct verbal notice or by the posting of 11 x 17 inch signs at each entrance saying "[Operator of the establishment] BANS GUNS ON THESE PREMISES," may well find himself asked to leave, and possibly charged with a violation if he does not.

If you don't leave when asked, the police can be summoned, and you can be charged with a petty misdemeanor trespassing violation, with a $25 fine for a first offense. Further offenses are treated more harshly.

The very interesting question of whether or not a business owner assumes responsibility for the safety of a permit holder when denying him or her the ability to carry a firearm at that place of business has yet to be addressed by the courts, although legal arguments could, and likely will, be made on both sides.

---

[58] If there was, Scott Adams of *Dilbert* fame would be out of business.

One thing is clear: if you are asked to leave, *do so*.

Still, if you're carrying your handgun properly concealed, it's unlikely that it will ever be noticed. Again, there are likely to be test cases on this, and the sensible thing to do is to avoid being involved in a test case.

Carrying without a permit

The MPPA did not change the situations in which it is lawful to carry a handgun without a permit. A loaded handgun may be carried at one's home, place of business, or when traveling between the two, although how directly you must travel is not clear from the case law.

As we mentioned earlier, case law is also not terribly informative as to what is considered a "place of business." State v. Palmer (636 N.W.2d 810 (Minn. App., 2001) makes it clear that a "place of business" must be a fixed location. Palmer, who carried a handgun as a courier, couldn't use his car as his place of business.

Realistically, anybody who wants to keep a firearm for personal protection, even if only at home, should apply for a carry permit. A permit will eliminate questions about "home" and "place of business" boundaries.

No permit is necessary to carry a firearm — even if loaded — to a place where it will be repaired.[59] In other situations, the gun must be transported "unloaded, contained in a closed and fastened case, gunbox or securely tied package."[60]

Naturally, these restrictions don't apply to permit holders.

Prohibited places

As a matter of policy, it's unwise to prohibit permit holders from carrying handguns anywhere, as those policies announce to criminals that such places are "disarmed victim zones," where they don't have to worry about being confronted by lawfully armed citizens. That said, both Minnesota state and US federal law do prohibit *even* permit holders from carrying in some places, and until those laws are changed, anybody violating them runs the risk of severe legal penalties.

Permit holders are *automatically* prohibited from carrying in the fol-

---

[59] However, explaining to a police officer that that's what you were doing is not likely to be a lot of fun.

[60] Many police officers believe that the case must also be locked, and that the gun must be secured in the trunk of the car. They're wrong.

lowing locations:

1. *Schools and day-care centers.* The only situations in which a permit holder can carry at a school or day care center (public or private) is when staying in the car or taking off the handgun to store it in the car while in the parking lot. You may also carry on school or day care grounds with the explicit, written permission of the school principal or day care center director.

2. *Federal courthouses.* Federal law prohibits citizens, even those with carry permits, from carrying guns in federal courthouses and this is not superseded by Minnesota law. There is no case law as to whether adjacent parking lots are also prohibited, but a conservative approach is best: park outside of the parking lot and secure your handgun in your car before going in.

3. *Courthouse complexes.* Minnesota Statute 609.66, Subdivision 1g, prohibits even permit holders from carrying in court buildings, unless the sheriff is notified. In theory, once the sheriff is notified, it's legal to carry in court buildings. In practice, courthouse guards and police will ask — insist, really — that a permit holder lock up his or her weapon in the secure storage area of a courthouse facility.

If you go into a state court building, such as the St. Paul City/County Center, just walk right up to the guard station. Show the guard your permit and ID, and ask for directions. You will permitted to secure your handgun in a strongbox. Naturally, all safety procedures should be followed at all times, including those for routine encounters with police. Never remove your handgun from your holster without explicit permission or instructions. Unload it, and verify that it is unloaded, before securing it in the lockbox.

It is nothing to be nervous about. The guards and police on duty at the court buildings generally have significant experience with people checking in their firearms, and will usually treat it as a routine matter.

It's reasonable to expect one or more test cases on this subject, as the standard practice is in conflict with Minnesota Statute 609.66. Once those test cases occur and work themselves through the courts, it should be possible for permit holders to carry in courthouse complexes in the same way they carry in the capitol and on its grounds, as described below, simply by giving notice.

In the meantime, it's best to avoid being the subject of a test case, no matter how clear the statute appears to be. Let somebody else deal with the hassle, and read about it on the AACFI website.

4. *The state capitol and buildings in the "capitol complex."* Minnesota Sta-

tute 609.66 Subdivision 1g also prohibits carrying handguns in the state capitol building, its grounds, and nearby buildings in the "capitol complex," with some exceptions. A citizen—with or without a permit—may receive written permission from the Commissioner of Public Safety to carry in these places. Realistically, this is a rarity. A simpler way is provided by Minnesota Statute 609.66. Rather than asking permission, if you're a permit holder, you can give written notice to the Commissioner of Public Safety that you intend to carry on the capitol grounds. This notification should be sent by certified mail, return receipt requested, and a copy of the letter and the return receipt should be kept by the permit holder.

Make the letter simple and businesslike. One sample letter by a permit holder reads as follows. Feel free to use it as a model:

March 21, 2007

Commissioner of Public Safety
Minnesota Department of Public Safety
444 Cedar Street
Saint Paul, Minnesota 55101

Via <u>certified mail with return receipt requested</u>

Dear Commissioner:

Minn. Stat. 609.66, Subdivision 1g specifies that a person who" possesses a dangerous weapon, ammunition, or explosives in any state building within the capitol area described in section 15.50, other than the National Guard Armory" is guilty of a felony, except for several classes of persons, including "persons who carry pistols according to the terms of a permit issued under section 624.714 and who so notify the sheriff or the commissioner of public safety, as appropriate." (Minn. Stat 609.66, Subd 1g, (b)(2))

As a citizen involved in the legislative process, I frequently visit buildings within the capitol area. As the holder of a Minnesota State Permit to Carry a Pistol, it is likely that when I do so, I will have my pistol in my possession.

Please consider this letter as the required notification, securing for me the exemption specified in Minn. Stat 609.66,Subd 1g, (b)(2). A copy of both the front and back of my current permit, which expires on February 21, 2010, is included, as is a copy of the front of my Minnesota driver's license.

Thank you for your attention to this matter.

Very truly yours,

It's a good idea, although not necessary, to carry a photocopy of the letter and the return receipt when visiting the capitol, just in case the issue comes up. If you're questioned by a security officer or state trooper, just be calm and responsive, as when dealing with a police officer on a routine matter.

Since all citizens should participate in the legislative process—at least, that's our opinion—sending out a notification like this one should be a regular part of holding a permit.

You should not, under any circumstances, go through a metal detector without notifying a capitol policeman or state trooper that you are a permit holder and have given notification to the commissioner.

It's no big deal. You'll be let through or, more likely, escorted around the metal detector.

Realistically, experienced police officers in and around the capitol have already encountered a number of permit holders who have given notification, and can be expected to behave calmly and professionally. One of the authors had a conversation with a senior officer in the Minnesota State Patrol assigned to the capitol area who said, chuckling, "Of all the things I worry about around here, it isn't permit holders."

5. *Correctional facilities, state hospitals, and jails.* Permit holders cannot carry in correctional facilities, state hospitals, or county jails, even with advanced notice. This is probably not a bad idea, all in all. If you have to visit somebody in one of these places, just store the gun in your car, properly secured.

6. *When hunting.* It is illegal to carry a handgun "while hunting big game by archery, except when hunting bear." While there's no case law on whether this prohibition is overruled by the possession of a valid carry permit, this is not likely to be a major issue for most permit holders, all in all. But, it's best to be safe. If you're hunting big game with a bow and arrow, leave your handgun at home—unless you're hunting bear.

On the other hand, with that specific exception, Minnesota laws about calibers used in hunting do not apply to permit holders carrying a handgun for personal protection. For example, it is illegal to hunt deer with a .45 ACP pistol, but it is not illegal for a permit holder hunting deer with a suitable rifle or shotgun to also carry a .45 ACP pistol for personal protection. Just don't shoot the deer with a pistol that isn't legal for deer.[61]

7. *Airports.* You may never walk through a security station or metal detector at an airport when carrying a gun, either on your body or unloaded and secured in a locked box. More on that below.

Airports

Airports need special attention. The general rule, which must be paid attention to, is that you may not, ever, walk through a security station or metal detector when carrying a gun, on the body or even unloaded and secured in a locked box.

That said, it's lawful to enter airports, whether to pick up or drop off passengers or to do business *outside* of the security zone while armed[62]. The experience of other states with modern, nondiscretionary permit laws, though, shows that a small number of permit holders occasionally forget they are carrying. You should never approach the security station of an airport—or any other metal detector or security station, anywhere—without first making utterly certain that you do not have a gun on you or in a briefcase, purse, or whatever. This applies to spare magazines, speed loaders, and loose ammunition, as well. Many permit holders get in the habit of carrying a spare magazine or speedloader in a pocket, purse, or briefcase.

It's good to get in the habit of making a short trip to the restroom before braving the security entrance, simply to check all pockets and bags. Yes, it would be embarrassing to have to miss a flight because you forgot that you'd locked your gun in your briefcase, and it would be annoying to have to figure out what to do with a spare magazine or speedloader, but being arrested for forgetting would be even more embarrassing, and worse in other obvious ways.

"I forgot" is not an explanation that will go over very well with the security people at the airports, or with a court later on. Besides civil fines, security violations may also lead to felony charges in federal court.

While lockers outside of the security zone in airports used to be commonplace, in the wake of modern security concerns, they've entirely

---

[61] If, on the other hand, you're attacked by a deer, in or out of hunting season, and have to use your .45 to defend yourself, you're probably okay, but we wish you the best of luck in explaining that to the DNR game officer.

[62] An airport may be "posted" property pursuant to PFPA section 11. In that event, the rules discussed above will apply.

vanished. If you go into the airport with the intention of going inside the security zone—say, if you're going to meet a friend at his gate—just lock the gun, all ammunition, and the holster (just as a matter of good practice) in the trunk of the car.

While there is nothing unlawful about carrying a holster inside the security zone, it's the sort of thing that's likely to draw excessive and unwanted attention from airport security officers, and should be avoided.

For more on traveling with handguns, see *Traveling outside of Minnesota*, starting on page 138.

Post offices and other federal facilities

Post offices and most other federal facilities need special attention, too, because they're a gray area.

The federal law (Title 18, United States Code, Sec. 930.—Possession of firearms and dangerous weapons in federal facilities) is very clear (the emphasis is added):

> Sec. 930. Possession of firearms and dangerous weapons in Federal facilities.
>
> **(a) Except as provided in subsection (d), whoever knowingly possesses or causes to be present a firearm or other dangerous weapon in a Federal facility (other than a Federal court facility), or attempts to do so, shall be fined under this title or imprisoned not more than 1 year, or both.**
>
> (b) Whoever, with intent that a firearm or other dangerous weapon be used in the commission of a crime, knowingly possesses or causes to be present such firearm or dangerous weapon in a Federal facility, or attempts to do so, shall be fined under this title or imprisoned not more than 5 years, or both.
>
> (c) A person who kills any person in the course of a violation of subsection (a) or (b), or in the course of an attack on a Federal facility involving the use of a firearm or other dangerous weapon, or attempts or conspires to do such an act, shall be punished as provided in sections 1111, 1112, 1113, and 1117.
>
> **(d) Subsection (a) shall not apply to:**
>
> (1)   the lawful performance of official duties by an officer,

agent, or employee of the United States, a State, or a political subdivision thereof, who is authorized by law to engage in or supervise the prevention, detection, investigation, or prosecution of any violation of law;

(2) the possession of a firearm or other dangerous weapon by a Federal official or a member of the Armed Forces if such possession is authorized by law; or

(3) the lawful carrying of firearms or other dangerous weapons in a Federal facility incident to hunting or other lawful purposes.

(e) (1) Except as provided in paragraph (2), whoever knowingly possesses or causes to be present a firearm in a *Federal court facility*, or attempts to do so, shall be fined under this title, imprisoned not more than 2 years, or both.

(2) Paragraph (1) shall not apply to conduct which is described in paragraph (1) or (2) of subsection (d).

(f) Nothing in this section limits the power of a court of the United States to punish for contempt or to promulgate rules or orders regulating, restricting, or prohibiting the possession of weapons within any building housing such court or any of its proceedings, or upon any grounds appurtenant to such building.

(g) As used in this section:

(1) The term "Federal facility" means a building or part thereof owned or leased by the Federal Government, where Federal employees are regularly present for the purpose of performing their official duties.

(2) The term "dangerous weapon" means a weapon, device, instrument, material, or substance, animate or inanimate, that is used for, or is readily capable of, causing death or serious bodily injury, except that such term does not include a pocket knife with a blade of less than 2 ½ inches in length.

(3) The term "Federal court facility" means the courtroom, judges' chambers, witness rooms, jury deliberation rooms, attorney conference rooms, prisoner holding cells, offices

of the court clerks, the United States attorney, and the United States marshal, probation and parole offices, and adjoining corridors of any court of the United States.

(h) Notice of the provisions of subsections (a) and (b) shall be posted conspicuously at each public entrance to each Federal facility, and notice of subsection (e) shall be posted conspicuously at each public entrance to each Federal court facility, and no person shall be convicted of an offense under subsection (a) or (e) with respect to a Federal facility if such notice is not so posted at such facility, unless such person had actual notice of subsection (a) or (e), as the case may be.

So it's lawful to carry in post offices and any other federal facilities, right? No.

Firstly, it's never lawful to carry into a federal *court* facility; that's illegal under another part of the statute, which limits carry to, basically, LEOs and military folks on active duty.

But does Title 18, Section 930 mean that it's legal to carry into, say, a post office? That's what the law says—carrying legally for somebody with a carry permit should be one of those "other lawful purposes" mentioned in the statutory exception. That's only common sense.

But the Postal Service, in particular, doesn't agree. They've posted signs that look like this:

Possession of Firearms and Other Dangerous Weapons on Postal Property is Prohibited by Law

18 U.S.C. Section 930.
Possession of Firearms and Dangerous Weapons in Federal Facilities

(a) Except as provided in subsection (d), whoever knowingly possesses or causes to be present a firearm or other dangerous weapon in a federal facility, or attempts to do so, shall be fined under this title or imprisoned not more than 1 year, or both.

(b) Whoever, with intent that a firearm or other dangerous weapon be used in the commission of a crime, knowingly possesses or causes to be present such firearm or dangerous weapon in a federal facility, or attempts to do so, shall be fined under this title or imprisoned not more than 5 years, or both.

39 CFR 232.1 (l).
Weapons and Explosives

No person while on postal property may carry firearms, other dangerous or deadly weapons, or explosives, either openly or concealed, except for official purposes.

Report all firearms violations immediately to the Postal Inspection Service

Poster 158. June 1999

You'll notice that when the Postal Service created this poster, they carefully left out the exemption for "other lawful purposes," and added a reference to the Code of Federal Regulations (CFR).

There's another problem with their theory: they left out the key section of the CFR on this subject:

> "Nothing contained in these rules and regulations shall be construed to abrogate any other Federal laws or regulations of any State and local laws and regulations applicable to any area in which the property is situated."

Or, to put it simply, the United States Code—the statute—*trumps* the agency's regulations.

But—and this is important—there have been no test cases on this. The Postal Service is under the probably mistaken impression that it's illegal for permit holders to carry in post offices, and just "doesn't notice" when off-duty cops or armed security guards (who have the same carry permits as others do) happen to wander in. For the rest of us, they would notice, and there would be trouble.

Do you want to be involved in a test case? Probably not.

Generating a test case is something that somebody with a strong will, a lot of money, and a willingness to spend up to a year in a federal penitentiary *might* think about doing.

For the rest of us, it's really simple: this is a gray area, and it's best to stay out of gray areas. Test cases are for other people.

Short form: it's probably legal to carry in the Post Office, but don't.

Churches

In late 2006, a Hennepin County District Court judge issued a permanent injunction in favor of the Edina Community Lutheran Church barring the state from enforcing:

(1) The statutory sign requirement for posting "religious property" (thus allowing other forms of notice),

(2) The prohibition of parking lot posting on "religious property" (thus allowing bans against employees and visitors), and

(3) The prohibition of bans on a tenant (or guest) carrying or possessing firearms on "religious property" (thus allowing bans against these persons).

The court opinion did, however, make it clear that the burden of providing *adequate* notice to each person who comes on the "religious property" is on the church. Under the 2005 act, (1) personal notice (direct, individual, and by personally addressed writing or verbally face-to-face) of the church's current policy is also sufficient but (2) a specific, individual, face-to-face "demand to leave" is still required.

As the edition goes to print, the state has appealed the lower court decision.

Carrying and drinking

The permit law that the MPPA replaced did not address the issue of drinking and carrying. Supposedly, the printed message on some of the old permits—which stated, without any support in the statute—"Not valid when consuming alcohol or drugs"—was an attempt to remedy that problem.

It didn't. Police departments are not allowed to write laws. That's for the legislature. The only reason this didn't create problems is that permit holders are a self-selected, responsible group of people.

It would have been illegal, for example, for a permit holder carrying in public to have a single sip of a friend's beer while, but it would have been lawful (stupid, but lawful) to drink oneself into a stupor first, and then stop drinking and start carrying.

Fortunately, permit holders have always been a responsible group. The MPPA is both more reasonable than the previous law, and very specific about carrying and drinking.

Carrying while "under the influence of alcohol or a controlled sub-stance" is prohibited. Technically, the MPPA sets the legal limit for blood alcohol content (BAC) of .04 (four hundredths of one percent)—half the legal limit for drinking and driving. It punishes carrying with a BAC of .04, .10 as a petty misdemeanor, and carrying with a BAC of .10 or more as a misdemeanor and, in either case, prescribes a suspension of the permit in addition to a fine or jail time.

Realistically, none of this should be a problem for a responsible permit holder. Even a relatively small man or woman can have one beer, a single glass of wine, or a single shot of whiskey without going near a BAC of .04, and most people's BAC will drop at about .02 per hour after they stop drinking.

It's legal for most people to have a small glass of wine, a beer, or a mixed drink—containing a single shot—once every couple hours over an evening. It's also possible to consult a standard blood alcohol table, and cross-check against sex, age, height, and body weight, in order to get closer to the legal limit without going over.

But we strongly recommend against it.

It's illegal to go over the limits, and it's unwise to try to get close.

When it comes to mixing drinking and carrying, it's best to avoid the whole thing. Alcohol mixes only a little worse with cars than it does with guns. Ideally, you should simply skip drinking entirely while carrying.

On the other hand, if you don't want to take that advice, we strongly recommend no more than a single drink—a glass of wine, a beer, or a single mixed drink—combined with food while carrying. The time to make decisions about combining alcohol and operating any possibly dangerous machine—whether it's a gun or a car—is before drinking.[63]

In a situation where you've decided to drink more than that, the best thing to do is to unload and secure the firearm in a locked case in the trunk before you do, just as it is to make sure there's a designated driver.

If you've decided that you really want to have that second drink (or third, or fourth), unload and secure the firearm first.

Traveling outside of Minnesota

Whether or not another state recognizes a Minnesota carry permit is entirely up to the legislature of that state. As of this writing, Minnesota carry permits are recognized by Arizona, Idaho, Indiana, Kentucky, Michigan, Missouri, Montana, South Dakota, Oklahoma, Tennessee, Utah, and Virginia. Minnesota permit holders may carry in those states, subject to those states' laws. Vermont and Alaska are special cases—no permit, from is necessary to carry in these states.

Minnesota carry law is similar to those other states, but law is subject to change at any time by the other states' legislatures, and you should learn about the current law in a given state before carrying there. For example, some states forbid carry in bars, although Minnesota law does not. Most states require that permit holders carry concealed, unlike Minnesota, and in some there are serious penalties for even accidentally displaying a firearm.

Generally speaking, it's lawful to travel with an unloaded gun, ammunition stored separately, locked in a case in the trunk, if one is simply traveling through a jurisdiction, rather than staying there. A special federal statute deals with this. Title 18 United States Code section 926A provides:

> Notwithstanding any other provision of any law or any rule or regulation of a State or any political subdivision thereof, any person who is not otherwise prohibited by this chapter from transporting, shipping, or receiving a firearm shall be entitled to transport a firearm for any lawful purpose from any place where he may lawfully

---

[63] Never forget that the effect of alcohol on your body is cumulative with everything else you have consumed, including over-the-counter and prescription medications, and medical conditions of which you may be unaware.

possess and carry such firearm to any other place where he may lawfully possess and carry such firearm if, during such transportation the firearm is unloaded, and neither the firearm nor any ammunition being transported is readily accessible or is directly accessible from the passenger compartment of such transporting vehicle: Provided, That in the case of a vehicle without a compartment separate from the driver's compartment the firearm or ammunition shall be contained in a locked container other than the glove compartment or console.

That aside, it is not legal to possess a handgun—even unloaded and locked in a case in the trunk of the car—while *remaining* in New York City, Chicago, the District of Columbia, or Massachusetts. And the same principles that apply to entering the security zone of the airport apply here: forgetting that you have a gun with you does not constitute an excuse if, for example, you decide to stay overnight.

Permit holders who want to travel with their handguns can consult the Attorney General's offices of the states through which they'll be traveling, though the websites at *www.packing.org* or *www.handgunlaw.us* provide largely reliable, generally up-to-date information about carry in the 50 states.

The National Rifle Association also regularly publishes a guide on traveling with firearms. See *www.nra.org*.

Traveling outside the United States

When traveling outside of the US, Mexico is the simplest case: Mexico forbids foreigners—including US citizens—to have firearms or ammunition, and it's both illegal and foolish to drive into Mexico with so much as a single .22 cartridge anywhere in the car.

On the other hand, while Canada forbids US citizens—and, generally, Canadian citizens—from traveling with handguns, Canadian law and Customs Canada regulations permit a visitor to Canada to declare and check in guns at the border, and then retrieve them when leaving.

The guns should be unloaded, in a case, and the ammunition stored separately. Just be sure to stop at a previous rest stop and make sure that's so.

When driving up to the Customs station, the Customs officer will generally ask a question such as, "Are you carrying any handguns for your own protection?"

As usual, the rules about routine police encounters apply. Just answer honestly, and—as an exception to the rule about not volunteering information—inform the Customs agent that the guns are unloaded and locked in cases with the ammunition stored separately, and then proceed as he or she directs you.

In the rare but occasional event that a Customs officer forgets to ask the gun question, and instead says something like "Welcome to Canada," urging you on, it's necessary to say something like, "I've got an unloaded handgun locked in a box in the trunk. May I check it in here?" before proceeding. The fact that a Customs agent has made a mistake isn't a defense in a Canadian court.

Regardless of how the issue is brought up, the Customs officers will either ask you to bring the cased guns inside, or will retrieve the case themselves. They will log in the guns and usually the ammunition, round by round, and then give you a receipt. Canadians tend to look at handgun ownership as a strange thing that US citizens do, but Customs Canada agents have long experience, both with Americans politely checking in firearms, and with a very few trying to sneak one or more through.

There's an important legal point about the ammunition. While Canadian law does not prohibit citizen possession of ammunition, it does prohibit the possession of *hollowpoint* ammunition, and should the Customs officers forget to ask the traveler to check in the ammunition—as sometimes happens—it's important to politely remind them that hollowpoint ammunition is prohibited, and to request that it be checked in as well.

The Canadian Customs station will hold the guns for up to forty days, during which time, upon leaving Canada, you just stop at the same Customs station and produce your picture ID and the receipt. They will give the guns back to you and ask you to sign a receipt.

You should then keep the guns cased and unloaded while proceeding down the road to US Customs. You don't have to declare your firearms when reentering the US, but if you find yourself involved in a Customs search, it's a good idea to politely inform the Customs agent that you have an unloaded firearm that you've just retrieved, and tell him where it is.

Traveling by air

It is both legal and entirely practical to bring a handgun along when traveling in the US by air, although there are a few pitfalls.

Know the local laws of your destination

The most important rule is to be sure, in advance, that you can lawfully possess the gun *at your destination*. If you're final destination is New York City or the District of Columbia[64], you may well be arrested at the airport, even with your gun in checked luggage. It is only lawful under very specific circumstances to pass through New York, New Jersey or Massachusetts with one. In February 2005, the US Department of Justice issued a letter clarifying the effect of 18 USC 926A on direct[65] travel to the airport. It can be found on the Internet at:

www.calgunlaws.com/Docs/TRANSPORTATION%20OF%20FIREARMS/Agenc y%20Opinion/FOPA-DOJltrTSA.pdf.

Again, to find out what the law in your destination is, check the NRA publication, *www.packing.org*, or *www.handgunlaw.us.*

Even if the state doesn't recognize Minnesota carry permits, you may be legally able to keep one in your rented car or hotel room—just be sure what the laws are in advance. While Florida does not accept Minnesota carry permits at the moment, they do have very generous rules for travelers (and will issue the widely-recognized Florida carry permit to non-residents). In Florida, it's not necessary to have a permit to carry a loaded firearm in a private vehicle, as long as the gun is "securely encased." This, under Florida law includes it being in the glove compartment (even if it's unlocked), in a zippered case, or any box with a lid—which includes, for example, a closed cigar box on the seat next to you in the car, or in a holster on the seat as long as you aren't wearing the holster. It just can't be on your person, unless you have a Florida carry permit.

---

[64] Just for your information, both major DC airports are in Virginia. But don't cross the river with your handgun.
[65] Stopping overnight in an unfriendly state, such as New York, is *not* protected by section 926A. Stopping for gas, toilet breaks, or lunch may be.

How to check in a firearm

The general procedure when checking in for a flight outside the security area is to orally declare the firearm to the airline ticket agent. The gun should be brought to the counter already unloaded and in a hard-sided case, and the ammunition should be stored separately, either in the same suitcase or another checked one. Tell the agent as you check in that you have a firearm in your *checked* baggage. Tell them you wish to sign an "orange firearms tag" (most airlines use orange tags; Alaska doesn't, but their agents know what you mean). Make certain that you sign the tag certifying that the firearms are unloaded. The agent initials and dates the tag, verifying that you did declare the firearm. The tag then goes inside the case with the firearm. At this time, lock the gun case and take the keys with you.

The firearm must be in a lockable, hard-sided case within your suitcase, in a soft container inside a lockable, hard-sided suitcase, or in a separate lockable, hard-sided guncase. You may transport a modest amount of ammunition in cardboard or plastic package (not a gun magazine) in the same suitcase. It is best to check the airline's web page or reservation agent shortly before you fly for information about their current limitations and procedures, which can be more stringent than the FAA/TSA regulations (every airline does things a bit differently and not every agent knows the rules). Print out and carry with you copies of both the TSA policies and the specific airline policies. If you have a problem with a ticket agent, don't argue. Instead, ask for a supervisor. In the author's experience, supervisors have been both knowledgeable and helpful.

The airline ticket agent will direct you in how to deal with the federal Transport Security Agency. TSA procedures vary from airport to airport and from day to day. Simply be prepared to follow the agent's directions.

For non-police, there is *no such thing* as a handgun or ammunition lawfully held in *carry-on* baggage.

Usually, the airline will have a baggage handler carry the luggage with the firearm in it over to the TSA screening point. Go with them. Follow the directions of the TSA agent. Sometimes they want to unlock the gun case, and sometimes they don't. The authors have observed various procedures at various airports.

Again, it's not a big deal, and it's nothing to worry about.

What not to do

There are two possible very serious pitfalls. If there is a stop or change of planes, it's important that you check the luggage through to the final destination. Regardless of how you acquire it, it is illegal for a citizen to possess a handgun *inside* the security zone of the airport, even when transporting luggage to be checked in for another leg of the trip.

This can be a problem, particularly when changing planes from different airlines. Some airlines don't have transfer agreements with others. In those cases—and sometimes, in the case of changes in routing on a single airline—travelers will be instructed to pick up their luggage from one baggage claim and check it in for the next leg of the flight.

Don't do this.

Ever.

Ticket agents will, under such circumstances, sometimes try to persuade you to do the transporting yourself.

Listen politely, but politely decline, and do not, under any circumstances, accept custody of the checked baggage containing either the handgun or ammunition. Don't so much as touch the bags. A ticket agent saying, "It's okay—people do this all the time," will not be a useful defense in court.

Ask for a supervisor, but, again: *do not accept possession of the suit-*case containing the gun or ammunition, not even for a moment.

If necessary—and it may well be—it's far safer to notify the airport police and ask to have them do the transfer than it is to put yourself in the position of possessing a gun in a zone where, even if it's unloaded and locked in a case, you can be convicted for doing so.

This simple, inviolable rule must be followed: do not, ever, have in your possession a handgun—or shotgun or rifle, or any ammunition—no matter how it's secured or packaged, and no matter who has reassured you that it won't be a problem, within the security zone of an airport.

In the very worst case, while abandoning a suitcase with a gun inside is a bad idea, it's a much worse idea to put yourself in the position of committing a felony for fear of losing property.

The same rule—make the airline keep it—applies if your plane is diverted to an unfriendly state such as New York, New Jersey, or Massachusetts (or you have to sleep in Chicago or Washington, DC). Taking your gun to your hotel room overnight will result in your arrest the next day when you try to declare it before your flight out. It's a trap, and the local police know it, but they like to hassle gun owners (if you avoid jail, you'll pay a big fine and someone will get your gun).

And remember: a gun never solves problems.

CHAPTER 8
The Mechanics of Everyday Carry

Carrying a firearm for personal protection certainly has legal implications, which we've addressed, and moral implications that you will have to consider for yourself.

This chapter is about societal considerations—a sort of communal agreement as to what is acceptable and tolerable in society. It isn't a legal issue. What, when, and how you carry may very well be within your legal rights, and you should defend them. But, as the Old West saying goes, "Don't scare the horses or the women."

This chapter is also about the practical aspects of carrying a firearm.

When should I carry?

It's up to you. You have to make your own decisions about when to carry. A carry permit gives you the right to carry a pistol, but it doesn't confer an obligation. As a matter of fact, some permit holders will carry a handgun rarely, if ever.

Carrying only when you feel that you're in danger simplifies the problem in some senses, but leaves you vulnerable to the unexpected. Realistically, any attack will be at least somewhat unexpected. Any sensible person who thinks that, say, he or she will be mugged when walking down the street at a given time will simply avoid being there at that time.

We recommend a simple practice: *carry everywhere it's permitted, all the time,* and be prepared to store the gun safely when it's not. (For more on safe storage while carrying, see *Storing when carrying* on page 164.)

That said, carrying a handgun in Minnesota presents some unusual challenges, largely because of the weather. Those new to Minnesota are often surprised how hot the summers are and how cold the winters can be as the wind comes whipping across the plains. The temperature in this state varies over the course of a year, typically by 100 degrees or more, and as the temperature changes, so does clothing. This is a major factor that must be considered when carrying a handgun, as reasonable clothing can range from a t-shirt and shorts to layers of clothing underneath a parka, with everything in between.

Choosing a carry method—or, more likely, a combination of carry methods—that will work across that broad spectrum of dress requires a fair amount of planning.

We'll get to that in a moment, but first, think about this: carrying a handgun is an intimidating experience, particularly at first. You have the sense that everybody sees the handgun; that they're looking right through your clothes.

That goes away after awhile. For the time being, following a few simple rules will minimize the chances of unintentionally frightening somebody.

Don't touch the gun

This isn't just the ordinary safety rule—although safety is always important—but refers to the tendency of somebody new to carrying to be constantly touching at the holster, perhaps through the covering garment, as though to make sure the gun is still there. We call this "pistol petting."

Don't do that. If it's necessary to adjust it or to move it, do it in private—ideally, say, in a locked bathroom, or at least a bathroom stall—rather than fiddling with it in public. If it's necessary to handle the gun other than in complete privacy (say, to move it from a hip holster to a coat pocket when getting out of the car), some advance practice with a gun *that you have repeatedly checked is completely unloaded* will show you that it's possible to do this in a parked car without displaying the handgun, even in the unlikely event that somebody is looking. With more practice, it's possible to quickly and discreetly move a handgun in a pocket holster from one pocket to another without drawing attention, even in public. The main trick is to grip the holstered gun in a way that conceals the butt of the gun in your hand. A casual observer will think it's a wallet or a leather pouch.

This shouldn't be a problem. It's illegal to threaten somebody with a gun, and whether someone feels threatened by an unintentional display is at their discretion. Therefore, it is generally unwise to actually reveal that you have one on you.

Still:

Do avoid exposing it unintentionally

A gun in a hip holster will be exposed if, for example, you sweep your jacket back to retrieve your wallet. It is much better to reach back, behind and underneath the hem of the jacket, and retrieve the wallet without exposing the handgun. This feels strange at first, but with a little practice it becomes natural. Even better is to get in the habit of carrying your wallet on the side opposite where you have your handgun.

Realistically, if you're using a good holster or some other reasonable carry method, it's unlikely that a handgun is going to tumble to the ground. But if it does, simply pick it up and replace it without a lot of glancing around or jerky movements that will make you look like you're doing something wrong. You aren't. Accidentally exposing a handgun isn't illegal, and deliberately exposing one, while unwise, isn't illegal either unless it constitutes a threat.

Still, the earlier caution still applies: if you show a handgun, even accidentally, while engaged in any sort of confrontation, persuading the police or the courts that it was an accident may be difficult.

The belt

One *non*obvious thing about carrying on a hip holster is the fact that *the belt itself is even more important than the holster*. Thin, flexible belts are perfectly adequate to keep a pair of pants from falling down, but they're not rigid enough to keep a piece of metal weighing a pound or more in a stable position. One of the few absolute certainties about carrying a handgun regardless of the method used is that it will never feel lighter as the day goes by.

Most commercial belts, even of the appropriate 1.5 to 1.75 inch width, don't have the required stiffness. Our recommended approach is to purchase one or more belts that have been specially designed to have the necessary rigidity. Most of these are leather belts with polymer inserts through ¾ of their length. The polymer insert prevents both twist and sag—the enemies of comfortable carry.

Aker and Uncle Mikes, for example, sell polymer insert dress belts for roughly $40 retail. Like most specially made gun belts, they are not only more rigid than dress belts, but they have a more dense arrangement of holes that allows for a more precise fit, which also helps to prevent the holster from flopping around.

Carry methods

There are several different basic carry methods and an almost unlimited number of combinations. Still, they can be reduced to the following categories: hip holster, shoulder holster, pocket holster, deep cover, off-body carry, and a few miscellaneous options.

Each of these has different advantages and problems, and we'll talk about each one in turn. Because of both physical and social differences between men and women, the subject of carry for women has some special issues, and we'll get to that in its own section.

Holsters

The most common way to carry a handgun is in a holster. All good holsters have a few things in common: they all cover the trigger guard completely, and all support the gun in precisely the same position each time, without letting it flop around.

Belt holsters

One good carry method that combines both security and availability is the hip holster, which holds the gun on the outside of the hip by a belt. Belt holsters are typically worn on the "strongside" hip (the right hip for right-handers; the left hip for lef-

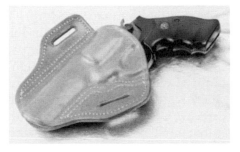

ties), at or behind the hip joint.

One obvious requirement of this method is that you must wear a covering garment over the belt—a coat, jacket, or at least a vest or loose shirt—in order to make concealment possible. While some hip holsters permit a shirt to be tucked around them (the Mitch Rosen "Workman" is probably the best example), for all but the smallest of handguns and the loosest of shirts or blouses, there will still be a noticeable bulge.

As long as you are wearing a covering garment that can be quickly brushed aside, this keeps the gun reasonably available and well-concealed. On the other hand, a gun on a belt holster that's under two sweaters and a zipped-up parka during winter will be anything but quickly available. It's something to think about.

There are all sorts of hip holsters. Some, like the one on the right, with re-taining devices such as "thumb break" snaps, will help to keep the gun in the holster. The key to making this method work is the belt, which should be as wide as is practical—at least 1.5 inches, al-though 1.75 inches is better—and as stiff as possible.

Holsters vary dramatically both in configuration and quality. We recom-mend a moderate approach—neither try-ing to get off as cheaply as possible, nor spending a lot of money on a top-of-the-line custom holster—at least at first. Even a well-made holster that's designed for the gun it's carrying may not quite fit right for a given person, since peoples' bodies and preferences vary.

The "holster drawer"—a sort of living graveyard for holsters that didn't quite work out—is a *very* common thing to have for people who carry handguns.

While there are far too many good on-the-belt holsters to list, among the very good and affordable choices are the Galco Fletch and FX for 1.75-inch belts, or their "Concealable" model for 1.5-inch belts. The Milt Sparks "55BN," a custom holster available in all belt sizes, the Desantis "Thumb Break Scabbard," and the Alessi "Belt Slide Unit" are also good holsters.

Prices for these holsters vary from about $50 to around $95, and they can be bought either at local stores, by mail order, or on the Internet.

For on-the-belt carry, high-tech plastics such as Kydex are often good choices. Plastic is less expensive and needs less care than leather. A particularly good choice for Glock owners is the minimalist Glock "Sport" holster, available for around $15. The only problem with this holster is that it leaves the muzzle of the gun exposed, and while the bottom of a closed leather or plastic holster might, if it shows, be mistaken for the bottom of a cell phone holster or something similar, the muzzle of a handgun is distinctive.

Inside the waistband

One very good kind of hip holster, which hides most of the barrel and muzzle, is what is called the "inside the waistband," or IWB, holster. Instead of riding on the outside of the belt, this holster is slipped inside the waistband of the pants and is generally still secured to the belt, which presses the holster and handgun into place.

We like IWB holsters a lot. The "tuckable" style, like the Comp-Tac "C-T.A.C." holster at the right, allows great flexibility in concealment clothing.

For many people, this has huge advantages. The covering garment doesn't need to extend past the bottom of the holster, as it, along with most of the gun itself, is concealed inside the trousers. Nothing but a strap or so is visible on the belt line, and somebody seeing the strap will most likely think it's a carrier for a pager or cell phone.

Further, the importance of the stiffness of the belt is diminished, since the belt is used to compress the holster up against the body rather than supporting the weight of the gun. And, as a temporary expedient, if it's necessary to remove the covering garment, you can pull your shirt or blouse out and tuck it around the holster, providing decent concealment.

As always, there are trade-offs. Unless you already have pants that fit loosely around the waist, you will be required to buy new trousers with an additional inch or two in the waistband. Some people, especially those with bad backs, find that the pressure against the side and back can become painful, particularly after a few hours.

And while high-tech plastics such as Kydex can be perfectly fine on the belt, the stiffness of the plastic tends to make them uncomfortable when they're pushed up strongly against the body.

Some IWB holsters are soft-sided, and the mouth of the holster will collapse when the gun is removed, making reholstering a complicated, two-hand operation that might require undoing the belt. This isn't particularly a problem for somebody who is keeping his gun on his hip all day, but presents ongoing difficulties for people who have to take the gun out to store it before going into a prohibited place. On the other hand, soft-sided holsters can be more comfortable.

We recommend hard-sided holsters for IWB carry.

Among the recommended holsters in this category are the Alessi "Talon Plus" (pictured at right), the Desantis "Inner Piece," the Galco "Summer Comfort," the Tucker Gunleather "Answer" and "Royal Guard," the Milt Sparks "Executive Companion," and the Mitch Rosen "ARG." One of the best Kydex designs is the "C-T.A.C." by *www.Comp-Tac.com*. One model of C-T.A.C. holster will hold all three lengths of Glock 9mm pistols, while another model will hold all three lengths of Colt .45 pistols.

Prices, by and large, are a little higher than for equivalent on-the-belt holsters.

Shoulder holsters

Shoulder holsters have some advantages, but also a lot of problems.

For obvious reasons, they always require a covering garment, and the vest or jacket or coat has to cover not only the gun itself, but all of the straps as well. The temporary expedient of pulling out the shirt that can work well for an IWB holster or even decently for an on-the-belt holster isn't available. If you have to take off your covering garment and don't want to expose your holster, you'll have to go off to the bathroom or some other private area, remove the whole thing, and then store it in a briefcase or bag.

Again, television is misleading: on TV, many policemen wear shoulder holsters and seem to have no trouble removing their handgun when they need it.

That's not usually true in real life. Since men tend to have arms that are shorter relative to their shoulder width than women do, it's often more difficult than it looks on television for men to reach under the armpit and retrieve the gun.

Shoulder holsters can be uncomfortable. If the straps are narrow, they'll tend to cut into the shoulders. Shoulder rigs with wider straps are more difficult to conceal, and more expensive.

Shoulder holsters, in general, are fairly expensive. Among the better commercial ones are the Galco "Miami Classic" and "Jackass," the Alessi "Guardian," and the Desantis "CEO Shoulder Rig," but even the least expensive of these costs more than $100. The price of shoulder holsters only goes up from there.

The "Rolls Royce" of domestic shoulder holsters is probably the Mitch Rosen "Stylemaster," but that starts at close to $400 — more if you want an exotic leather.

On the positive side, by carrying the handgun on one side and spare magazines or speedloaders on the other side, shoulder holsters balance well and keep the handgun reasonably available while seated or driving. A jacket or coat doesn't have to be completely unzipped or unbuttoned to make the gun available.

One major limitation of most shoulder holsters is that they are, like belt holsters, one-handed. Only a contortionist can quickly reach up with the right hand to where the gun is under the left armpit, open the thumb-break closure, and remove the handgun at all, much less quickly. Furthermore, when you draw, your arm is out there in front of your body begging a close assailant to grab it. To add to the problems of shoulder holsters, the horizontal variety insure that the gun is always pointed at someone, or at least part of someone. That's usually a "no-no."

Drawing from a shoulder holster generally means sweeping a large area or number of people before the gun is trained on the attacker. The majority of the time, the strong-side hand removes the handgun from the holster and sweeps an area of from 90 to 180 degrees before the gun can be leveled at the target. Everything and everyone is an unintended target as the firearm moves towards the assailant. Great for TV; not so good for real life.

For revolvers, there is another option, although it's not a common one. Shoulder holsters based on the classic Berns-Martin design, popularized by the James Bond books, hold revolvers in a butt-down position by a spring built into the holster itself, which clamps around the cylinder. It looks strange — the barrel of the gun seems to point directly up toward the armpit—but it's actually quite practical for revolvers.

These are not made by any of the main commercial manufacturers these days, but Ken Null of KL Null Holsters (*www.klnullholsters.com*) makes what he calls his "City Slicker," a plastic version of the classic Berns-Martin. The particular advantages of these holsters are that they permit the handgun to be retrieved by either hand, and the durability and moisture-resistance of the plastic, combined with his particularly low-profile harness, permits them to be worn under loose-fitting shirts.

Still, the problems with shoulder holsters remain.

All in all, our recommendation is that shoulder holsters be thought of as special-purpose holsters and not be a prime candidate for day-to-day carry, particularly for men.

Pocket holsters

All three of the contributors to this book like pocket holsters.

Pocket holsters are a terrific choice for many people, particularly those carrying smaller guns. Anything other than overly tight trousers makes them very concealable, and the ability to reach into a pocket without doing anything dramatic permits you to, if necessary, get a grip on the handgun without having to commit yourself to displaying it. Pocket holsters also have the advantage of being able to fit into different kinds of pockets—the same holster can work in the pants pocket, a coat pocket, or even in the chest pocket of a parka, if it's large enough.

The price of a good pocket holster also tends to be much lower than for other kinds of holsters. The Uncle Mike's Pocket Holster series, like the holster shown above, starts at about $10, and is perfectly adequate for pants pocket carry, especially for smaller semiautos. The fact that the pocket itself is helping to hold the gun prevents the necessity of the holster fitting tightly around the gun. The suede strap stitched into the outside of the holster will keep the holster in the pocket when the gun is drawn.

For guns that are going to be carried in a coat or jacket pocket at least some of the time, a more rigid pocket holster is a better idea. These are more expensive but, again, prices are relatively low compared with belt holsters.

Galco, Milt Sparks, Desantis, and many other quality manufacturers make good-fitting, rigid pocket holsters, all of them designed to permit you to draw the gun while leaving the holster in the pocket where it belongs. These run from $40 to around $70. An excellent pocket holster, in our opinion, is the KD Holsters "Pocket Defender."

Even the Kramer Pocket Holster, at the upper end, goes for only around $85, and the leather square stitched to the outside of the holster gives it the outline of a wallet even in a tight pants pocket.

For people new to carrying a handgun, we recommend a combination of a small hammerless revolver and a rigid pocket holster as a good starting point. Many experienced permit holders will find that it's not only a good starting point, but a completely satisfactory permanent carry method. The holstered gun can be carried in a pants pocket and easily transferred to and from a coat pocket. With a little practice, this can be done in public without drawing any attention to yourself. The hand conceals the butt of the handgun, and if somebody notices the leather square of holster, it just looks like a wallet or case for an electronic device.

One huge advantage of a pocket holster is that it enables you, in a stressful situation, to get your handgun *in your hand* without committing yourself to drawing it or displaying it at all. Instead of sweeping back your jacket (as you'd have to with a belt holster) or shoving your hand into your jacket (as you'd need to with a shoulder holster), all you have to do is stick your hand in your pocket. That's something people do all the time, and it doesn't draw attention — unless you want it to.

As we discuss later, it may be reasonable under some situations (say, when walking to your car in a darkened parking lot late at night) to actually carry your handgun in your hand, on the grounds that, while you're probably not going to need it, if you do need it, you'll need it now, and not have to get involved in trying a fast draw out of the movies or television.

With a pocket holster, you can already have the firearm *in hand* and can get it out a lot more quickly, without doing anything threatening in advance, should it be necessary to bring it out.

Consider two similar scenarios in that darkened parking lot. In both cases, you're walking to your car, and somebody starts to approach you from across the parking lot. You're nervous about him — there's something about his appearance and manner, and the fact that you're alone. The only car around is yours, and he's walking in a way to intercept you, rather than just cutting across the parking lot.

Naturally, the first thing you do is thrust out your left hand, palm out, and say, "Please stop. Stay where you are." While that isn't normally a polite thing to do, an isolated, dark parking lot is one of the places where you've got enough reason to worry about your security to give up being polite for the moment. Innocent people will, by and large, not only respect your request and your personal space, but will understand it and apologize for violating it as they move away.

In the first scenario, you're carrying a full-sized semiauto on a hip holster, under your jacket.

In the second, you've got a small revolver in a pocket holster.

Bill Jordan, the legendary Border Patrolman, was capable of drawing and firing in a measured .270 seconds, but his reflexes were almost inhumanly fast, and he spent thousands of hours practicing. Even so, Jordan said on more than one occasion that "if you don't have your gun in your hand when the trouble starts, you probably never will get to it." A good pocket holster — one that covers the trigger guard, and prevents you from accidentally putting your finger on the trigger — lets you have your gun in your hand well before trouble starts, and without any danger of frightening innocents.

We think that's a terrific advantage.

The only possible disadvantage it has is that it has no "macho value" at all.

That's as it should be.

Deep cover

Beyond standard holsters, there's a whole variety of "deep cover" alternatives, and some of these can be very useful.

One common type of holster in this category is what's called the "belly band." This is basically a broad elastic bandage with an attached holster, and it is worn under the shirt. It does conceal very well, but it's necessary to either unbutton the shirt or yank it up in order to get at the gun. It works best for people with flat stomachs, as otherwise the holster tends to flop around.

Kramer Leather makes what they call their "Confidant Shirt Holster." Basically, it's an armless t-shirt with a built-in elastic holster under each armpit. It's worn much as a t-shirt is, under any shirt or other clothing and, just as is true for the belly band, it can make retrieving a gun very difficult, but it conceals very well. The only additional disadvantage is that the t-shirt itself is, for structural reasons, made from poly-

propylene rather than cotton and can be very uncomfortable, particularly when worn for extended periods of time. Particularly with heavier
guns, the pressure of the straps on the shoulders can be painful.

Still, it does provide excellent concealment.

Perhaps the strangest but possibly the most useful "deep cover" carry method is the under-the-pants pouch, sold by the brand names of
Thunderwear™ or Thunderbelt™. The gun is carried in a breathable
plastic or denim pouch on the front of the waist—just over the crotch, or
slightly to the side—with the butt either under the belt or the belt resting
on the butt of the gun.

The real problem with Thunderwear and similar holsters is safety,
for obvious reasons. Either holstering or retrieving the gun requires
pointing it at your crotch, and that violates the safety principle of "never
point a gun at anything you're not willing to destroy."

Almost everybody who uses one of these devices finds the whole
process somewhat nerve-wracking at first, and it's absolutely necessary
to spend a lot of time—with a many-times checked, unloaded gun—
holstering and unholstering before considering this as an actual carry
method.

That aside, there are some definite advantages to these devices. Since
they come with a built-in elastic belt to hold the pouch in place, you're
not dependent on your own belt to hold up the weight of the gun. They
can work perfectly well under, say, a loose pair of running shorts, trousers and slacks with a shirt or blouse, a three-piece suit with either a belt
or suspenders, or, for women, either a dress or a skirt. Because of how
well the shape of the body and drape of all but the tightest clothing tend
to conceal the handgun, they offer excellent concealment, usually with
an undetectable bulge. And since it's both rare and impolite to stare at
somebody's crotch, even a modest bulge will rarely draw attention.

Retrieving the handgun is simply a matter of reaching the thumb
down the front of the pants or skirt—or, in the case of a dress, yanking
up the dress—pulling the gun butt up with the thumb until you can get
a full grip on the handgun, and withdrawing it. None of that looks particularly graceful or becoming, of course, but a life-threatening situation
is not the time to worry about that sort of thing.

It should be noted that, in the case of any carry method, but particularly for Thunderwear, there may be a situation where it is necessary to
get the gun out quickly, but there is never a time when it's necessary to
put it away quickly. You should make a habit, even when using weapons that are known to be unloaded, to be very, very slow and delibe-

rately careful when inserting the gun into such holsters.

Thunderwear and other pouches can be a reasonable choice for those people for whom a compromise between deep concealment and fast access is important, but we caution that such holsters should only be used after much practice with a repeatedly checked, unloaded weapon.

Miscellaneous carry methods

Some miscellaneous carry methods have been around for a while. An ankle holster is one. At first glance, it does have some advantages. For example, the trouser leg covers the pistol and relieves concerns about brushing back a covering garment or having a bulge in your shirt. The main problem with ankle holsters is that they put the gun as far away from the hand as it can be and still be on the body. While it may be reasonably accessible when seated in a chair, when standing it's necessary to stoop over — not a good idea in a dangerous situation — before getting the gun in hand. Even when seated in a car, particularly from behind the steering wheel, it's difficult for all but the most limber to get at the ankle, and the holster

Ankle holsters are a bad idea for your primary gun.

Still, as long as there are people, there will be new ideas, and some newer ideas are useful. One unusual holster is called the "Pager Pal™." It's a pager, either real or phony, which is firmly attached to a flat leather holster. The holster itself slides inside the pants, similar to an IWB holster, with the pager hanging it on the belt. To retrieve the gun, it's a matter of pulling the holster at least partway out by the pager.

Also in the miscellaneous carry category — and more useful — are the various "fanny packs" specifically designed for guns. There is usually a concealed compartment, closed either by a zipper or Velcro fastenings, which — *importantly* — keeps the gun separate from other things being carried. Those where the gun compartment is sealed with a zipper often permit the use of a small padlock to seal the compartment shut, making storage much safer. For people who already carry fanny packs, this is obviously a good choice. The gun is reasonably accessible, and the fanny pack is also useful for things like keys, wallets, change and cell phones. All of the major holster manufacturers — including Bianchi, Galco, and others — make some form of these, with prices ranging from around $20 to around $50.

Fanny packs are definitely handy—and not just for handguns—but they're not for everybody or every situation. For one, they look distinctly out of place in most office or more formal settings. The general rule for using a fanny pack to carry a handgun is that it should be used only where fanny packs are already common. You'll find them in abundance at the malls, or on people taking walks in parks, and so forth.

The main problem with fanny packs used for handguns is what to do when you take them off. That issue will be addressed more generally in *Storing when carrying*, starting on page 164, but as a matter of safety and common sense, either the gun or the fanny pack—or, better, both—must be secured when it's not on the body.

Holsters to avoid

One apparently convenient idea is the small-of-the-back (SOB) holster. Instead of being placed on or just behind the hip, the holster—usually with a dramatic cant—goes on the belt in the middle of the back.

There is an obvious advantage to this mode of carry. There's little danger of a covering garment being inadvertently swept so far aside that the firearm is revealed.

The main problem with it is one of safety. Putting a piece of hard metal—even inside a holster—up against the spine isn't a good idea. When sitting, the back of the chair or car seat will press the handgun up against the back, and a fall—whether on an icy sidewalk or if being attacked—can slam the holstered firearm against your spine, doing a horrible amount of damage.

Small-of-the-back carry is only a good idea if you've got a spare spine.

Another option—less problematic, but still recommended against—is the cross-draw holster. Instead of being on or behind the strongside hip, the holster sits on the weakside of the belt, with the butt canted toward the strong hand. The main problem with this is concealment. For anybody with arms shorter than an orangutan's, the holster will have to be placed in front of the hip, making it more difficult to keep the firearm and holster concealed under the covering garment, and making unintentional display more likely. This is a common carry mode for plainclothes police, but on-duty police officers—uniformed or plainclothes—don't have as much need to avoid having the fact that they're carrying a handgun being noticed as sensible citizens do.

Cross-draw holsters have an advantage for those who spend most of their time sitting while carrying, such as truck drivers or anyone confined to a wheel chair. Anyone else would be well advised to try a different method first.

Carry without a holster

It's also possible—although generally *not recommended*—to carry a handgun without any holster at all. Depending on body type, gun shape, and the tightness of the belt, it's possible to simply insert a pistol or revolver inside the waistband of the pants and have the belt itself hold it in place. Similarly, pocket carry without a pocket holster is possible, particularly for revolvers, which tend to ride properly barrel-down, as opposed to the relatively butt-heavy semiautos, which tend to shift around.

One particularly neat and inexpensive device is the "Barami Hip Grip." These are replacement grips for small revolvers that incorporate a small flange. The gun is inserted into the waistband, with the flange preventing the gun from slipping down into the pants.

The main disadvantage to carrying in any of these ways is that the trigger is not covered. That's a particular problem with pocket carry. It's possible—and has happened—that something like a set of keys carried in the same pocket can become wedged in front of the trigger, causing an unintentional discharge when the gun is removed from the pocket. If you do carry a handgun in a pocket without a pocket holster, be sure to put nothing else in that pocket. Still, all in all, we recommend against holsterless carry methods, particularly for those new to handguns.

That said, it's not impossible. With some practice and experience, holsterless carry can be done. Small revolvers and smaller semiautos can simply be slipped into a pocket or under a sufficiently tight belt, with the pressure of the belt holding the gun in place.

Again, it's not recommended, but is not utterly beyond reasonable consideration, either.

Off-body carry

There's not a lot of good to be said about off-body carry, except that it's sometimes necessary. It's important that, when you're carrying a handgun in public, *it be under your personal control at all times*, and that's difficult to do unless it's on your body.

That said, there are quite a few devices that can be used at those times when carrying on the body is impractical. For women, some manufacturers make purses with hidden compartments. Others make daily planners with a hidden compartment. Similarly, compartments in briefcases specifically designed for handguns, or even ordinary ones, can be used. A photographer's bag can easily conceal a handgun in one of its compartments.

The problem with any form of off-body carry is that, in an emergency situation, it's very easy for the gun owner to be separated from whatever it is that's carrying the gun.

Our suggestion — our strong suggestion — is that the only good places for a self-defense handgun are on the body or secured. This applies also to women and purses.

The bathroom

One problem that those who are new to carrying a handgun in public will have to deal with is the rest room, as indelicate as it is to mention.

In the case of single-user rest rooms with a lock on the door, there is no problem. You simply remove the handgun from the holster, perhaps placing it on an edge of the sink, and use the facility. When you have finished, you readjust your clothing and replace the handgun in the holster. The only possible pitfall is in forgetting the handgun in the bathroom — *don't do that.*[66]

Typical public bathrooms, though, don't provide that level of privacy. What's to be avoided is to have a person in the next stall seeing a handgun — or even a holster — lying on the floor. Part of carrying a concealed handgun is *keeping* it concealed.

For men using a urinal, it's fairly simple to manipulate the zipper without brushing the covering garment aside, although those men who typically loosen their belt when using a urinal will need to stop doing that. The clunk of a handgun hitting the floor, either still in the holster or after having fallen out, will draw attention.

From time to time, men as well as women will need to use restroom stalls. Typical stalls are open at the bottom, and it's obviously undesira-

---

[66] One permit holder, who found himself halfway out of the bathroom with the handgun still on the sink, has ever since made it a habit when using public bathrooms to remove one shoe and put the handgun in it.

ble for the person in the next stall to be able to see trousers or slacks down around the ankles, with a firearm and holster in clear view.

Obviously, this isn't a problem for those using shoulder holsters. For those who carry via a belly band or Thunderwear, the solution is easy: the belly band or Thunderwear can simply be left in place, and the clothing adjusted before leaving the stall. Similarly, for pocket carry, it's just a matter of making sure, when lowering the trousers, that the holster doesn't show.

With belt holsters, the problem remains.

One obvious way to handle the problem is to hang the holster — or the handgun itself — on the hook of the stall.

It's obvious, but it's a *bad* idea for several reasons. For one thing, it removes the handgun from your immediate control, if only by a few feet. Thieves have been known to reach over the top of restroom stalls and steal purses and other bags, and it's hard to imagine any good coming out of one stealing a handgun under that sort of circumstance.

A little foresight, as usual, helps. It's possible, and unlikely to draw any attention, to bring a briefcase or other bag into the restroom stall, keep it between your feet while using the facility, and put the handgun in that, with the trousers or slacks arranged to conceal the holster.

Failing that, arranging the lowered trousers or slacks to cover the handgun, while it remains in a belt holster, is something that takes only a little practice.

If necessary, the pistol can be removed from the holster and placed in a pants pocket or kept in the lap while using the toilet.

The bottom line on carrying and using the bathroom is: develop a procedure, dependent upon your style of carry, that allows you to safely conceal the firearm and holster from view and prevent theft. Use your procedure consistently to prevent accidents (with the firearm) and to avoid accidentally leaving the handgun in the restroom.

Carrying for women

Women have special issues when it comes to carrying self-defense handguns, both for cultural and physiological reasons.

As a historical matter, most belt holsters were designed for men. Because of generally different shapes in the hip area, and where the waist of women's slacks or skirts are relative to men's, a handgun carried in a typical belt holster will have the muzzle pushed out by the swell of a woman's hip. This tilts the gun so that the butt digs into a woman's side which, while not dangerous, is decidedly uncomfortable.

For police-service holsters for women, the problem has been solved by spacers, which push the top of the holster further out from the hip. That's a fine solution for uniformed women police officers—but uniformed police officers, both male and female, don't carry concealed. The butt of the pistol sticks out significantly, and that's the sort of bulge that will be noticed under any covering garment.

For women carrying concealed, spacers won't do.

There are some belt holsters designed specifically for women. Perhaps the best known is the Mitch Rosen "Nancy Special," which tilts the grip forward and out just a little, rotating the barrel of the firearm out of the way to prevent the butt pressing in on the side. Take a look at the holster at the right. It's got that extra tilt, and it's not pressing the handgun into the side of the woman wearing it.

Still, there's the question of dress.

Men generally wear shirts and trousers, with the trousers secured by a belt. A slightly wider than normal belt is unlikely to draw much attention.

Women generally wear skirts and blouses or dresses. In both cases, the typical belts are usually rather thin, and a covering garment—a jacket or vest—is not worn as routinely as it is for men. For women wearing jeans or slacks and some sort of jacket or vest, a belt and holster combination—as long as it's the right holster—is every bit as practical as it is for men. Similarly, for those women who wear suited skirts and similar attire, the matter of the belt and holster can be handled by proper selection of both. Galco, for example, makes a concealment belt that, while wide at the sides and back, is tapered to an inch or so in front. Under a jacket or vest, it looks like a one-inch belt.

But for women wearing more typical clothes—either a skirt and blouse, or a dress—without a covering garment, belt holsters are a problem.

Shoulder holsters, when a covering garment is worn, are far more practical for women than they are for men. Generally speaking, women's arms are much longer in relation to the width of their shoulders, and it's usually much easier for a woman to reach across the chest and acquire the grip of a pistol in a shoulder holster than it is for a man.

Still, the rest of the limitations apply: shoulder holsters must be covered by some garment, and the sort of temporary expedient possible with belt holsters — untucking a shirt to cover the handgun and holster — just isn't possible.

That said, for women who wear sufficiently loose blouses or shirts, it is possible to wear one of the KL Null shoulder holsters under the blouse or shirt. Since the strap of the harness is thin and white, should the strap show at some point, it's likely to be mistaken for a bra strap.

But it won't work under a tight blouse, or one of sheer material.

The obvious place for many women — and some men — to carry a handgun is in a purse or the equivalent, and many manufacturers make purses with concealed pockets for handguns.

We recommend against this. Even the most alert people occasionally lapse in attention for just a moment, and a purse snatching is a bad enough thing in itself without making it worse by giving the criminal a handgun.

In the case of a violent attack, anything carried — including a purse — is likely to be knocked away. During the day at work, it's often necessary, if the gun is in the purse, to lock the entire purse in a desk drawer, leaving it available to anybody who has the key to the desk. It's simply *not acceptable* to leave a gun with a purse in it on the desk unattended. Permit holders must keep their firearms either secured or under their personal control at all times.

All in all, we strongly advocate in favor of on-the-body carry, both for men and women. Those women who can't find another suitable on-the-body carry method should seriously consider Thunderwear, the Kramer Confidant t-shirt holster, or a belly band.

There are intermediate steps possible, particularly if you have a place to lock up the firearm at work.

One female permit holder has made it a habit to carry her pistol in her coat pocket, in a pocket holster, both to and from work. When she gets to the place she works, she immediately proceeds to the women's room, with her briefcase, where she takes her gun from her coat and locks it in a small case, which she keeps in a locked bank deposit bag. The locked bag is then locked in her desk drawer throughout the day until it's time to leave, at which time she reverses the process.

In this case, her employer does have a generalized policy against carrying in the office, but it's been specifically waived for her, with the understanding that she'll keep the firearm secured while she's at work and not scare anybody with it. In her case, it's not been a problem.

For more on work-related issues, see *Carry at work* commencing on page 124.

Storing when carrying

There are often times when it may be necessary to store a gun while away from home: you may need to enter a prohibited place like a school, you may not be able to carry at work, you may decide to go out for a few beers with a friend, or any of a myriad of other things.

When you do that, the gun must be securely stored, and it's important to decide how to do that in advance.

We recommend securing the gun in a lockable container inside a locked car. If your evening out includes drinking alcohol, we recommend unloading the gun before locking it up.

The important thing is preventing the gun from being stolen. Simply leaving it in a car is a bad idea. Most cars can be broken into quickly by experienced thieves, and the locks on most cars' glove compartments (if even equipped with a lock) are remarkably weak. The Secure-It from *www.aacfi.com/products/secureit.shtml* is designed to reduce the possibility of theft from a vehicle. The lockable metal box is small enough to be hidden under the seat, and it comes with a strong cable that can be attached to a seat support or other permanent structure of the vehicle. It is inexpensive to boot.

The trunk was once a good place, but today most cars come with a trunk-opening latch or button in the passenger. A gun stored in the trunk must also be in a locked container.

You can get a specially made gun box to bolt into the trunk of your car. These aren't terribly expensive, either. You can buy them for around $60 and up, and they can be installed in either the passenger compartment of the car or the trunk. Or, you can use the Secure-It discussed above.

Some of these lockboxes come with Simplex push-button locks, which enable keyless access. Push-button locks are also useful for storing guns in the home, combining reasonable security with reasonably quick access — and, of course, if quick access is an issue, it's perfectly reasonable to leave the gun fully loaded in a lockbox that's been bolted in place, whether that place is the car or against the bedroom wall.

When traveling, stay at hotels with in-room safes or bring a Secure-

It. The key point is this: when you're carrying in public, maintaining control of your handgun is your responsibility. It needs to be either on your person, or secured.

That's just plain good sense, and good safety.

Specifics of Minnesota law

There are a few things about Minnesota law that affect issues surrounding everyday carry.

Let's take a look at them.

Carrying openly

Minnesota law is unusual in that it allows both open and concealed carry with a permit. Some states require, by law, that permit holders carry in a way that an average person can't tell they are carrying. The only thing that makes concealment required in Minnesota is common sense.

If you have a carry permit, you are theoretically allowed to strap a cowboy-style sixgun belt around your hips and walk around in public. But *don't*. You'll scare people, and you'll get a lot more attention from the police than you care for.

You'll also make the whole permit-holding community look irresponsible, and you'll help nervous anti-self-defense types persuade your city or county government to prohibit open carry.

Minnesota Statute 609.66 is clear:

> "Whoever does any of the following is guilty of a crime and may be sentenced... (1) recklessly handles or uses a gun or other dangerous weapon or explosive so as to endanger the safety of another; or (2) intentionally points a gun of any kind, capable of injuring or killing a human being and whether loaded or unloaded, at or toward another."

"Brandishing" is prohibited by other sections — as is harming or threatening someone, either by word or pointing. But simply holding a gun isn't illegal, provided it's not pointed at someone or part of a threat.

That said, there are times when it may be prudent to carry a handgun openly, but discreetly — even in your hand.

Obviously, this the sort of thing that should be done in high-risk, isolated situations while obeying the safety rules (say, while walking to the car in a parking lot or ramp late at night). This is not reckless and, in the dark, it's very likely that it won't be noticed, if you do it discreetly.

The word "discreetly" is used deliberately. While it's not illegal in and of itself, it could be misinterpreted by somebody who sees the gun, and could, at least conceivably, lead to a misdemeanor charge of disorderly conduct.

Number and type of guns carried

Minnesota law does not limit the number of handguns a permit holder can carry at the same time, or at different times. It's perfectly lawful, though silly, to carry a dozen guns at once—but don't.

Most sensible people will carry a small, easily accessible pistol or revolver and leave it at that. At most, you may want to carry a larger firearm and a single backup.

With the expiration of the so-called "assault weapons ban" in 2004, there is no legal restriction on having "pre-ban" or "law enforcement only" magazines, which hold more than ten rounds.

Handguns vs. long guns

In terms of carrying a gun, Minnesota law does not distinguish between handguns and long guns.

While Minnesota Statute 624.7181 makes it illegal for most people to carry a rifle, shotgun, or BB gun in public, it also expressly excludes permit holders: a permit holder can carry a rifle or shotgun anywhere that he or she can carry a pistol or revolver. The sole exception is carrying a long gun in the passenger compartment of a motor vehicle; a practice that is forbidden due to a hunting law.[67]

Carrying a long gun is, in theory, like strapping a cowboy sixgun belt around your waist and going for a walk in public. Yes, it's legal to sling your shotgun over your shoulder and go shopping—after all, with a proper sling, it won't be pointed at anybody—but don't.

The police would, no doubt, find some theory that you wouldn't like.

In practice, of course, permit holders will not be carrying rifles or shotguns around in public.

---

[67] This is the DNR's interpretation of Minnesota Statute 97B.045.

Loaded guns and children

Section 609.666, Subdivision 2 of the Minnesota statutes makes it a crime for someone who "negligently stores or leaves a loaded firearm in a location where the person knows, or reasonably should know, that a child is likely to gain access, unless reasonable action is taken to secure the firearm against access by the child."

While there is no specific law on the storage of unloaded firearms, any negligent storage may leave a gun owner subject to other criminal penalties, such as child endangerment, or to civil charges if somebody misuses one of the guns.

What is "reasonable action"? We don't know. The people who wrote the law intended for it mean either securing all firearms, or teaching gun safety to children who are old enough—but there aren't any appellate cases where it's been decided if safety instruction is enough.

Realistically, the Minnesota law is no more stringent than the requirements of good gun safety (see *Gun Safety, On and Off the Range* on page 169), and people who resolutely follow sound safety practices will not find themselves at risk.

And remember: a gun never solves problems.

Everything You Need to Know About (Legally) Carrying a Handgun in Minnesota

CHAPTER 9
Gun Safety, On and Off the Range

Safety is a vital component of AACFI's and this book's orientation. The safety rules are simple and few. In truth, it's quite possible to neglect all but any one of them without something really bad happening.

But *don't neglect any of them*. Ever!

Make a firm commitment to obey *all* the rules, *all* the time. People do make mistakes at times, but if you make a conscious effort to follow all of the safety rules all of the time, the odds that you'll ever hurt someone with a negligent discharge of your firearm are very close to zero.

There is a simple problem with all firearms: after a bullet leaves the barrel, there is no way to call it back. Your first protection against causing harm to yourself and others is to make sure no bullet is ever fired from your gun unless you intend for it to happen. Your second protection is to make sure that, even if a bullet is fired unintentionally, it goes somewhere harmless.

Basic safety rules

The four basic safety rules are straightforward. We have changed their original order for the simple reason that you cannot verify a firearm is unloaded until you have picked it up. While checking it, it must be pointed in some direction, so we address the rules in the order in which they become operable.

1. Always keep your finger outside the trigger guard until you're ready to shoot

Beginners seem to have more trouble with this rule than any other. Whether that's due to the influence of toy guns, the natural ergonomics of handguns, or television and movies isn't clear.

Regardless, it's extremely important. Most trainers advocate keeping the index finger pointed straight forward, parallel with the barrel. Others, like Massad Ayoob, favor pressing the tip of the index finger against the frame of the handgun, above and forward of the trigger. Either method is fine. The important point is that you keep your finger off the trigger, even when the gun is pointed at a target, until you're actually ready to shoot.

In a defensive shooting situation, this rule has benefits beyond safety. Placing your finger along the frame acts as a pointing aid. By pointing your trigger finger at the target, you improve your hand-eye coordination and improve your accuracy. Go ahead and try it.

A second benefit is that it gives you a bit more time (if even a millisecond) to make the final shoot-no-shoot decision before placing your finger on the trigger. Under the stress of an attack, once you put your finger on the trigger, it is highly likely the gun will be fired. Keeping your finger off the trigger until the last possible moment provides a bit more time to make a final decision.

2. Always keep every firearm pointed in a safe direction

Pretend there is a laser beam shining out through the barrel, destroying everything it touches. Whenever you're handling a firearm, make sure the imaginary laser beam never shines on another person, or a window, or anything else you're not willing to destroy. Even when holstering a handgun, do it (if possible, and it usually is) without pointing the muzzle toward any part of your own body, even for a moment, and always do it without pointing the muzzle at someone else.

This has to be done actively. Imagine a situation where you are holding an unloaded handgun, pointed in a safe direction, and somebody starts to walk in front of it. You must take the responsibility to make sure it doesn't point at that person. Whether you do it by persuading him not to walk in front of it or by pointing it in another direction doesn't matter. What does matter is that you make absolutely sure that, at no moment — not even for a split second — does the firearm actually point at him.

3. Always treat every firearm as though it's loaded

The main cause of firearms accidents is assuming that a gun is unloaded when it isn't. If you make it a policy to treat a firearm as though it's loaded — even when you're utterly certain that you unloaded and checked it even a moment before — you won't be involved in that type of accident.

Since AACFI's primary focus is self-defense training, we know that all self-defense handguns are *always* loaded. Therefore, we alter this rule to say that *Every gun is loaded until it is proven unloaded.* To do this, you perform a clearing procedure (more on that in a moment).

4. Always know your target and what's beyond it

When you pull the trigger, you are responsible for sending a bullet from the barrel at extremely high speed. You are responsible for where the bullet goes and what it hits. There are no two ways about it — you fire the gun, you own the results. Add to this the fear and excitement of having to defend yourself and, all of the sudden, how comfortable you are with your gun, how safely you handle it, and how well-practiced you are for accuracy become even more important.

The best way to deal with this rule is to maintain a constant awareness of your surroundings and those around you. Being aware of your physical situation, as well as your options, allows you to plan ahead. When you are in *Condition Yellow* (see page 27), consider how best to avoid a problem, what steps can be taken to retreat or call for assistance, and whether introducing a firearm will be useful at all. If you step back to the left or right as you draw, will the background be clear? Will the introduction of your firearm make the tactical situation better or worse? Get in the habit of thinking through the costs and benefits of drawing your gun before a situation ever presents itself. "Be prepared" isn't just a motto for scouts.

Your situational awareness is part of the mental preparedness that backs up your split-second, "shoot-no-shoot" decision. That decision is not as simple as it sounds. In milliseconds, you need to process the potential legalities of your actions and the likelihood that you will be able to justifiably hit only what you need to hit. It demands both mental preparedness and physical practice.

Sally, a fictional soccer mom enjoying the afternoon sun outside her favorite java hut, doesn't deserve to have her day or life ruined because you missed your target. You may not have any legal issues as a result of hitting Sally accidentally, but the trauma of hurting an innocent bystander will remain with you forever.

Know your target, know what's beyond your target, and don't shoot unless you are confident that you will hit only your target.

Rules for handling guns

Beyond the four basic safety rules, the next in importance are the rules for handling firearms.

Let's take each in turn.

1. Every time you pick up or are handed a firearm, make sure it is unloaded

New gun owners are often surprised to see experienced gun owners constantly opening actions and checking firearms, as though they're nervous or unsure about whether or not the guns are loaded. They're not nervous, they're just practicing good safety. Even if you've just handed an unloaded gun to your best friend and he's had it for only a second, the moment he hands it back, you must open the action and check it. Each check is a form of *clearing procedure* (a process to verify that a firearm is unloaded).

For revolvers, it's a matter of swinging out the cylinder—at which point the revolver, even if the chambers are loaded, can't fire—and looking into each chamber. Although simple, opening the cylinder and focusing on the chambers to be sure they are empty is a two-step clearing procedure.

Semiautos are more complicated, which is one of the reasons we recommend revolvers for those new to firearms.

Semiautos can have rounds in the magazine, in the chamber, or both. While pulling (racking) the slide will almost always eject a round from the chamber, releasing the slide will chamber another round if there's a loaded magazine in the pistol.

So it's important to follow all the steps, *in this order*, every time:

1.   First, remove the magazine, and either set it aside or hold it in

your hand.

2. Second, rack the slide *three times*. Pull the slide all the way back and let it go. Don't worry about doing it gingerly; the gun can handle it. It does so every time it is fired.

3. Third, pull the slide all the way back and look carefully inside the pistol, making sure there is no round in the chamber or somewhere in the magazine well.

4. Fourth, uncock the gun. If the pistol has a hammer, lower it by pointing the pistol in a safe direction and the decocker or decocking safety. Or, you can simply pull the trigger with chamber empty. Then — and *never* until then — reinsert the magazine.

This is the same semiauto clearing procedure taught to air marshals, federal flight deck officers (armed pilots), and other federal law-enforcement officers. It works for them. Make it work for you, too.

If you do the steps in the wrong order — say, racking the slide before removing the magazine — you will have chambered a round, which is why we recommend racking the slide *three times*. Ejecting three live cartridges in a row should give you a clue that something is wrong with your clearing procedure.

And if you uncock the gun by pulling the trigger without verifying that the chamber is empty, you may, a few milliseconds later, put a hole in something. *Do not make this unfortunate error!*

Almost everyone who has seen a cartridge ejected from a supposedly unloaded pistol has experienced a momentary surge of adrenaline and fear!

2. Practice safe gun handling

Before you hand a firearm to someone else, make it a point to verify that the gun is unloaded and the action is open.

A revolver with an empty cylinder swung out, or a semiauto with the slide locked back and the magazine removed, simply can't fire at that moment, and won't be able to until several things happen.

Make it a habit, when handing a firearm to somebody else, to do it just like this. In addition to being the safest way to hand off a firearm, it also shows consideration and respect for the recipient.

3. If somebody wants to hand a firearm to you, ask that he unload it and open the action

There are very few situations when this rule and the rule above don't apply, but don't go looking for them.

4. Don't leave firearms unattended, loaded or not

The reasons for this are obvious. Firearms that are not under your immediate control should be secured. If they're not being kept for self-protection, they should be unloaded as well.

5. Think before you act—take your time

If you're at the range, and your handgun has failed to fire when you've pulled the trigger, there's no reason at all to rush. If you're shooting from behind a bench — the usual situation — the first thing you should do is just set the gun down, with the muzzle pointed downrange (in a safe direction), and think about it for a moment. Wait at least sixty seconds before opening the action[68]; there's no hurry. If you're concerned about what to do next, this gives you an opportunity to call the range officer or a knowledgeable friend over.

In self-defense situations, unfortunately, speed and haste may be necessary. At the range, neither is ever necessary, so take your time.

Safety when shooting

Beyond gun handling are issues around actually shooting. Most shooting, of course, should and will take place on the range.

If you're careful and lucky, none of your shooting will ever take place anywhere else, but the same rules apply.

1. Keep your finger off the trigger until you're ready to shoot

Yes, we know we're repeating ourselves, but this rule is critically important.

Even on those very rare occasions when a handgun is being brought out "for real," you still need to keep your finger off the trigger until you're ready to shoot. That's the very *last*

---

[68] There could be a delayed ignition of the cartridge. You don't want that to happen while it's in your hand.

step before firing, and you need to consider other matters first.

You must assume that, under the stress of a life-threatening situation, what would normally feel like just resting a finger on the trigger is very likely to send a bullet moving downrange at extremely high speed the moment you touch your finger to the trigger. The adrenaline dump we discussed in a previous chapter will seriously affect you, and you simply can't count on the sort of fine motor control you normally have. Also, when you have tunnel vision—which is, as you've seen, likely to be the case in a life-threatening situation—you can trip over things, or have a "startle reflex," and your hands can clench. If that happens when your finger is on the trigger, you'll likely fire the gun.

2. Be sure you know where your bullet will go

The range is the place to find out if your firearm shoots where you point it. Before selecting a particular handgun for carry, be sure it points well for you. If a particular revolver shoots to the right of where you point it, you want to find that out at the shooting range and not in the street.

Don't shoot before considering what happens if you miss, or if the bullet over-penetrates your target.

Formal ranges have massive backstops behind the target area. Even so, at indoor ranges, note that the ceiling above the target is often marred by bullets that didn't go where they were supposed to.

At an indoor range, that's sloppy shooting and likely to irritate the range owner. Outdoors, it can be much worse. A round that's fired above the backstop can go a terribly long distance—a mile or more, in some cases—and, while most well-designed outdoor ranges have a large enough "dead area" behind the backstop, that's often not the case with informal ranges. Be sure that you know where your bullet is going to go, not only if you hit the target, but if you miss it.

In a self-defense situation, you may not have as much choice as you would like but, when practicing, you always have the option to stop for a moment and think about it.

Even in the gravest extreme, you are obligated—both legally and morally—to consider what might happen if you miss.

It's not okay to miss your assailant by an inch and send a 125-grain bullet whizzing across a busy street and into a schoolyard, and it's foolish to think that even frequent practice can guarantee that you'll be able to put a bullet into a human-sized target from even a few feet away.

We advocate firing at the center of mass (COM) during a defensive shooting. Aiming or pointing toward the middle of the chest means that you may be able miss your target by as much as a foot or more horizontally and even more vertically and not send a bullet past the assailant.

Further, the torso is the thickest part of the human body. It's not unknown for relatively powerful handgun bullets to penetrate all the way through the chest or belly and come out the other side, but it's incredibly rare for all but the most powerful rounds.

3. Don't drink before shooting

This should be obvious.

An afternoon at the range, followed by dinner and a few drinks with friends — after the guns have been cleaned and put away — is a fine thing, just as a few beers around the cabin or campfire after a day of hunting is.

It's *the order* that is important. Reverse the order — drink before shooting — and you're asking for trouble. Guns and alcohol just don't mix, and that includes cleaning as well as shooting.

The same thing obviously applies to any drug (prescription or nonprescription) that affects your judgment or perception. We're not suggesting any silliness here. A diabetic can, of course, take insulin or metformin at regular times during the day, even when going to the range, but mixing firearms and recreational drugs isn't only illegal, it's stupid.

Remember that many nonprescription drugs contain alcohol and that some can affect judgment and perception. Some common antihistamines can have dramatic effects. If in doubt, don't go shooting until you've consulted with a physician or pharmacist.

A few miscellaneous safety issues:

Cleaning guns

Most of the time, being shot or shooting somebody else while cleaning a gun is fiction (a lie).

It was either suicide or reckless gun handling.

The first step when cleaning a firearm is to make sure it's unloaded, and a detailed cleaning of most semiautos and rifles requires that the firearm actually be disassembled first, which makes it literally incapable of being fired. For some firearms — Glocks, for example — the first step in disassembly is to dry-fire it: pull the trigger with the internal mechanism cocked, but the chamber empty. Always make sure that the firearm is unloaded before doing that, and point it in a safe direction while dry-firing it.

Realistically, most "gun cleaning" accidents are either suicide or the result of playing with guns, while ignoring more than one safety rule.

Don't ignore safety rules. When cleaning a firearm, make sure it's unloaded and remove any ammunition from the immediate area.

Storage

Firearms that are not being kept for self-defense should be unloaded and secured, with the ammunition stored separately. This is one of the few things that responsible gun owners and anti-gun hysterics actually agree on. You're simply not likely to need, say, your .22 target rifle in a hurry; targets will wait patiently.

When it comes to self-defense weapons, storage options are less obvious and require some careful thought.

A self-defense handgun will be either not needed at all, or needed immediately and when you are under stress. In real life, it's not likely that you will think, "Gee, I'm going to need a handgun—and need it badly—in about five minutes." If a handgun is needed, *it's needed now.*

If it's not needed immediately, there are almost certainly better ways to handle the situation than by using a handgun. If you've got five minutes, you can just drive away or even run away. If you've got half an hour, there's probably enough time for the police to arrive.

An intruder in your home won't give you an opportunity to find your keys, retrieve a self-defense handgun or shotgun from the gun safe, and then retrieve your ammunition and load your gun.

Granted, it will probably take much less time to do all that than it will for the police to respond to a 911 call, but still, it's clearly not an adequate solution to an immediate problem.

How to store your defensive guns depends on your situation. Some gun owners without children leave a loaded handgun in or on a bedside nightstand, some all of the time and some only at night.

We recommend against this practice. A home is not a safe, and burglars can break in at night or during the day. The most likely place for a burglar to look for a handgun is near the bed and, whether you're at home or at work, you don't want to provide an intruder with a loaded firearm.

One inexpensive and reasonable solution is the Secure-It, a small metal lockbox with a steel cable that can be used to attach it to a bed frame or other solid object. It can also be mounted permanently to a shelf or drawer. It's available from *www.aacfi.com/products/secureit.shtml*.

Other options include small fire safes and insulated file boxes with combination or key locks. Besides storing important papers, a loaded gun can be kept inside. With one of these, it's important to unlock it every night before going to bed, and lock it again every morning.

For those with children, a system like this may be inadequate. Odds are that you will eventually forget to lock it, leaving a loaded handgun in a place where a child can get at it. The same argument applies to any gun box with a keyed lock.

We prefer specially designed gun boxes that have simple push-button locks—either an electronic lock or the mechanical Simplex lock—that can, after a little practice, be quickly opened in the dark. The big name in electronic gun boxes is Gun Vault, and several well-known manufacturers use the mechanical, push-button Simplex lock, including Amsec, Cannon, and R&D Enterprises.

A three-pound gun box is, of course, not a substitute for a five hundred pound safe. Still, it can be counted on to keep a loaded self-defense gun away from a thief or child in the short term.

How to store a handgun inside a gun box is another consideration. Perhaps out of fear of liability, many manufacturers recommend against storing guns in a condition in which it will take just a trigger pull to fire the gun.

We recommend storing a self-defense handgun in precisely the same state that you carry it.

And, as a matter of safe gun handling, every time you remove the handgun from the box—no matter how much or how little time has passed since you put it in there—be sure to check whether or not it's loaded. Yes, you'll treat it as loaded regardless, but you do need to *know*, not remember or assume.

Wash your hands

The chemical components that make up modern propellants aren't terribly toxic, but they are not intended for human consumption. And the lead in bullets is very definitely toxic. After shooting, be sure to wash your hands thoroughly before doing anything else.

Wear safety glasses and hearing protection

This should be obvious, but we'll say it anyway: loud sharp sounds can damage your hearing severely. Be sure to have your hearing protection in place *before* you step out on the range. Hearing protection can consist of specially made earplugs or headsets that clamp over the ears. In some cases, wearing both is preferable. Earplugs are usually available for under $1 per set, and headsets start at around $10.

There are also very effective electronic sound-canceling headsets that use high-tech computer circuitry to cancel out loud sounds while letting ordinary sounds—like conversation—through. These can be purchased for about $40 at *www.aacfi.com/products/HearingProtection.shtml.*

Hot gases and particles that are kicked up by shooting can be bad for your eyes. For those who don't wear glasses normally, eye protectors are necessary. For those who do, eye protectors that fit over glasses add protection and are strongly recommended.

Gun safety and children

For those with children, the most important part of gun safety is education. Teaching your children the gun safety rules for children is essential

The NRA "Eddie Eagle" program recommends teaching children to do the following if they see a firearm:

STOP!
DON'T touch.
LEAVE the area.
TELL an adult.

Beyond this mantra, teaching children about the proper handling of firearms under an adult's supervision is certainly a good idea, as is having children help to clean the guns. There's nothing better for taking the wonder and excitement out of firearms than helping to run a few dozen patches of foul-smelling cleaning solution through the barrel of a disassembled firearm, and then having to scrub up later.

Keep all firearms either on your person or secured. Obviously, firearms being kept for self-protection can't be kept unloaded with the ammunition stored separately, but they can be secured in a holster on your body or in a locked gun box. Firearms not being kept for self-protection should be unloaded and secured.

Hiding guns with the hope that children won't find them is unsafe and risky unless the child is an infant. Yes, putting the firearm on the top shelf of the closet is fine if your child is in a bassinet. If you're going to rely on training your children as a means to ensure their safety, assume that they know where the guns are.

We recommend the NRA "Eddie Eagle" program very strongly. With hundreds of millions of firearms in tens of millions of households in the US, it's important for all children to know what to do if they see a firearm: *Stop! Don't touch. Leave the area. Tell an adult.* This training will be useful not only in your own home, but can save a life should your children visit the home of someone who pays less attention to safety than you do.

Gun accidents

In 2000, there were around 600 fatal gun accidents in the US, according to the National Safety Council — more than six times that number of people drowned. In that year, the largest group to die in fatal gun accidents were adults 25-44 years of age.

In reality, the number of gun accidents in the US is at a hundred-year low and continues to fall almost every year, both in total numbers and on a per-capita basis. Despite the increasing population and the increasing numbers of firearms in the US, fatal accidents have fallen by more than 60% over the past quarter century. Maintaining that trend is primarily a matter of education and of following all of the safety rules, all of the time.

Be part of the solution, not part of the problem. Please.

And remember, a gun never solves problems.

CHAPTER 10
Shooting, on the Range and on the Street

When you take your carry permit course, whether from an AACFI instructor or somebody else, shooting should be a relatively small part of your training. And that's why this chapter is short.

The reason is simple: most of what's important about the responsibilities of a permit holder are the day-to-day things: staying out of trouble, avoiding conflict, and so forth. Most permit holders, as we've said, will never have to so much as take out their handgun "for real" — and that's just fine.

But if you're going to carry a self-defense handgun, you must know how to shoot it. While we're going to discuss some of the details of that here, you really do need some one-on-one instruction if you're not already very familiar with handguns. Even then, more instruction is a good idea.

Training in gun safety and handling is part of the AACFI's *Basic Handgun* course. It's intended to get you ready for the AACFI *Carry Permit Course*. See the AACFI website at *www.aacfi.com* for details.

This is not to say that the AACFI is the only group whose certified instructors can teach beginners about safe gun handling and basic shooting skills. There are also many gun clubs in Minnesota that give introductory courses in firearms handling and shooting, and they're generally very good.

That said, there is a very large difference between target shooting—the focus of much other training—and self-defense shooting, which is the concern of AACFI Carry Permit training.

Target shooting vs. self-defense shooting

Target shooting is, among other things, fun—although some people never do take to it. At a range, you stand behind a shooting bench in a well-lighted area when you shoot. You take your time settling into whatever position you like, take a breath and let half of it out, focus carefully on the sights and gently squeeze the trigger until the gun fires. If you've done it right, there's a nice round hole in the paper target, or perhaps you've knocked over a tin can, or turned a stale cookie into a cloud of rapidly expanding crumbs.

The point is that, when target shooting, you can take your time, are not under real stress, and can easily see not only your target, but also your sights.

A self-defense shooting is going to be *different* in almost every respect.

Most self-defense shootings take place in low-light conditions, making both the sights and the target—your assailant—difficult to see. No self-defense shooting allows a lot of time for thought: if you have a lot of time to think about it, you've probably got enough time to escape.

And then there's the stress. As discussed previously, the stress of a life-threatening situation causes physiological changes that have serious implications.

While some training courses have students do things to increase their heart rate (e.g., running in place or doing pushups), an increase in heart rate is only part of what you'll experience when you're frightened—although trying to hit a target with your heart pounding from exercise can be humbling.

Still, it's not possible to duplicate the actual stress of a life-threatening event on the shooting range.

What is possible to do—and what AACFI-certified instructors teach—is self-defense shooting, as opposed to target shooting. We start with how you stand, moving to how you hold your firearm and finally, to how you point it—and we emphasize *point* when shooting in self-defense.

Three basic stances are taught in modern handgun self-defense courses, and our recommendation of the Isosceles stance combined with point shooting needs some explanation.

Let's start with the stance: how you stand when you're shooting in self-defense or practicing on the range.

The Weaver

In the Weaver stance, the body is turned slightly away from the target as the pistol is brought up to eye level—so that the sights can be used—in a two-handed grip, with the strong arm slightly flexed and the weak arm flexed more. The strong arm pushes out on the pistol, while the weak arm pulls in, creating a tension that helps the shooter quickly return the pistol to the same position after each shot. It feels a little awkward at first, but with some practice it's possible to quickly fire multiple accurate shots at a target.

The Chapman

The Chapman stance, or Modified Weaver, is similar. The main difference is that the strong arm is kept as straight as possible, ideally with the elbow locked. In effect, the strong arm becomes a human rifle stock. Again, the strength of the upper body is used to bring the sights back on target, and the target is not faced quite directly.

With either the Weaver or the Chapman stance, the head is usually turned slightly to the side to bring the dominant eye in line with the sights.[69]

There's no question that both of these two stances permit fast, repeated, sighted fire at many distances. There's also no question that mastering either of these stances requires a lot of time and effort.

---

[69] People vary. Some right-handed people use their left eye for aiming and shooting; some use their right. The same is true for lefties.

The problem is that many people (we think almost all) who have been thoroughly trained in either of these stances simply won't use it when under the stress of an attack. We've seen videos of police shootings — and encourage you to do the same — on any of the television programs that show such things. How many times do you see police officers taking up a Weaver or Chapman stance? How often do you see them cocking their head to one side to bring the dominant eye in line with the sights?

At best, it's a rarity.

The Natural Isosceles

The Isosceles stance is different; it's more instinctive. You face the target directly, with your strongside leg taking half a step back, as though trying to back away from the threat. This is what people do naturally when faced with a threat. They face it squarely, and at least start to back away.

The handgun is thrust out, either at chest- or eye-level, as though using the gun to push the threat away.

For reasons discussed in a previous chapter, a violent confrontation is physiologically different than shooting on the range. The massive adrenaline dump makes it almost impossible for most people to use the sights or take up anything other than an instinctive stance.

This is not a new insight.

Colonel Rex Applegate, who spent much of WWII training OSS agents, argued over many years that, "most shooters, no matter how well trained in the Weaver [stance] instinctively revert to the Isosceles when faced with life threatening situations... he instinctively faces the threat with both eyes open focusing on the target."

Videos of police shootings bear this out. Police are, by and large, *not* trained to step back on the strongside leg, and they *are* trained to use their sights. Nevertheless, in video after video, you can see that the officers are stepping back on the strongside leg and focusing on the assailant instead of their sights.

Even in the famous 1986 FBI Miami shooting, one of the FBI agents—a champion in FBI pistol competitions—was shot dead while standing and looking at his assailant, unable to focus on his sights.

Realistically, even if you *can* look at the sights, they may not do you any good—anywhere from 80% to 90% of self-defense shootings take place in low light or worse. This is why we emphasize that your carry handgun must *point* well for you. *Point shooting is aimed shooting.* You are just using your body and stance to index on the target rather than the sights of your gun.

Bruce K. Siddle's 1998 paper, *Scientific and Test Data Validating the Isosceles and Single Hand Point Shooting*, presents data supporting the notion that, under stress, almost all people will square off against the threat and not turn their body away from it even a little, regardless of what they're trained to do.

It would be hard to argue that, in good light and with enough time to assume a trained stance, and given the ability to remember to do so, careful sighted fire from either the Weaver or the Chapman stance wouldn't be more accurate than point-shooting from an instinctive stance. It probably would. But if highly trained police officers can't and don't, can you?

Probably not.

The late Julio Santiago of Burnsville, Minnesota, a veteran of the US Army and twenty-five years as a Deputy Sheriff, was one of the first trainers to note this. He spent much of his life teaching the importance of point shooting, particularly in low-light situations where the sights won't be useful.

Of course, you could train both methods and hope that you will be able to choose between the two in a life-threatening emergency. We prefer, as usual, to keep things simple and use what's instinctive as the basis for defensive shooting. Massad Ayoob teaches advanced students that it's possible, from the Isosceles stance, to raise the handgun high enough to use the sights. We see no problem in doing this if you can.

Most self-defense shootings take place at close distances where point shooting works. Beyond close range, distance yields time, and with that time you can transition to sighted fire, or maybe even escape without having to fire. If you can escape, you probably should.

Take a look around your home. Unless your house has very large rooms, it's difficult to envision a situation where you could be more than 20 or so feet away from an assailant.

This is why self-defense firearms training takes place at very close distances. Many AACFI trainers do all their shooting training and qualifications at 15 feet which, in terms of real-life self-defense distances, is fairly long. But by far the majority of self-defense shootings take place within just a very few feet or at actual contact distances.

We think that you should initially plan on putting in a lot of range time, both by yourself and under formal or informal instruction, using the Isosceles stance.

To assume an Isosceles stance, grip the handgun with your strong hand (finger off the trigger) and support it with your weak hand. Bring it up to chest level and thrust it straight out toward the target, as though trying to push it away with the muzzle of the firearm. Look at the target and not your sights.

If the pistol points right for you, when you shoot, a hole will appear near the middle of the target, what would be the center of mass of an assailant. If you keep firing in this way, a number of holes will appear near the center of the target.

It's aimed fire with your body and stance doing the target indexing for you. It's really that simple.

If you want to use the sights, just raise the handgun to eye level. Most people will need to turn their heads slightly to bring the dominant eye in line with the sights, but don't close the other eye. You won't do it in a self-defense situation, and it's best to practice what you would actually do.

Most people, of course, simply won't be able to focus on the sights. Look at the picture on the right. Would you be looking at your sights or at the assailant?

What could go wrong?

A lot, actually. If you're thinking too much instead of just pointing, you might be relying on bad habits. This is particularly true for experienced target shooters who often find themselves "betwixt and between" — half sight-shooting, half point-shooting, and mostly missing.

If the gun doesn't point right for you, you're likely to see a grouping of shots above, below, or to one side of the center of the target. At the range, it's an easy matter to adjust that, but in the dark, under stress, it almost certainly won't be. It may be that you need to change the way you grip the handgun rather than the grips themselves. Still, the important thing about instinctive point-shooting is that you shouldn't have to remember anything. It should work even (or particularly) when you have a spastic, life-and-death grip on the handgun.

If your shots are scattered all over the target, it may be that you're flinching or that the firearm just does not shoot to point of aim. It's fairly easy to discover the problem — just have a friend shoot the handgun. If your friend manages to group shots well, the problem is almost certainly that you're flinching.

This can be overcome with practice[70], or with the "dirty trick" exercise at the shooting range.

The "dirty trick" exercise is simple to perform, particularly with revolvers. With your back turned, have a friend load some of the chambers with live rounds and the others with empty shells or with "snap caps,"[71] then place the revolver, pointed downrange, on the shooting bench. You then pick it up,[72] assume an Isosceles stance,

---

[70] Some trainers recommend "dry fire" practice, in which a handgun that you've repeatedly verified to be unloaded is pointed in a safe direction, and then fired. The idea is to teach you that there's not necessarily going to be any recoil when you pull the trigger, and to help you stop anticipating it and therefore flinching. We would be less suspicious about "dry fire" practice if we didn't know of somebody who tried it while sitting in front of his television, and unwittingly put a bullet through the television. We recommend that if you're going to engage in "dry fire" practice, just do it on the range, just as you would the "dirty trick" test.

[71] "Snap caps" are dummy rounds that are intended to make "dry fire" practice safer—for the pistol, that is, as some pistols can be damaged by repeated dry firing. While using snap caps, follow *all* of the gun safety rules, particularly about keeping your handgun pointed in a safe direction.

[72] This is one of the rare occasions when you don't check to see if the handgun is loaded. You do, however, keep it safely pointed downrange.

and slowly squeeze off a shot. If there's just a click (because you've dropped the hammer on a dummy round), but your hand jerks, you know the problem is flinching. Repeating the exercise will eventually cure you of that. You can even do the "dirty trick" test on yourself: put one or two live rounds in a revolver, fill the rest of the chambers with dummy rounds, and spin the cylinder before closing it, deliberately not looking at which chambers contain the live rounds and which contain the empty shells.

Doing the exercise with a semiauto is a little different, more time-consuming, and can't be done solo. For each shot, your friend has to either chamber or not chamber a round, and you've got to be sure that not only don't you see what he's doing, but also that you don't hear whether the slide is racked before or after the magazine is clicked into place, unless you're using "snap caps."

Practicing

New permit holders should make practice a regular part of their lives, and even experienced shooters shouldn't neglect a regular trip to the range. At least once a month at first—the more the better.

But *what* you practice is as important as *how often* you practice. Plinking at long-distance targets with a .22 target pistol can be fun, but it isn't self-defense practice.

Practice at realistic self-defense distances—21 feet at most, and there's nothing wrong with using a target only five or six feet away.

You can add realism in various ways. For example, use two targets and have a friend shout "left" or "right" after you line up on one of them. Or, once in awhile, your friend might shout "don't shoot" after you've lined up on a target. Remember, you have to stay active and constantly evaluate the situation as it develops.

Most people will instinctively take up a stance similar to the Natural Isosceles stance, with the handgun thrust out at chest level, and that's what we think most of you should practice. If you can persuade the range owner to turn the lights down for your practice—and some will, particularly if the range isn't busy—that's all the better.

Practice often.

A good way to combine your need for regular practice with your need to take precautions against legal liability is to follow this plan: once a month, go to the range and shoot up all the ammo in your carry gun, all the ammo in your ready-to-use magazines, and the rest of the ammo in the box you loaded up with. That should be 50 rounds—a good test for your gun and yourself. Then clean the gun and fully reload the firearm and magazines from a fresh box of ammunition. That will leave you with the original manufacturer's box with the ammunition lot number stamped on it and a number of unused rounds.

The clean gun with fresh ammunition goes in your holster, and the box and extra rounds go in your ammo storage container. If you have to use your gun defensively during the next month, your lawyer will be able to establish the characteristics of your ammo.

Practice, fresh ammo, and identified samples—all in one monthly exercise.

And remember: a gun never solves problems.

THE DIFFERENCE BETWEEN
A VICTIM AND A SURVIVOR

IS OFTEN SMALL &
WELL-CONCEALED

CHAPTER 11
Training

If you've decided to pursue a concealed carry permit, your next step is to get training. This will include both classroom training and a shooting qualification. If you pass the course, you will be certified by a trainer as eligible to apply.

Where to get training

Under the MPPA, sheriffs—the issuing authority—can accept a training certificate from anyone they choose. By law, however, they must accept certificates issued by an instructor training organization approved by the Commissioner of Public Safety pursuant to the 2005 act. The American Association of Certified Firearms Instructors (AACFI) is recognized by the Department of Public Safety (DPS). Certificates of course completion issued by AACFI-certified instructors *must* be accepted by all Minnesota sheriffs as proof of the MPPA's required training.

Obviously, we think the AACFI courses have much to offer. For example, our training materials, like this book, were written with Minnesota statutes, case law, and culture in mind. AACFI trainers offer both introductory courses, which are suitable for those new to handguns, and the AACFI Carry Course, which presumes at least some familiarity with firearms.[73] Go to *www.aacfi.com* for more information.

We strongly encourage you to look around and decide which courses best suit your needs. If you want to complete a non-AACFI course, just be sure in advance that your local sheriff will accept the certificate.

Qualifications

Regardless of which training you choose, all courses must, as per the MPPA, include:

- Instruction in the basics of using a handgun
- Successful completion of a shooting qualification exercise
- Instruction in the legal aspects of handgun possession, carry, and use
- Instruction in self-defense law and restrictions on the use of deadly force.

The instructor must provide you with a certificate or affidavit as to your completion of the course. If the course skips even one of the required topics, it is not valid.

And remember: a gun never solves problems.

---

[73] Although, as a matter of policy, no AACFI course assumes familiarity with firearms *safety.*

CHAPTER 12
Applying for a Minnesota Carry Permit

Once you've passed a training course, the next step is to apply for your carry permit. By design, this is a straightforward process, and for most applicants, it won't require more than filling out a form and making one visit to the local sheriff's office.

In order to be eligible, you must—in addition to having passed an approved training course and having gotten your certificate:

- Be at least 21
- Be either a citizen or a permanent resident of the US
- Have and be able to show qualifying ID (a driver's license or Minnesota ID card are the usual ones; a US passport is acceptable)
- Not be disqualified by reason of having been convicted of any of various serious crimes, or adjudged mentally incompetent. For the full list of disqualifying crimes, see *Appendix C* on page 223.

Where to apply

If you're a Minnesota resident, you must apply at the sheriff's office in the county where you live. If you're not a Minnesota resident, you can apply at any sheriff's office. Regardless, you do have to apply in person.

Call your local sheriff's office and ask where to apply—sheriffs are permitted to contract out the application process to local police chiefs, and some may tell you to go there, instead.

How to apply

Applications are available at all sheriff's offices, or can be downloaded from the Internet. the Commission of Public Safety must make them available.

For your convenience, there's always a copy of the current application form available for free download at *www.aacfi.com*. To make things easier, before making that trip to the sheriff's office, make copies of your driver's license, state ID or the photo page of your passport, and of your graduation certificate from your training course. (If the training course took isn't from one of the groups whose certification is automatically accepted, the sheriff can ask for additional information about it, and then decide for himself whether or not to accept your certification. It's up to him.)

Filling out the application is straightforward. All of the information must be provided, and must be accurate—it's a crime to deliberately provide inaccurate information.

You must submit your application in person, along with a check, cash, or money order for $100, although the sheriff can set a lower fee.

What happens next

After submitting your application, the sheriff will run a standard computerized background check on you to see if you are disqualified. They may conduct a more thorough check if they choose, calling your friends, neighbors, employer, your local police, or whoever they want, although they're unlikely to bother. It's nothing to be concerned about, either way.

They have thirty days from the day on which you submit your application to either deny or grant the permit. That's thirty calendar days, not business days—if, say you submit your permit application on December 20th, their time is up on January 20th, regardless of time out for the holidays.

They will usually mail your permit to you. If they mail you your permit, proceed to the next step, *When the permit is granted*. If they deny your permit—which they must do in writing, specifying reasons for the denial — proceed to *If the permit is denied.*

Don't call and ask about the status of your permit at least until the thirty days have elapsed. It's wise to wait an additional day or two, just to be sure that a denial letter hasn't been sent on the final day.

Why? If they don't deny the application within the statutory time, they have to give you the permit. If they do deny it, they're committed to (read: "stuck with") defending the reasons they give in the denial letter. If you can successfully dispute those, they have to give you the permit.

If you haven't heard by thirty-two days or so, then it's time to call the sheriff's office and ask about your permit status. If you're told that they're still investigating, politely remind the sheriff, deputy, or clerk that the statutory period has elapsed, and ask that the permit be issued immediately.

If they don't immediately agree to issue the permit, consider it denied.

When the permit is granted

When you have your permit, you may begin carrying a handgun in public. Your permit is valid for five years from the date it was issued. (For more on renewal and refresher courses, see *Prepare to renew your permit*, starting on page 212.)

Congratulations — and, again, please do your best to keep out of trouble (see *Chapter 14.*)

If the permit is denied

If your permit application is denied, there are three steps to take: evaluate, negotiate, and litigate.

Let's take them one at a time.

Evaluate

The first thing to do is to look at the letter and see why the sheriff has denied your permit. Minnesota law requires the sheriff to give specific reasons and a factual basis for any denial. Look at what was written.

There are really only four reasons you can be denied: (1) you're prohibited by statute from possessing a handgun, (2) there's some flaw — real or perceived — in your paperwork, (3) the sheriff has decided not to accept the certification your trainer gave you, or (4) the sheriff has determined that you're a dangerous person who just hasn't gotten around to being convicted or committed quite yet.

If you really are prohibited by law from possessing a handgun, there's nothing you can do to get a permit until that prohibition is removed. Until those disqualifications can be removed, you won't—and can't—be granted a permit. If you want to take it further, see an attorney.

If the sheriff has *mistakenly* decided that you're prohibited by statute—say, he thinks that you're Bob Smith the convicted bank robber, rather than Bob Smith the never-been-convicted-of-anything insurance salesman—all you should need to do is call the sheriff's office, politely explain the situation, and ask him to recheck the records. That should solve the problem.

The fourth reason that a permit may be denied is, as we said, because the sheriff thinks he has good reasons based on evidence (not just a prejudice or dislike of the notion of lawfully armed citizens) to believe that you are likely to be dangerous if given permission to carry a firearm in public.

If that's the reason your permit has been denied, you should begin by asking yourself an obvious question:

Is the sheriff right?

If you decide that he is, doesn't it seem reasonable not to take on the responsibility of carrying a handgun in public? If you agree that he's right, and you really ought not to be carrying a handgun, let it drop.

If you decide that the sheriff is wrong, the question then becomes a legal one: Does the sheriff have sufficient evidence that you're likely to be dangerous? His denial, again, has to be based not on his feeling, but on evidence. He has good reasons not to play fast-and-loose in choosing to view minor issues as evidence that you'd be dangerous.

If he doesn't have persuasive enough evidence and you win, he will be embarrassed, at least, and significantly out of pocket if you can show that his denial was "arbitrary and capricious."

So, assuming that you think that the sheriff is both wrong and doesn't have enough evidence of your supposed danger to society, you should hire a lawyer and have him file a lawsuit, yes?

Negotiate

No, not yet. You may not have to. It may be possible to solve the problem with a phone call or letter. Why sue when you can negotiate?

That aside, if this does go to a hearing officer's review, district court or beyond (and it may), the judge will look more favorably on you and perhaps even on your demand for attorney's fees if you can show that you made a sincere effort to resolve the problem without going to court. Judges don't like people rushing to court when they can settle their disputes among themselves. The courts are busy enough with controversies that can't be settled otherwise, after all.

You have two options at this point. One is to negotiate by yourself — and provide documentation, say, that you're Bob Smith the insurance salesman, and not Bob Smith the felon. Another is to get an attorney and have him negotiate for you or advise you how to do it yourself.

Which option makes the most sense depends on you and your situation. It won't be wrong to contact an attorney (see *Finding an attorney* on page 199), although it may not be necessary. If you can easily afford it, that may be the best way to go. If all it takes is a couple of attorney's phone calls and perhaps a letter, it's not likely to be terribly expensive.

But let's assume that you're capable of making a calm phone call and writing a sensible letter, and the denial was based, at best, on weak evidence of something that wouldn't, even if true, actually disqualify you.

In this hypothetical example, the denial letter from the sheriff says the investigation revealed — accurately, in this example — that earlier this year, you and your next door neighbor had a shouting match over where a fence was placed, and the sheriff has decided that this constitutes evidence that you're likely to be dangerous if given a permit to carry.

You might write a letter something like this:

Dear Sheriff Smithers:

Thank you for your letter of September 1, denying my August 20th Application for a Minnesota State Permit to Carry a Pistol.

You give as the sole reason for your denial your evaluation of an incident on July 1, 2003, involving an argument with my next-door neighbor, Alphonse Hornsby, over the placement of a border fence.

There are two points about this incident that make it clearly insufficient as grounds for a denial.

1. No violence was committed by me, or threatened by me, in

this incident.

2. Not only was there no conviction—of either Mr. Hornsby or
    myself—for anything, but there was no arrest made, nor were
    any charges filed, nor a police report made. The police were
    not even summoned, as it was merely a minor, if perhaps noi-
    sy, disagreement, that has nothing at all to do with carrying
    guns in public, as my part of the argument took place entirely
    from my back yard, and no firearms were involved at all. As
    your denial is clearly not permitted under Minnesota Statutes,
    section 624.714, subdivision 12, should we need to go to court
    on this, your denial would be overruled by the court, and a writ
    of mandamus issued, requiring you to issue me the permit, and
    an order would be issued for court costs and attorney's fees
    awarded to me as per the statute.

I would rather we save the county the expense and both the county
and myself the annoyance of unnecessary litigation. Please issue my
permit within five (5) business days of the date of this letter.

Thank you for your prompt attention to this matter.

Very truly yours,

Bob Smith

One important point about this letter: it deals *only* with the reason
the sheriff gave for denying your permit. Should this go to beyond district court—and in this hypothetical case, it's unlikely to—your attorney
will prevent the sheriff from raising other issues.

If the sheriff can't establish that his reason holds water, the court will
order him to issue your permit. That might not be the case if you'd
brought up extraneous matters, so don't. Stick to the subject, which isn't
whether or not you ought to have a carry permit, but only that the specific reason he gave for denying you isn't sufficient.

Send the letter to the sheriff by certified mail, return receipt requested, and save a copy of the letter and the receipt. If you'd like, fax an
additional copy to the sheriff.

If he doesn't, within the five business days you've given him, instruct you to come down and pick up your permit or mail it to you, it's
time to go to court.

Now, you'll need an attorney.

Litigate

The world is full of non-attorneys who think that they can play lawyer. They're almost always wrong. If you need to go to court, get an attorney.

Finding an attorney

The language of the Minnesota carry law was written with the intent that any competent attorney should be able to handle an appeal of a license denial. While there's no substitute for an experienced criminal attorney when charged with a crime, many attorneys without any particular expertise in this area will be able to handle this sort of appeal.

If you already have a good attorney, criminal or otherwise, he or she is probably a good place to start, if only for a recommendation. Friends who have been through the process before may be able to advise you, as should contacts at your local gun range, gun club, or gun store. And, of course, a quick email or phone call to your trainer should provide you with a good starting point.

Ask around.

After finding an attorney and getting him or her to agree to take the case, it's important to remember the basic rule: your attorney is on your side. Nothing you say about what you've done can be used against you, or even repeated without your permission. On the other hand, anything you say to your attorney that is either false or incomplete can very seriously damage your situation.

Answer your attorney's questions completely, and *never, ever* lie to him or her. Your relationship with your attorney is in some ways the opposite of your relationship with the police in a criminal investigation — anything you *don't* say can come back to bite you.

Most attorneys will listen to your situation for a brief period of time without charging you, and advise you how to proceed.

Listen carefully. If your attorney says that yours is a borderline case, you should accept that there's a real possibility you'll not only be without a permit, but may also be out several thousands of dollars in attorney's fees and court costs. And, unless the sheriff is shown to have acted in bad faith, you'll not get those costs back even if you do win.

Best of luck.

The appeals process

The appeals process is simple. Your attorney will file papers with the court, asking for a "Writ of Mandamus," a fancy way of asking the court to tell an official to do something—in this case, to issue your permit. You'll be the "plaintiff" (the person filing the suit) and the sheriff is the "respondent"(the person being sued).

The sheriff's lawyer—a lawyer from the County Attorney's office—will respond, explaining to the judge why he thinks there's sufficient evidence that the sheriff's reason for your disqualification is not true but, by law, disqualifies you.

And then your attorney goes to court. He or she may want you to come along, or not.

Because of the way the MPPA was written, the burden of proof is on the sheriff—and, in practice, his attorney. They must produce evidence that you are disqualified. The evidence must not be merely enough to show that there's more likelihood than not that you'd be dangerous if issued a permit or are otherwise disqualified, but be "clear and convincing."

If the sheriff's attorney doesn't produce sufficient evidence, your attorney doesn't have to produce any at all or—at least in theory—say a word. The judge will order the sheriff to issue your permit. Even if the sheriff's attorney does produce evidence, you—through your attorney—have the right to challenge it, to show that it's insufficient, inaccurate, or irrelevant, or even to move to have it discarded as inadmissable. Your attorney may want to call you to testify, or call other witnesses, or produce documents—it all depends on the situation.

The example we gave above is the sort of thing that's unlikely to go past the negotiation stage.

But if it does, and it gets to court, it should be an easy win for you and your attorney, and a fairly expensive lesson for a sheriff.

And remember: a gun never solves problems.

CHAPTER 13
Out-of-state Permits: Not Just for Those From Other States

Out-of-state permits

The MPPA provides for recognition of carry permits issued by other states. If recognized, the permit is treated as a Minnesota permit for all purposes. Minnesota Statute 624.714, subdivision 16 provides:

> Subdivision 16. **Recognition of permits from other states.**
>
> (a) The commissioner must annually establish and publish a list of other states that have laws governing the issuance of permits to carry weapons that are not substantially similar to this section. The list must be available on the Internet. A person holding a carry permit from a state not on the list may use the license or permit in this state subject to the rights, privileges, and requirements of this section.
>
> (b) Notwithstanding paragraph (a), no license or permit from another state is valid in this state if the holder is or becomes prohibited by law from possessing a firearm.
>
> (c) Any sheriff or police chief may file a petition under subdivision 12 seeking an order suspending or revoking an out-of-

state permit holder's authority to carry a pistol in this state on the grounds set forth in subdivision 6, paragraph (a), clause (3). An order shall only be issued if the petitioner meets the burden of proof and criteria set forth in subdivision 12. If the court denies the petition, the court must award the permit holder reasonable costs and expenses including attorney fees. The petition may be filed in any county in the state where a person holding a license or permit from another state can be found.

(d) The commissioner must, when necessary, execute reciprocity agreements regarding carry permits with jurisdictions whose carry permits are recognized under paragraph (a).

Although the Minnesota legislature set a standard of only *similarity*, the Department of Public Safety requires *identical* provisions and practices. Under this narrow approach, only four states have qualified for recognition. The DPS lists them on its website at:

www.dps.state.mn.us/bca/CJIS/Documents/CarryPermit/States.html.

The number of states that recognize the Minnesota permit to carry continues to increase. However, some states require reciprocity before Minnesota residents will be allowed to carry under their home state's permit.

Out-of-state permits *for* Minnesota residents

Getting an out-of-state permit also serves as a workaround for some Minnesota residents. If you travel and don't want to wait until your favorite destination state recognizes your home state permit, you still have some options.

Many other states have had carry laws for years. The agreements are already in place for most of these states regarding recognition (one state automatically honoring another's licenses) or reciprocity (each state must recognize the other for the licenses to be valid in the other state).

Sometimes it takes awhile for a new state law to be recognized in other states; agreements must be made. Other times, reluctant government officials will do nothing until someone asks. Still other officials will not act to support law-abiding permit holders because they do not like guns and do not want to see carry laws expanded in any way.

A similar workaround may help everyone in these situations: get an out-of-state permit from another state.

Some states, like Washington, require you to apply in person, and that's probably a reasonable option only if you're already going there for some other reason.

But several states allow you to apply by mail without having to leave Minnesota. The four obvious options—although there are others—are Pennsylvania, Florida, New Hampshire, and Utah.

Pennsylvania

The Pennsylvania permit application process is simple, inexpensive, and—at least in theory—straightforward. You get the permit application from any Pennsylvania sheriff, fill it out, and send it in along with a recent photo; the name, address, and phone numbers of two references; and a check for $19.

The only problem is that Pennsylvania requires you to send along a copy of your carry permit if you're able to get one in your home state, and some Pennsylvania sheriffs aren't willing to issue permits to Minnesota residents now that a carry law is in effect in Minnesota.

The simple way to find out if a given sheriff will issue a permit to a Minnesota resident is to call and ask. Or, if you have Internet access, browse to *www.wmsa.net*, which keeps track of such things, or *www.packing.org*, which is the gold standard of carry permit information on the Internet.

Florida

For most people who need an out-of-state permit, Florida is probably a better choice. It costs more, and it takes more time than the Pennsylvania permit, but it's certainly quicker than waiting for Minnesota to reach agreements with other states.

As with a Minnesota permit, you have to take training with a certified instructor. You'll want to be sure that your instructor is certified by the American Association of Certified Firearms Instructors or the National Rifle Association, or has received recognition from the Florida Department of Agriculture and Consumer Affairs as a carry permit instructor.

And yes, it's possible for your Minnesota instructor to be certified for Florida. All AACFI Minnesota instructors are recognized by Florida, and your course completion certificate should say so.

You'll need to get an application packet from the Florida Department of Agriculture and Consumer Affairs. You can contact them at:

Department of Agriculture and Consumer Affairs
Division of Licensing
Post Office Box 6687
Tallahassee, Florida 32314-6687

Phone: (850) 487-0482
Fax: (850) 488-2789

Or, you can order the forms online at:
http://licgweb.doacs.state.fl.us/weapons/index.html.
They'll be sent out promptly and at no charge.

After that, it's only slightly more complicated than Minnesota, and the costs are slightly higher up front—$117 for a five-year permit rather than $100 for a Minnesota permit. In addition to the application, you have to include a photo and a fingerprint card. It also takes up to 90 days to get your Florida permit, so be patient.

The Florida non-resident permit is good in at least the **27** reciprocity states listed at *http://licgweb.doacs.state.fl.us/news/concealed_carry.html*, and in a few other states as well. For permit holders of states without reciprocity with Florida, you may only carry in Florida under a Florida non-resident permit. For permit holders of states *with* reciprocity, Florida allows you to carry under the permit from your state of residence. For example, Minnesota permit holders with a New Hampshire non-resident permit must still apply for a Florida permit to carry in Florida. Florida does not honor Minnesota's permit and only allows New Hampshire residents to carry in Florida under a New Hampshire permit.

New Hampshire

The New Hampshire permit application process is simple, inexpensive, and straightforward. You get the permit application from the New Hampshire State Police. At this time, you will have to call them for the application, as it is not available electronically. Fill it out and send it in along with a permit to carry from any other state (it does not have to be from your home state)[74] and a check for $20.

The New Hampshire permit is one of the easiest to get once you have a permit to carry from any other state. No additional training is

---

[74] Effective 10/21/04, you must have a permit to carry from *any* state before New Hampshire will issue you a non-resident pistol/revolver license.

required. However, as with any state, you must know the applicable laws dealing with the threat and use of deadly force, along with the carry laws for that state.

You can contact the New Hampshire State Police at:

Division of State Police
Permits and Licensing Unit
33 Hazen Drive
Concord, NH 03301

Phone: (603) 271-3575
Fax: (603) 271-1153

www.nh.gov/safety/divisions/nhsp/

Note: A concealed carry permit with restrictions will be accepted by New Hampshire, and they will issue you a non-resident license even with a restricted carry permit from another state.

Utah

Utah is another good option for most people who need an out-of-state permit. As with a Minnesota permit, you need to complete training with a certified instructor to obtain a Utah permit. Be sure your instructor is certified by the Utah Bureau of Criminal Apprehension. Many AACFI instructors have been certified as Utah carry permit instructors, and it's possible that your Minnesota instructor is certified for Utah. If not, once you have completed the AACFI Minnesota Permit to Carry course, you may take an addendum course from another AACFI instructor who is certified in Utah.

You'll need to get an application from the Utah Bureau of Criminal Apprehension. You can contact them at:

Licensing Authority:
Utah DPS (Bureau of Criminal Identification)
3888 W. 5400 S.
Salt Lake City, Utah 84114-8280
Phone: (801) 965-4445

Or, you can download the forms online at:
www.bci.utah.gov/CFP/CFPHome.html.
They'll be sent out promptly and at no charge.
After that, the process is similar to Florida's, except that it costs a lit-

tle less up front—$59 for a five-year permit. In addition to the application, you have to include a photo and a fingerprint card. The Utah nonresident permit is good in at least **28** states.

And remember: a gun never solves problems.

CHAPTER 14
What to Do After You've Gotten Your Permit

First of all, of course, *stay out of trouble*.

Look at it this way: most people who got permits have already gone their entire lives without needing to point a gun at another human being, and it's obviously best to keep it that way. If you haven't been persuaded by the chapters about the use of lethal force and what happens after producing a handgun—even if you've not so much as pointed it at anybody—read them again.

If you're even idly considering the idea that now is a good time to go down to that bad neighborhood you've been avoiding, or to head over to your neighbor's house and straighten him out about his dog voiding itself on your lawn, think again. Repeat as necessary, think all you want—just don't do it. The carry endorsement on your driver's license or nondriver's identification card is just that: it's an endorsement of your right to carry a handgun in public. It doesn't make you bulletproof, attack-proof, arrest-proof, or lawsuit-proof.

And of all the many things it's not, the foremost among them is a reason to go looking for trouble.

Decide on your own personal carry strategy

There's no question that some permit holders rarely, if ever, carry handguns in public. Some people take out a permit as insurance against a possible threatening situation and don't actually intend to carry their handguns in public until they find themselves faced with one. Others simply make it a policy to carry most of the time — everywhere it's legally permitted.

Still others pick a middle-of-the-road policy — carrying when they feel like it, and not bothering when they don't.

It's up to you, but it's worth thinking through. Some very ordinary sorts of problems can be complicated by the mere presence of a handgun, even if it's never deliberately pointed at somebody or even drawn from the holster.

Let's take an example: you're having an argument with a mechanic, as you think (correctly, as it turns out) that he's replaced your broken alternator with a used one, rather than the new one you've been billed for. Having a carry permit, you're wearing your gun (in this example, on your strongside hip, concealed by your jacket), and you unintentionally put your hands on your hips, brushing your jacket back and revealing that you're armed.

Two things are likely to happen, very quickly.

The first is that he's likely to immediately back down and admit that you are right. The second is that he's going to dial 911 for the police at the first moment he thinks it's safe to do so.

Did you mean to threaten him? Absolutely not.

Have you committed a crime? No.

Are you going to have an unpleasant learning experience?

Absolutely.

You head home, but before going more than a few blocks, a police cruiser, lights flashing, responding to a "man with a gun" call, pulls you over. Two policemen leap out with their pistols drawn and instruct you to get out of the car.

Since you know enough to cooperate with the police, you find yourself kneeling on the ground with your hands clasped behind your head. You're disarmed, handcuffed, taken to jail, and charged with any number of crimes, including the all-purpose "breach of peace."

Since you know enough not to get involved in a discussion with the police, you call your lawyer. If you're lucky, he'll able to arrange for the minimal bail that day. If you can't post the whole bail amount, you'll pay ten percent of it to a bondsman and never see it again.

And then, if you're lucky — and haven't said anything that can possibly be construed as an admission of guilt — your lawyer will persuade the prosecutor to drop the charges. Perhaps you won't be that lucky. The best he may be able to do is get the prosecutor to reduce the charges and arrange for you to plead guilty to a misdemeanor and pay a fine, leaving you several thousand dollars poorer, without a carry permit, and with a misdemeanor conviction on your record.

Or you can fight the charges — after all, you didn't threaten the dishonest mechanic — and hope that the judge or jury will see it that way, with the certainty that you'll spend several thousand dollars on lawyer's fees when it goes to trial.

And all because you innocently put your hands on your hips while involved in an ordinary argument.[75]

This point needs to be emphasized because it's important: when you're carrying a handgun, *you have to take extra precautions – not fewer – to avoid trouble.*

Your permit and handgun aren't for settling disputes. Your handgun is for saving your life, and your permit is what makes it legal for you to carry it in public. *Period.*

That said — even though it's your choice — we feel we owe you a recommendation for a personal carry strategy, and here it is:

We think it makes sense for anybody who is willing to make strong and continuous efforts to stay out of trouble, to carry his or her handgun everywhere it's legal and permitted, and nowhere else. *The thing about life-threatening emergencies is that they tend to be unpredictable.* There is no guarantee, we're sorry to say, that having your handgun will be able to protect you in that sort of situation, but even the FBI reports show that the single most effective thing you can do if attacked is to produce a handgun.

Spend time at the range with your carry handgun

A handgun is a tool. As with most tools, the more you use it, the more comfortable you become with it, and the more likely that, even under stress, you'll use it properly. Particularly at first, you should plan on

---

[75] If you find yourself in a situation like that, the best thing for you to do is back down, even if you're right. "I'm sorry," you should say. "Of course it's a new alternator, and I apologize for suggesting otherwise."

making regular trips to the range and practicing point-shooting at close targets. If you can convince the range master to lower the lights so you can practice in low-light or darkness, that's all the better.

Remember: keep it simple. Target shooting with aimed fire is a lot more fun for most folks than thrusting out a handgun at chest level from an Isosceles stance, but the idea is practice, not fun.

Recycle your carry ammunition

Modern ammunition can last a long time—it doesn't tend to "go bad." That said, nothing lasts forever. One occasional mistake new gun owners make is to clean their ammunition with various chemicals suitable for cleaning the handgun. Don't do that; it can ruin the primers.

If you're practicing with your carry ammunition, just start off by using it—point-shooting from an Isosceles stance—at the target, and put new ammunition in when you leave the range.

Clean your carry handgun

Handguns are machines, and machines need care and maintenance. People adopt different policies about how often and how thoroughly to clean their handguns. Some take the position that the handgun should be clean enough to "eat off of"—although how they'd do that, we don't know—and perform a full, detailed disassembly and cleaning of their guns after every shooting session. That's not wrong, although it might be excessive. And, in the case of some semiautos, it raises the question of whether or not the pistol was reassembled properly and will perform if needed.

After a detailed cleaning of a handgun, we recommend running another magazine full of your carry ammunition through it. Or you can, after making *very* sure that it's *completely* unloaded (no rounds in the cylinder of a revolver, no ammunition in a semiauto), cock it, insert a pencil (eraser first) down the barrel, point it in a safe direction, and "fire" it. If the pencil pops out, it means that at least the firing mechanism is working.

We recommend giving semiautos and revolvers a light cleaning after every shooting session.

Take additional training

There is no such thing as too much education, and that applies to permit holders and the carrying of handguns as much as anything else. Consider taking an advanced course from AACFI or any other reputable training organization.

Keep up with changes in the law

There are lots of minor issues that Minnesota courts haven't had to address yet, but they will. You can expect that there will be test cases, for example, involving carrying in courthouses—right now, the law permits permit holders to just give notification to the sheriff and carry in courthouses, but the practice is to have permit holders lock up their firearms. You can expect that some lawyers with carry permits will be challenging this.

Employers, as we've said, do have the right to forbid per-mit holders to carry at work—but when they do that, are they responsible for an injury that happens to an employee who wasn't able to defend himself or herself? We don't know; there haven't been any test cases on that, as of yet. You can expect there to be test cases, for example, involving employers. Employers have the right to forbid permit holders to carry at work, but when they do that, are they responsible for an injury to an employee who wasn't able to defend him- or herself? Nobody knows; there haven't been any test cases on that yet.

The only way you ever want to be involved in a test case, of course, is to read about it. So do.

Beyond that, there's the legislature. As Judge Gideon J. Tucker said in 1866, "No man's life, liberty, or property is safe while the legislature is in session." Keep an eye on them.

Check out the AACFI website

Make it a habit to consult the AACFI website at *www.aacfi.com* to keep up with any test cases that happen and how they're resolved, and with any pending bills in the legislature that might affect your rights as a permit holder and a gun owner.

Also keep an eye out for the next edition of this book. As the case law develops, we will be updating and expanding it.

Prepare to renew your permit

There's no rush; the "Minnesota State Permit to Carry a Pistol" is valid for five years. Renewing it is, basically, the same procedure as getting one in the first place. You'll have to take a refresher course within a year prior to your renewal, and the maximum fee for a permit renewal is $75 instead of $100. AACFI and other organizations will announce refresher courses as that time approaches.

It's nothing to worry about, but it is something to plan for. With the many permits issued in 2003, the first year of the MPPA, it's a safe bet that in 2008 there will be some of the same problems in scheduling training sessions—schedule yours early and plan to apply for your renewal two months or so before your permit expires. Your renewal will be effective as of the last valid date of your original permit, so there's no waste in applying a little early.

Support the individuals and groups that made it possible for you to get your carry permit

The battle to change Minnesota's antiquated, bureaucrats-know-best permit law to the modern, mainstream, moderate MPPA was a long and difficult one, and it didn't happen all by itself.

Among elected officials, the legislative battle was fought tirelessly by the chief authors of the bill—Representative Lynda Boudreau in the Minnesota State House, and Senator Pat Pariseau in the Senate. If you appreciate the hard work they've done, please drop them a thank-you note. And the same goes for all of the legislators in both the Minnesota House and Senate who voted for the MPPA—their names are in *Appendix D, Minnesota Legislators Who Supported You*, on page 245.

And it wasn't by any means just two legislators—nor even all the legislators, of all three parties, who voted for the bill. The National Rifle Association put a lot of effort into the lobbying process in Minnesota, as it has in the other states that have passed "shall issue" laws. Please consider joining the NRA if you haven't already—you can join at their website at *www.nra.org*.

But the majority of the work was done by a grassroots group called Minnesota Concealed Carry Reform Now!, otherwise known as CCRN, a division of GOCRA, the Gun Owners Civil Rights Alliance. The contribution of the volunteers of CCRN/GOCRA, over quite literally years of working on the legislation and lobbying for its passing, can't be overstated.

Please consider supporting and joining CCRN/COCRA — their website is at *www.mnccrn.org*.

But, mainly, the most important thing to do is just to go on with your life, living it as well as you can, and hope that — like the fire insurance on your home — the combination of your carry permit and your carried handgun is something you'll never have to use.

We hope so, too.

And, for one last time, remember:

a gun never solves problems.

APPENDIX A
Necessary Equipment

Carrying a handgun isn't, or shouldn't be, just a matter of having a handgun and carry permit. We think there are several other items that a permit holder should definitely have, and others that are a good idea to have, depending on your budget.

Minimum equipment

- An utterly reliable handgun that points well for you.
- A pocket holster, or some other carry method or combination of carry methods, that works for you throughout the varying seasons.
- Your carry permit, or driver's license or nondriver's license with its carry endorsement.
- A cell phone.
- A gun box or some other method to secure your firearm, whether you're out in public or at home, should you need to. At a minimum, have a trigger lock or padlock.
- A gun cleaning kit.
- The phone number of a good criminal lawyer, just in case.

Recommended equipment

- A flashlight. (We recommend a Xenon flashlight, available at *www.aacfi.com/products/XenonFlashlight.shtml*)
- A spare handgun.
- A spare magazine for a semiauto, or a speedloader for a revolver.
- A spare wallet containing some expired credit cards and around $20 in small bills—you can throw it to a mugger as you run in the opposite direction.

APPENDIX B
IACP "Officer-Involved Shooting Guidelines"

In 1998, the International Association of Police Chiefs, through its Psychological Services Section, adopted the following guidelines to help police officers through the traumatic event of being involved in a shooting. While citizens can't expect this sort of treatment, it's worth knowing how stressful the IACP thinks a shooting is for the survivor of it, and the sort of gentle and thoughtful care that such an officer needs. It's also worth noting guideline 6, which suggests that, to avoid "legal complications," the officer should avoid discussing the shooting before the investigation.

In the case of citizens, realistically, the only person you can turn to to provide anything like this is your attorney.

Officer-Involved Shooting Guidelines

Adopted by the IACP Police Psychological Services Section in 1998

These guidelines were developed to provide information and recommendations on constructively supporting an officer(s) involved in a shooting. In the past, officers involved in on-duty shootings were often subjected to a harsh administrative/investigative/legal aftermath that compounded the stress of using deadly force. A "second injury" can be created by insensitively and impersonally dealing with an officer who has been involved in a critical incident.

Field experience of members of the Police Psychological Services Section of the IACP suggests that following these guidelines can reduce the probability of long-lasting psychological and emotional problems resulting from a shooting. However, these guidelines are not meant to be a rigid protocol. These guidelines work best when applied in a case-by-case manner appropriate to each unique situation.

1. At the scene, show concern. Give physical and emotional first aid.

2. Create a psychological break; it is advisable to get the officer away from the body and suspect(s) or remove the officer completely from the immediate scene. Shielding the officer from media attention is essential. The officer should stay with a supportive peer or supervisor and return to the scene only if necessary.

3. Explain to the officer what will happen administratively during the next few hours and why. It is recommended that an administrator brief the officer again sometime in the next two days regarding the entire process of investigation, media interaction, grand jury, review board, and any other potential concerns that might be encountered after a shooting.

4. If the firearm is taken as evidence, replace it immediately or when appropriate (telling the officer it will be replaced). Officers, especially when in uniform, may feel extremely vulnerable if they are left unarmed. Immediate replacement of a firearm also communicates support for the officer, rather than miscommunicating that an administrative action is being taken. If the firearm must be removed at the scene and cannot be replaced, it is desirable to assign an armed companion officer to stay with the involved officer.

5. If possible, the officer can benefit from some recovery time before detailed interviewing begins. This can range from a few hours to overnight, depending on the emotional state of the officer and the circumstances. Officers who have been afforded this opportunity to calm down are likely to provide a more coherent and accurate statement. Providing a secure setting, insulated from the press and curious officers, is desirable during the interview process.

6. Totally isolating the officer breeds feelings of resentment and alienation. The officer may benefit from being with a supportive friend or

peer who has been through a similar experience. (To avoid legal complications, the shooting should not be discussed prior to the preliminary investigation.)

7. If the officer is not injured, either the officer or a department representative should contact the family with a telephone call first, perhaps followed up with a personal visit, and let them know what happened before other rumors and sources reach them. If the officer is injured, a department member known to the family should pick them up and drive them to the hospital. Offer to call friends, chaplains, etc., to make sure the family has support.

8. Personal concern and support for the officer involved in the shooting, communicated face-to-face from high-ranking administrators, goes a long way toward alleviating future emotional problems. The administrator does not have to comment on the situation, or make further statements regarding legal or departmental resolution, but can show concern and empathy for the officer during this stressful experience.

9. It is desirable to give the officer a few days of administrative leave to deal with the emotional impact. Make sure the officer understands this is an "administrative leave," not a "suspension with pay." It may well be in the best interests of the officer and the agency to keep the officer off the street until the criminal investigation, internal shooting review board, grand jury, coroner's inquest, and district attorney's statement have all been completed. This avoids placing the officer in potential legal and emotional double binds from being involved in another critical incident before the first one has been resolved, or being further involved with suspects or witnesses while working.

10. Departments may wish to screen all emergency service personnel at the scene (including dispatchers) for their reactions and give administrative leave or the rest of the shift off, if necessary.

11. It is advisable that a confidential debriefing with a licensed mental health professional be scheduled for all involved personnel within 72 hours. While this can be a group session, it may not be legally or emotionally appropriate to include the officer(s) who did the shooting in a debriefing with others, as actually doing the shooting creates different issues. A one-on-one debriefing with a licensed mental health professional is recommended for the officer(s) who did the shooting prior to or in place of a group debriefing. Follow-up sessions for any personnel involved in the shooting may be appropriate.

It was the majority consensus of members of the IACP Police Psychological Services Section that debriefings be mandatory for all involved in a shooting incident. The Section recognizes there are a few departments with well-established police psychology programs who have positive results with voluntary briefings. In the absence of this type of program, it is advisable that debriefings be mandatory.

It needs to be made very clear to all involved personnel and supervisors that debriefings are separate and distinct from any fitness-for-duty assessment, and administrative or investigative procedures. It is extremely inappropriate to use information from a debriefing in any manner other than to help the individuals involved in the incident deal with psychological or emotional issues.

12. Opportunities for family counseling and/or family group debriefings (spouse, children, significant others) should be made available.

13. If the officer has a published home telephone number, it may be advisable to have a friend or telephone answering machine screen telephone calls, since there are sometimes threats to the officer and his or her family.

14. When possible, an administrator should tell the rest of the department (or at least the supervisors and the rest of the officer's team) what happened so the officer does not get bombarded with questions and rumors are held in check. Screen for vicarious thrill seekers to protect the officer and the situation.

15. Expedite the completion of administrative and criminal investigations and advise the officer of the outcomes. Lengthy investigations can stimulate a secondary injury.

16. Consider the officer's interest in preparing media releases.

17. The option of talking to peers who have had a similar experience can be quite helpful to personnel at the scene. Peer counselors can also be an asset participating in group debriefings in conjunction with a mental health professional, and in providing follow-up support.

    Family members may also greatly benefit from the peer support of family members or other officers who have been involved in critical incidents. The formation and administrative backing of peer support teams for officers and family members will prove a wise investment during the stress of a critical incident.

18. It is advisable not to force a return to full duty before the officer indi-

cates readiness. Allow a paced return, perhaps allowing the officer to "team" with a fellow officer, or work a shorter or different "beat" or shift.

19. Prior to any event, attempt to train all officers, supervisors, and family members in critical incident reactions and what to expect personally, departmentally, and legally.

20. Shootings are complex events often involving officers; command staff; union representatives; internal affairs; peer support teams; district attorneys; investigators; city, town, or county counsel; personal attorneys; city, town or county politicians; media; and others. It is recommended that potentially involved parties meet to establish locally acceptable procedures and protocols on handling these stressful, high-profile events to avoid conflict among the many different interests. It is recommended that they continue to communicate regularly to ensure smooth functioning and necessary adjustments.

APPENDIX C
Selected Minnesota Statutes

Authorized Use of Force

609.06 AUTHORIZED USE OF FORCE.

Subdivision 1. When authorized. Except as otherwise provided in subdivision 2, reasonable force may be used upon or toward the person of another without the other's consent when the following circumstances exist or the actor reasonably believes them to exist:

(1) when used by a public officer or one assisting a public officer under the public officer's direction:

    (a)   in effecting a lawful arrest; or

    (b)   in the execution of legal process; or

    (c)   in enforcing an order of the court; or

    (d)   in executing any other duty imposed upon the public officer by law; or

(2) when used by a person not a public officer in arresting another in the cases and in the manner provided by law and delivering the other to an officer competent to receive the other into custody; or

(3) when used by any person in resisting or aiding another to resist an offense against the person; or

(4) when used by any person in lawful possession of real or personal property, or by another assisting the person in lawful possession, in resisting a trespass upon or other unlawful interference with such property; or

(5) when used by any person to prevent the escape, or to retake following the escape, of a person lawfully held on a charge or conviction of a crime; or

(6) when used by a parent, guardian, teacher, or other lawful custodian of a child or pupil, in the exercise of lawful authority, to restrain or correct such child or pupil; or

(7) when used by a school employee or school bus driver, in the exercise of lawful authority, to restrain a child or pupil, or to prevent bodily harm or death to another; or

(8) when used by a common carrier in expelling a passenger who refuses to obey a lawful requirement for the conduct of passengers and reasonable care is exercised with regard to the passenger's personal safety; or

(9) when used to restrain a person who is mentally ill or mentally defective from self-injury or injury to another or when used by one with authority to do so to compel compliance with reasonable requirements for the person's control, conduct, or treatment; or

(10) when used by a public or private institution providing custody or treatment against one lawfully committed to it to compel compliance with reasonable requirements for the control, conduct, or treatment of the committed person.

Subd. 2. Deadly force used against peace officers. Deadly force may not be used against peace officers who have announced their presence and are performing official duties at a location where a person is committing a crime or an act that would be a crime if committed by an adult.

History: 1963 c 753 art 1 s 609.06; 1986 c 444; 1993 c 326 art 1 s 4; 1996 c 408 art 3 s 12; 2002 c 221 s 46

Basic Carry Law

624.714 CARRYING OF WEAPONS WITHOUT PERMIT; PENALTIES.

Subdivision 1.[Repealed, 2003 c 28 art 2 s 35; 2005 c 83 s 1]

Subd. 1a. **Permit required; penalty.** A person, other than a peace officer, as defined in section 626.84, subdivision 1, who carries, holds, or possesses a pistol in a motor vehicle, snowmobile, or boat, or on or about the person's clothes or the person, or otherwise in possession or control in a public place, as defined in section 624.7181, subdivision 1, paragraph (c), without first having obtained a permit to carry the pistol is guilty of a gross misdemeanor. A person who is convicted a second or subsequent time is guilty of a felony.

Subd. 1b. Display of permit; penalty.

(a) The holder of a permit to carry must have the permit card and a driver's license, state identification card, or other government-issued photo identification in immediate possession at all times when carrying a pistol and must display the permit card and identification document upon lawful demand by a peace officer, as defined in section 626.84, subdivision 1. A violation of this paragraph is a petty misdemeanor. The fine for a first offense must not exceed $25. Notwithstanding section 609.531, a firearm carried in violation of this paragraph is not subject to forfeiture.

(b) A citation issued for violating paragraph (a) must be dismissed if the person demonstrates, in court or in the office of the arresting officer, that the person was authorized to carry the pistol at the time of the alleged violation.

(c) Upon the request of a peace officer, a permit holder must write a sample signature in the officer's presence to aid in verifying the person's identity.

(d) Upon the request of a peace officer, a permit holder shall disclose to the officer whether or not the permit holder is currently carrying a firearm.

Subd. 2. Where application made; authority to issue permit; criteria; scope.

(a) Applications by Minnesota residents for permits to carry shall be made to the county sheriff where the applicant resides. Nonresidents, as defined in section 171.01, subdivision 42, may apply to any sheriff.

(b) Unless a sheriff denies a permit under the exception set forth in subdivision 6, paragraph (a), clause (3), a sheriff must issue a permit to an applicant if the person:

    (1)   has training in the safe use of a pistol;

    (2)   is at least 21 years old and a citizen or a permanent resident of the United States;

    (3)   completes an application for a permit;

    (4)   is not prohibited from possessing a firearm under the following sections:

        (i)   518B.01, subdivision 14;

        (ii) 609.224, subdivision 3;

        (iii) 609.2242, subdivision 3;

        (iv) 609.749, subdivision 8;

        (v) 624.713;

        (vi) 624.719;

        (vii) 629.715, subdivision 2;

        (viii) 629.72, subdivision 2; or

        (ix) any federal law; and

    (5)   is not listed in the criminal gang investigative data system under section 299C.091.

(c) A permit to carry a pistol issued or recognized under this section is a state permit and is effective throughout the state.

(d) A sheriff may contract with a police chief to process permit applications under this section. If a sheriff contracts with a police chief, the sheriff remains the issuing authority and the police chief acts as the sheriff's agent. If a sheriff contracts with a police chief, all of the provisions of this section will apply.

Subd. 2a. Training in the safe use of a pistol.

(a) An applicant must present evidence that the applicant received training in the safe use of a pistol within one year of the date of an original or renewal application. Training may be demonstrated by:

   (1) employment as a peace officer in the state of Minnesota within the past year; or

   (2) completion of a firearms safety or training course providing basic training in the safe use of a pistol and conducted by a certified instructor.

(b) Basic training must include:

   (1) instruction in the fundamentals of pistol use;

   (2) successful completion of an actual shooting qualification exercise; and

   (3) instruction in the fundamental legal aspects of pistol possession, carry, and use, including self-defense and the restrictions on the use of deadly force.

(c) The certified instructor must issue a certificate to a person who has completed a firearms safety or training course described in paragraph (b). The certificate must be signed by the instructor and attest that the person attended and completed the course.

(d) A person qualifies as a certified instructor if the person is certified as a firearms instructor within the past five years by an organization or government entity that has been approved by the Department of Public Safety in accordance with the department's standards.

(e) A sheriff must accept the training described in this subdivision as meeting the requirement in subdivision 2, paragraph (b), for training in the safe use of a pistol. A sheriff may also accept other satisfactory evidence of training in the safe use of a pistol.

Subd. 3. **Form and contents of application.**

(a) Applications for permits to carry must be an official, standardized application form, adopted under section 624.7151, and must set forth in writing only the following information:

   (1) the applicant's name, residence, telephone number, if any, and driver's license number or state identification card number;

(2) the applicant's sex, date of birth, height, weight, and color of eyes and hair, and distinguishing physical characteristics, if any;

(3) the township or statutory city or home rule charter city, and county, of all Minnesota residences of the applicant in the last five years, though not including specific addresses;

(4) the township or city, county, and state of all non-Minnesota residences of the applicant in the last five years, though not including specific addresses;

(5) a statement that the applicant authorizes the release to the sheriff of commitment information about the applicant maintained by the commissioner of human services or any similar agency or department of another state where the applicant has resided, to the extent that the information relates to the applicant's eligibility to possess a firearm; and

(6) a statement by the applicant that, to the best of the applicant's knowledge and belief, the applicant is not prohibited by law from possessing a firearm.

(b) The statement under paragraph (a), clause (5), must comply with any applicable requirements of Code of Federal Regulations, title 42, sections 2.31 to 2.35, with respect to consent to disclosure of alcohol or drug abuse patient records.

(c) An applicant must submit to the sheriff an application packet consisting only of the following items:

(1) a completed application form, signed and dated by the applicant;

(2) an accurate photocopy of the certificate described in subdivision 2a, paragraph (c), that is submitted as the applicant's evidence of training in the safe use of a pistol; and

(3) an accurate photocopy of the applicant's current driver's license, state identification card, or the photo page of the applicant's passport.

(d) In addition to the other application materials, a person who is otherwise ineligible for a permit due to a criminal conviction but who has obtained a pardon or expungement setting aside the conviction, sealing the conviction, or otherwise restoring applicable rights, must submit a copy of the relevant order.

(e) Applications must be submitted in person.

(f) The sheriff may charge a new application processing fee in an amount not to exceed the actual and reasonable direct cost of processing the application or $100, whichever is less. Of this amount, $10 must be submitted to the commissioner and deposited into the general fund.

(g) This subdivision prescribes the complete and exclusive set of items an applicant is required to submit in order to apply for a new or renewal permit to carry. The applicant must not be asked or required to submit, voluntarily or involuntarily, any information, fees, or documentation beyond that specifically required by this subdivision. This paragraph does not apply to alternate training evidence accepted by the sheriff under subdivision 2a, paragraph (d).

(h) Forms for new and renewal applications must be available at all sheriffs' offices and the commissioner must make the forms available on the Internet.

(i) Application forms must clearly display a notice that a permit, if granted, is void and must be immediately returned to the sheriff if the permit holder is or becomes prohibited by law from possessing a firearm. The notice must list the applicable state criminal offenses and civil categories that prohibit a person from possessing a firearm.

(j) Upon receipt of an application packet and any required fee, the sheriff must provide a signed receipt indicating the date of submission.

Subd. 4. Investigation.

(a) The sheriff must check, by means of electronic data transfer, criminal records, histories, and warrant information on each applicant through the Minnesota Crime Information System and, to the extent necessary, the National Instant Check System. The sheriff shall also make a reasonable effort to check other available and relevant federal, state, or local record-keeping systems. The sheriff must obtain commitment information from the commissioner of human services as provided in section 245.041 or, if the information is reasonably available, as provided by a similar statute from another state.

(b) When an application for a permit is filed under this section, the sheriff must notify the chief of police, if any, of the municipality where the applicant resides. The police chief may provide the sheriff with any information relevant to the issuance of the permit.

(c) The sheriff must conduct a background check by means of electronic data transfer on a permit holder through the Minnesota Crime Information System and, to the extent necessary, the National Instant Check System at least yearly to ensure continuing eligibility. The sheriff may conduct additional background checks by means of electronic data transfer on a permit holder at any time during the period that a permit is in effect.

Subd. 5.[Repealed, 2003 c 28 art 2 s 35; 2005 c 83 s 1]

Subd. 6. **Granting and denial of permits.**

(a) The sheriff must, within 30 days after the date of receipt of the application packet described in subdivision 3:

   (1) issue the permit to carry;

   (2) deny the application for a permit to carry solely on the grounds that the applicant failed to qualify under the criteria described in subdivision 2, paragraph (b); or

   (3) deny the application on the grounds that there exists a substantial likelihood that the applicant is a danger to self or the public if authorized to carry a pistol under a permit.

(b) Failure of the sheriff to notify the applicant of the denial of the application within 30 days after the date of receipt of the application packet constitutes issuance of the permit to carry and the sheriff must promptly fulfill the requirements under paragraph (c). To deny the application, the sheriff must provide the applicant with written notification and the specific factual basis justifying the denial under paragraph (a), clause (2) or (3), including the source of the factual basis. The sheriff must inform the applicant of the applicant's right to submit, within 20 business days, any additional documentation relating to the propriety of the denial. Upon receiving any additional documentation, the sheriff must reconsider the denial and inform the applicant within 15 business days of the result of the reconsideration. Any denial after reconsideration must be in the same form and substance as the original denial and must specifically address any continued deficiencies in light of the additional documentation submitted by the applicant. The applicant must be informed of the right to seek de novo review of the denial as provided in subdivision 12.

(c) Upon issuing a permit to carry, the sheriff must provide a laminated permit card to the applicant by first class mail unless personal delivery has been made. Within five business days, the sheriff must submit the information specified in subdivision 7, paragraph (a), to the commissioner for inclusion solely in the database required under subdivision 15, paragraph (a). The sheriff must transmit the information in a manner and format prescribed by the commissioner.

(d) Within five business days of learning that a permit to carry has been suspended or revoked, the sheriff must submit information to the commissioner regarding the suspension or revocation for inclusion solely in the databases required or permitted under subdivision 15.

(e) Notwithstanding paragraphs (a) and (b), the sheriff may suspend the application process if a charge is pending against the applicant that, if resulting in conviction, will prohibit the applicant from possessing a firearm.

Subd. 7. Permit card contents; expiration; renewal.

(a) Permits to carry must be on an official, standardized permit card adopted by the commissioner, containing only the name, residence, and driver's license number or state identification card number of the permit holder, if any.

(b) The permit card must also identify the issuing sheriff and state the expiration date of the permit. The permit card must clearly display a notice that a permit, if granted, is void and must be immediately returned to the sheriff if the permit holder becomes prohibited by law from possessing a firearm.

(c) A permit to carry a pistol issued under this section expires five years after the date of issue. It may be renewed in the same manner and under the same criteria which the original permit was obtained, subject to the following procedures:

   (1) no earlier than 90 days prior to the expiration date on the permit, the permit holder may renew the permit by submitting to the appropriate sheriff the application packet described in subdivision 3 and a renewal processing fee not to exceed the actual and reasonable direct cost of processing the application or $75, whichever is less. Of this amount, $5 must be submitted to the commissioner and deposited into the general fund. The sheriff must process the renewal application in accordance with subdivisions 4 and 6; and

   (2) a permit holder who submits a renewal application packet after the expiration date of the permit, but within 30 days after expiration, may renew the permit as provided in clause (1) by paying an

additional late fee of $10.

(d) The renewal permit is effective beginning on the expiration date of the prior permit to carry.

Subd. 7a. Change of address; loss or destruction of permit.

(a) Within 30 days after changing permanent address, or within 30 days of having lost or destroyed the permit card, the permit holder must notify the issuing sheriff of the change, loss, or destruction. Failure to provide notification as required by this subdivision is a petty misdemeanor. The fine for a first offense must not exceed $25. Notwithstanding section 609.531, a firearm carried in violation of this paragraph is not subject to forfeiture.

(b) After notice is given under paragraph (a), a permit holder may obtain a replacement permit card by paying $10 to the sheriff. The request for a replacement permit card must be made on an official, standardized application adopted for this purpose under section 624.7151, and, except in the case of an address change, must include a notarized statement that the permit card has been lost or destroyed.

Subd. 8. Permit to carry voided.

(a) The permit to carry is void at the time that the holder becomes prohibited by law from possessing a firearm, in which event the holder must return the permit card to the issuing sheriff within five business days after the holder knows or should know that the holder is a prohibited person. If the sheriff has knowledge that a permit is void under this paragraph, the sheriff must give notice to the permit holder in writing in the same manner as a denial. Failure of the holder to return the permit within the five days is a gross misdemeanor unless the court finds that the circumstances or the physical or mental condition of the permit holder prevented the holder from complying with the return requirement.

(b) When a permit holder is convicted of an offense that prohibits the permit holder from possessing a firearm, the court must take possession of the permit, if it is available, and send it to the issuing sheriff.

(c) The sheriff of the county where the application was submitted, or of the county of the permit holder's current residence, may file a petition with the district court therein, for an order revoking a permit to carry on the grounds set forth in subdivision 6, paragraph (a), clause (3). An order shall be issued only if the sheriff meets the burden of proof and criteria set forth in subdivision 12. If the court denies the petition, the court must award the permit holder reasonable costs and expenses, including attorney fees.

(d) A permit revocation must be promptly reported to the issuing sheriff.

Subd. 8a. **Prosecutor's duty.** Whenever a person is charged with an offense that would, upon conviction, prohibit the person from possessing a firearm, the prosecuting attorney must ascertain whether the person is a permit holder under this section. If the person is a permit holder, the prosecutor must notify the issuing sheriff that the person has been charged with a prohibiting offense. The prosecutor must also notify the sheriff of the final disposition of the case.

Subd. 9. **Carrying pistols about one's premises or for purposes of repair, target practice.** A permit to carry is not required of a person:

(a) to keep or carry about the person's place of business, dwelling house, premises or on land possessed by the person a pistol;

(b) to carry a pistol from a place of purchase to the person's dwelling house or place of business, or from the person's dwelling house or place of business to or from a place where repairing is done, to have the pistol repaired;

(c) to carry a pistol between the person's dwelling house and place of business;

(d) to carry a pistol in the woods or fields or upon the waters of this state for the purpose of hunting or of target shooting in a safe area; or

(e) to transport a pistol in a motor vehicle, snowmobile or boat if the pistol is unloaded, contained in a closed and fastened case, gunbox, or securely tied package.

Subd. 10. **False representations.** A person who gives or causes to be given any false material information in applying for a permit to carry, knowing or having reason to know the information is false, is guilty of a gross misdemeanor.

Subd. 11. **No limit on number of pistols.** A person shall not be restricted as to the number of pistols the person may carry.

Subd. 11a. **Emergency issuance of permits.** A sheriff may immediately issue an emergency permit to a person if the sheriff determines that the person is in an emergency situation that may constitute an immediate risk to the safety of the person or someone residing in the person's household.

A person seeking an emergency permit must complete an application form and must sign an affidavit describing the emergency situation. An emergency permit applicant does not need to provide evidence of training. An emergency permit is valid for 30 days, may not be renewed, and may be revoked without a hearing. No fee may be charged for an emergency permit. An emergency permit holder may seek a regular permit under subdivision 3 and is subject to the other applicable provisions of this section.

Subd. 12. **Hearing upon denial or revocation.**

(a) Any person aggrieved by denial or revocation of a permit to carry may appeal by petition to the district court having jurisdiction over the county or municipality where the application was submitted. The petition must list the sheriff as the respondent. The district court must hold a hearing at the earliest practicable date and in any event no later than 60 days following the filing of the petition for review. The court may not grant or deny any relief before the completion of the hearing. The record of the hearing must be sealed. The matter must be heard de novo without a jury.

(b) The court must issue written findings of fact and conclusions of law regarding the issues submitted by the parties. The court must issue its writ of mandamus directing that the permit be issued and order other appropriate relief unless the sheriff establishes by clear and convincing evidence:

   (1) that the applicant is disqualified under the criteria described in subdivision 2, paragraph (b); or

   (2) that there exists a substantial likelihood that the applicant is a danger to self or the public if authorized to carry a pistol under a permit. Incidents of alleged criminal misconduct that are not investigated and documented may not be considered.

(c) If an applicant is denied a permit on the grounds that the applicant is listed in the criminal gang investigative data system under section 299C.091, the person may challenge the denial, after disclosure under court supervision of the reason for that listing, based on grounds that the person:

   (1) was erroneously identified as a person in the data system;

   (2) was improperly included in the data system according to the criteria outlined in section 299C.091, subdivision 2, paragraph (b); or

(3)   has demonstrably withdrawn from the activities and associations that led to inclusion in the data system.

(d) If the court grants a petition brought under paragraph (a), the court must award the applicant or permit holder reasonable costs and expenses including attorney fees.

Subd. 12a. Suspension as condition of release. The district court may order suspension of the application process for a permit or suspend the permit of a permit holder as a condition of release pursuant to the same criteria as the surrender of firearms under section 629.715. A permit suspension must be promptly reported to the issuing sheriff. If the permit holder has an out-of-state permit recognized under subdivision 16, the court must promptly report the suspension to the commissioner for inclusion solely in the database under subdivision 15, paragraph (a).

Subd. 13. Exemptions; adult correctional facility officers. A permit to carry a pistol is not required of any officer of a state adult correctional facility when on guard duty or otherwise engaged in an assigned duty. **Subd. 14. Records.**

(a) A sheriff must not maintain records or data collected, made, or held under this section concerning any applicant or permit holder that are not necessary under this section to support a permit that is outstanding or eligible for renewal under subdivision 7, paragraph (b). Notwithstanding section 138.163, sheriffs must completely purge all files and databases by March 1 of each year to delete all information collected under this section concerning all persons who are no longer current permit holders or currently eligible to renew their permit.

(b) Paragraph (a) does not apply to records or data concerning an applicant or permit holder who has had a permit denied or revoked under the criteria established in subdivision 2, paragraph (b), clause (1), or subdivision 6, paragraph (a), clause (3), for a period of six years from the date of the denial or revocation.

Subd. 15. Commissioner; contracts; database.

(a) The commissioner must maintain an automated database of persons authorized to carry pistols under this section that is available 24 hours a day, seven days a week, only to law enforcement agencies, including prosecutors carrying out their duties under subdivision 8a, to verify the validity of a permit.

(b) The commissioner may maintain a separate automated database of denied applications for permits to carry and of revoked permits that is available only to sheriffs performing their duties under this section containing the date of, the statutory basis for, and the initiating agency for any permit application denied or permit revoked for a period of six years from the date of the denial or revocation.

(c) The commissioner may contract with one or more vendors to implement the commissioner's duties under this section.

Subd. 16. **Recognition of permits from other states.**

(a) The commissioner must annually establish and publish a list of other states that have laws governing the issuance of permits to carry weapons that are not substantially similar to this section. The list must be available on the Internet. A person holding a carry permit from a state not on the list may use the license or permit in this state subject to the rights, privileges, and requirements of this section.

(b) Notwithstanding paragraph (a), no license or permit from another state is valid in this state if the holder is or becomes prohibited by law from possessing a firearm.

(c) Any sheriff or police chief may file a petition under subdivision 12 seeking an order suspending or revoking an out-of-state permit holder's authority to carry a pistol in this state on the grounds set forth in subdivision 6, paragraph (a), clause (3). An order shall only be issued if the petitioner meets the burden of proof and criteria set forth in subdivision 12. If the court denies the petition, the court must award the permit holder reasonable costs and expenses including attorney fees. The petition may be filed in any county in the state where a person holding a license or permit from another state can be found.

(d) The commissioner must, when necessary, execute reciprocity agreements regarding carry permits with jurisdictions whose carry permits are recognized under paragraph (a).

Subd. 17. **Posting; trespass.**

(a) A person carrying a firearm on or about his or her person or clothes under a permit or otherwise who remains at a private establishment knowing that the operator of the establishment or its agent has made a reasonable request that firearms not be brought into the establishment may be ordered to leave the premises. A person who fails to leave when so requested is guilty of a petty misdemeanor. The fine for a first offense must not exceed $25. Notwithstanding section 609.531, a firearm carried in violation of this subdivision is not subject to forfeiture.

(b) As used in this subdivision, the terms in this paragraph have the meanings given.

(1) "Reasonable request" means a request made under the following circumstances:

(i) the requester has prominently posted a conspicuous sign at every entrance to the establishment containing the following language: "(INDICATE IDENTITY OF OPERATOR) BANS GUNS IN THESE PREMISES."; or

(ii) the requester or the requester's agent personally informs the person that guns are prohibited in the premises and demands compliance.

(2) "Prominently" means readily visible and within four feet laterally of the entrance with the bottom of the sign at a height of four to six feet above the floor.

(3) "Conspicuous" means lettering in black arial typeface at least 1-1/2 inches in height against a bright contrasting background that is at least 187 square inches in area.

(4) "Private establishment" means a building, structure, or portion thereof that is owned, leased, controlled, or operated by a nongovernmental entity for a nongovernmental purpose.

(c) The owner or operator of a private establishment may not prohibit the lawful carry or possession of firearms in a parking facility or parking area.

(d) This subdivision does not apply to private residences. The lawful possessor of a private residence may prohibit firearms, and provide notice thereof, in any lawful manner.

(e) A landlord may not restrict the lawful carry or possession of firearms by tenants or their guests.

(f) Notwithstanding any inconsistent provisions in section 609.605, this subdivision sets forth the exclusive criteria to notify a permit holder when otherwise lawful firearm possession is not allowed in a private establishment and sets forth the exclusive penalty for such activity.

(g) This subdivision does not apply to:

(1)   an active licensed peace officer; or

(2)   a security guard acting in the course and scope of employment.

Subd. 18. Employers; public colleges and universities.

(a)   An employer, whether public or private, may establish policies that restrict the carry or possession of firearms by its employees while acting in the course and scope of employment. Employment related civil sanctions may be invoked for a violation.

(b)   A public postsecondary institution regulated under chapter 136F or 137 may establish policies that restrict the carry or possession of firearms by its students while on the institution's property. Academic sanctions may be invoked for a violation.

(c)   Notwithstanding paragraphs (a) and (b), an employer or a postsecondary institution may not prohibit the lawful carry or possession of firearms in a parking facility or parking area.

Subd. 19. Immunity. Neither a sheriff, police chief, any employee of a sheriff or police chief involved in the permit issuing process, nor any certified instructor is liable for damages resulting or arising from acts with a firearm committed by a permit holder, unless the person had actual knowledge at the time the permit was issued or the instruction was given that the applicant was prohibited by law from possessing a firearm.

Subd. 20. Monitoring.

(a)   By March 1, 2004, and each year thereafter, the commissioner must report to the legislature on:

(1)   the number of permits applied for, issued, suspended, revoked, and denied, further categorized by the age, sex, and zip code of the applicant or permit holder, since the previous submission, and in total;

(2)   the number of permits currently valid;

(3)   the specific reasons for each suspension, revocation, and denial and the number of reversed, canceled, or corrected actions;

(4)   without expressly identifying an applicant, the number of denials or revocations based on the grounds under subdivision 6, paragraph (a), clause (3), the factual basis for each denial or revocation, and the result of an appeal, if any, including the court's findings of fact, conclusions of law, and order;

(5) the number of convictions and types of crimes committed since the previous submission, and in total, by individuals with permits including data as to whether a firearm lawfully carried solely by virtue of a permit was actually used in furtherance of the crime;

(6) to the extent known or determinable, data on the lawful and justifiable use of firearms by permit holders; and

(7) the status of the segregated funds reported to the commissioner under subdivision 21.

(b) Sheriffs and police chiefs must supply the Department of Public Safety with the basic data the department requires to complete the report under paragraph (a). Sheriffs and police chiefs may submit data classified as private to the Department of Public Safety under this paragraph.

(c) Copies of the report under paragraph (a) must be made available to the public at the actual cost of duplication.

(d) Nothing contained in any provision of this section or any other law requires or authorizes the registration, documentation, collection, or providing of serial numbers or other data on firearms or on firearms' owners.

Subd. 21. **Use of fees.** Fees collected by sheriffs under this section and not forwarded to the commissioner must be used only to pay the direct costs of administering this section. Fee money may be used to pay the costs of appeals of prevailing applicants or permit holders under subdivision 8, paragraph (c); subdivision 12, paragraph (e); and subdivision 16, paragraph (c).

Fee money may also be used to pay the reasonable costs of the county attorney to represent the sheriff in proceedings under this section. The revenues must be maintained in a segregated fund. Fund balances must be carried over from year to year and do not revert to any other fund. As part of the information supplied under subdivision 20, paragraph (b), by January 31 of each year, a sheriff must report to the commissioner on the sheriff's segregated fund for the preceding calendar year, including information regarding:

(1) nature and amount of revenues;

(2) nature and amount of expenditures; and

(3) nature and amount of balances.

Subd. 22. **Short title; construction; severability.** This section may be cited as the Minnesota Citizens' Personal Protection Act of 2003. The legislature of the state of Minnesota recognizes and declares that the second amendment of the United States Constitution guarantees the fundamental, individual right to keep and bear arms. The provisions of this section are declared to be necessary to accomplish compelling state interests in regulation of those rights. The terms of this section must be construed according to the compelling state interest test. The invalidation of any provision of this section shall not invalidate any other provision.

Subd. 23. **Exclusivity.** This section sets forth the complete and exclusive criteria and procedures for the issuance of permits to carry and establishes their nature and scope. No sheriff, police chief, governmental unit, government official, government employee, or other person or body acting under color of law or governmental authority may change, modify, or supplement these criteria or procedures, or limit the exercise of a permit to carry.

Subd. 24. **Predatory offenders.** Except when acting under the authority of other law, it is a misdemeanor for a person required to register by section 243.166 to carry a pistol whether or not the carrier possesses a permit to carry issued under this section. If an action prohibited by this subdivision is also a violation of another law, the violation may be prosecuted under either law.

History: *1975 c 378 s 4; 1976 c 269 s 1; 1977 c 349 s 3; 1983 c 264 s 10; 1986 c 444; 1992 c 571 art 15 s 8,9; 1993 c 326 art 1 s 32; 1994 c 618 art 1 s 45,46; 1994 c 636 art 3 s 38-40; 1998 c 254 art 2 s 69; 2003 c 28 art 2 s 4-28,34; 2005 c 83 s 1,3-10*

Carrying while intoxicated

624.7142 CARRYING WHILE UNDER THE INFLUENCE OF ALCOHOL OR A CONTROLLED SUBSTANCE.

Subdivision 1. **Acts prohibited.** A person may not carry a pistol on or about the person's clothes or person in a public place:

(1) when the person is under the influence of a controlled substance, as defined in section 152.01, subdivision 4;

(2) when the person is under the influence of a combination of any two or more of the elements named in clauses (1) and (4);

(3) when the person is knowingly under the influence of any chemical compound or combination of chemical compounds that is listed as a hazardous substance in rules adopted under section 182.655 and that affects the nervous system, brain, or muscles of the person so as to impair the person's clearness of intellect or physical control;

(4) when the person is under the influence of alcohol;

(5) when the person's alcohol concentration is 0.10 or more; or

(6) when the person's alcohol concentration is less than 0.10, but more than 0.04.

Subd. 2. **Arrest.** A peace officer may arrest a person for a violation under subdivision 1 without a warrant upon probable cause, without regard to whether the violation was committed in the officer's presence.

Subd. 3. **Preliminary screening test.** When an officer authorized under subdivision 2 to make arrests has reason to believe that the person may be violating or has violated subdivision 1, the officer may require the person to provide a breath sample for a preliminary screening test using a device approved by the commissioner for this purpose. The results of the preliminary screening test must be used for the purpose of deciding whether an arrest should be made under this section and whether to require the chemical tests authorized in section 624.7143, but may not be used in any court action except: (1) to prove that the test was properly required of a person under section 624.7143, or (2) in a civil action arising out of the use of the pistol. Following the preliminary screening test, additional tests may be required of the person as provided under section 624.7143. A person who refuses a breath sample is subject to the provisions of section 624.7143 unless, in compliance with that section, the person submits to a blood, breath, or urine test to determine the presence of alcohol or a controlled substance.

Subd. 4. **Evidence.** In a prosecution for a violation of subdivision 1, the admission of evidence of the amount of alcohol or a controlled substance in the person's blood, breath, or urine is governed by section 169A.45.

Subd. 5. **Suspension.** A person who is charged with a violation under this section may have their authority to carry a pistol in a public place on or about the person's clothes or person under the provisions of a permit or otherwise suspended by the court as a condition of release.

Subd. 6. **Penalties.**

(a) A person who violates a prohibition under subdivision 1, clauses (1) to (5), is guilty of a misdemeanor. A second or subsequent violation is a gross misdemeanor.

(b) A person who violates subdivision 1, clause (6), is guilty of a misdemeanor.

(c) In addition to the penalty imposed under paragraph (a), if a person violates subdivision 1, clauses (1) to (5), the person's authority to carry a pistol in a public place on or about the person's clothes or person under the provisions of a permit or otherwise is revoked and the person may not reapply for a period of one year from the date of conviction.

(d) In addition to the penalty imposed under paragraph (b), if a person violates subdivision 1, clause (6), the person's authority to carry a pistol in a public place on or about the person's clothes or person under the provisions of a permit or otherwise is suspended for 180 days from the date of conviction.

(e) Notwithstanding section 609.531, a firearm carried in violation of subdivision 1, clause (6), is not subject to forfeiture.

Subd. 7. **Reporting.** Suspensions and revocations under this section must be reported in the same manner as in section 624.714, subdivision 12a.

History: 2003 c 28 art 2 s 29,34; 2005 c 83 s 1

624.7143 CHEMICAL TESTING.

Subdivision 1. **Mandatory chemical testing.** A person who carries a pistol in a public place on or about the person's clothes or person is required, subject to the provisions of this section, to take or submit to a test of the person's blood, breath, or urine for the purpose of determining the presence and amount of alcohol or a controlled substance. The test shall be administered at the direction of an officer authorized to make arrests under section 624.7142. Taking or submitting to the test is mandatory when requested by an officer who has probable cause to believe the person was carrying a pistol in violation of section 624.7142, and one of the following conditions exists:

(1)   the person has been lawfully placed under arrest for violating section 624.7142;

(2)   the person has been involved while carrying a firearm in a firearms-related accident resulting in property damage, personal injury, or death;

(3)   the person has refused to take the preliminary screening test provided for in section 624.7142; or

(4)   the screening test was administered and indicated an alcohol concentration of 0.04 or more.

Subd. 2. **Penalties; refusal; revocation.**

(a)   If a person refuses to take a test required under subdivision 1, none must be given but the officer shall report the refusal to the sheriff and to the authority having responsibility for prosecution of misdemeanor offenses for the jurisdiction in which the incident occurred that gave rise to the test demand and refusal. On certification by the officer that probable cause existed to believe the person had been carrying a pistol on or about the person's clothes or person in a public place while under the influence of alcohol or a controlled substance, and that the person refused to submit to testing, a court may impose a civil penalty of $500 and may revoke the person's authority to carry a pistol in a public place on or about the person's clothes or person under the provisions of a permit or otherwise for a period of one year from the date of the refusal. The person shall be accorded notice and an opportunity to be heard prior to imposition of the civil penalty or the revocation.

(b) Revocations under this subdivision must be reported in the same manner as in section 624.714, subdivision 12a. Subd. 3. **Rights and obligations.** At the time a test is requested, the person must be informed that:

(1) Minnesota law requires a person to take a test to determine if the person is under the influence of alcohol or a controlled substance;

(2) if the person refuses to take the test, the person is subject to a civil penalty of $500 and is prohibited for a period of one year from carrying a pistol in a public place on or about the person's clothes or person, as provided under subdivision 2; and

(3) that the person has the right to consult with an attorney, but that this right is limited to the extent it cannot unreasonably delay administration of the test or the person will be deemed to have refused the test.

Subd. 4. **Requirement of blood or urine test.** Notwithstanding subdivision 1, if there is probable cause to believe there is impairment by a controlled substance that is not subject to testing by a breath test, a blood or urine test may be required even after a breath test has been administered.

Subd. 5. **Chemical tests.** Chemical tests administered under this section are governed by section 169A.51 in all aspects that are not inconsistent with this section.

History: *2003 c 28 art 2 s 30; 2005 c 83 s 1*

APPENDIX D
Minnesota Legislators Who Supported You

The following Minnesota legislators—in both House and Senate—voted for the MPPA, which was signed by Governor Tim Pawlenty on April 28, 2003. If you're grateful for the change in Minnesota's former antiquated, bureaucrats-know-best carry law to a moderate, mainstream, modern, "shall-issue" one, please do say "Thank you," to at least some of them, whether by letter, email, or phone call.

Minnesota House

1. Jim Abeler
2. Peter Adolphson
3. Bruce Anderson
4. Irv Anderson
5. Jeff Anderson
6. Michael Beard
7. Greg Blaine
8. Dick Borrell
9. Lynda Boudreau
10. Fran Bradley
11. Laura Brod
12. Marks Buesgens
13. Tony Cornish
14. Gregory Davids
15. Chris DeLaForest
16. Randy Demmer
17. Jerry Dempsey
18. David Dill
19. Dan Dorman
20. Rob Eastlund
21. Kent Eken
22. Sondra Erickson
23. Brad Finstad
24. Doug Fuller
25. Chris Gerlach
26. Bob Gunther
27. Bill Haas
28. Tom Hackbarth
29. Elaine Harder
30. Bud Heidgerken

31. Mary Liz Holberg
32. Joe Hoppe
33. Larry Howes
34. Carl Jacobson
35. Jeff Johnson
36. Al Juhnke
37. Tony Kielkucki
38. Karen Klinzing
39. Jim Knoblach
40. Lyle Koenen
41. Paul Kohls
42. Philip Krinkie
43. William Kuisle
44. Bernie Lieder
45. Doug Lindgren
46. Arlon Lindner
47. Eric Lipman
48. Doug Magnus
49. Paul Marquart
50. Denny McNamara
51. Doug Meslow
52. Mary Murphy
53. Carla Nelson
54. Peter Nelson
55. Bud Nornes
56. Stephanie Olsen
57. Mark Olson
58. Lynne Osterman
59. Mary Ellen Otremba
60. Dennis Ozment

61. Erik Paulsen
62. Maxine Penas
63. Duke Powell
64. Tom Rukavina
65. Connie Ruth
66. Char Samuelson
67. Alice Seagren
68. Marty Seifert
69. Anthony Sertich
70. Dan Severson
71. Dean Simpson
72. Steve Smith
73. Judy Soderstrom
74. Loren Solberg
75. Doug Stang
76. Steve Strachan
77. Steve Sviggum
78. Howard Swenson
79. Barb Sykora
80. Kathy Tingelstad
81. Dean Urdahl
82. Ray Vandeveer
83. Dale Walz
84. Lynn Wardlow
85. Andrew Westerberg
86. Torrey Westrom
87. Tim Wilkin
88. Kurt Zellers

Minnesota Senate

1. Michel Bachmann
2. Thomas M. Bakk
3. Dick Day
4. Steve Dille
5. Michell Fischbach
6. Dennis R. Fredericson
7. David Gaither
8. David Hann
9. Debbie J. Johnson
10. Michael J. Jungbauer
11. Bob Kierlin
12. Sheila Kiscaden
13. Dave Kleis
14. David L. Knutson
15. Paul E. Koering
16. Cal Larson
17. Keith Langseth
18. Brian LeClair
19. Warren Limmer
20. Mike McGinn
21. Thomas M. Neuville
22. Sean R. Nienow
23. Gen Olson
24. Julianne E. Ortman
25. Mark Ourada
26. Pat Pariseau
27. Mady Reiter
28. Claire A. Robling
29. Julie A. Rosen
30. Carrie L. Ruud
31. Dallas C. Sams
32. Tom Saxhaug
33. LeRoy A. Stumpf
34. David H. Senjem
35. David J. Tomassoni
36. Jim Vickerman
37. Betsy L. Wergin